Palgrave Studies in Accounting and Finance Practice

More information about this series at
http://www.palgrave.com/gp/series/16220

Lazaro A. Mederos

The Future of Outsourcing

Strategic Outsourcing Controls and the Backsourcing Evolution

palgrave
macmillan

Lazaro A. Mederos
Miami, FL, USA

ISSN 2524-8251 ISSN 2524-826X (electronic)
Palgrave Studies in Accounting and Finance Practice
ISBN 978-3-030-71406-2 ISBN 978-3-030-71407-9 (eBook)
https://doi.org/10.1007/978-3-030-71407-9

This Palgrave Macmillan imprint is published by the registered company Springer Nature Switzerland AG
The registered company address is: Gewerbestrasse 11, 6330 Cham, Switzerland

Series Editors' Foreword

At the start of this book project, we thought that there was something at odds with management currents. It is because backsourcing against outsourcing could be counterintuitive. Later, we were convinced that the outsourcing wave could not last forever and that there would be a need for backsourcing for some activities. We saw this in the context of the current pandemic. Confronted with a shortage of facemasks imported from China at a high price, governments in developed countries realized that national sovereignty would require some degree of backsourcing. Consequently, this book became unpredictably timely.

Not just is Lazaro Mederos' book timely, it is a perfect instance of what we want to promote in this series. Lazaro has spontaneously and brilliantly met our requirements. First, this book has been written to be read by both practitioners and researchers. The former should be fulfilled by the cases being reflected on two backsourcing models: the Mederos Quadrant and the Lazarus Weighted Model. The latter is fulfilled as it fills a blind spot of management studies which is the lack of research on backsourcing and as it rests upon its own philosophy which is different from that of outsourcing. Secondly, this book is built upon the ideas of Porterian and Transaction Costs Economics and takes a strategic perspective through an examination of a value chain and its implications for management structuring and controls.

All this has been possible because Lazaro Mederos bears a dual capacity. He has worked for many years as an outsourcing consultant at IBM by which he has substantially professed the topic area. After his tenure at IBM, his former clients wanted his service on backsource activities. This involvement was accelerated by the COVID-19 pandemic making him a leading Backsourcing consultant in the market. But Lazaro is not just an experienced consultant—his employer had encouraged him to ground his work in research leading him to complete a DBA. This book reflects on this great combination.

Le Blanc, France — Vassili Joannidès de Lautour
Glasgow, UK — Danture Wickramasinghe
Antibes, France — Aude Deville

Contents

List of Figures

List of Tables

CHAPTER 1

The Outsourcing Manifesto: The History, Rise, and Potential Fall of the Outsourcing Industry

This chapter provides a historical perspective not often shown where we can see aspects of outsourcing found throughout modern economics long before it came to be an industry on its own. The evolutionary story of outsourcing will be told within three main sections. The **first** section will connect key economists through how their theories kept building upon one another to ultimately help create a new outsourcing industry. The **second** section will showcase how the accounting evolution provided additional building blocks and management controls. This second section explores the four stages of management accounting and their synergy with outsourcing by providing the transferable controls that allowed outsourcing to thrive. The **third** and final section of this chapter takes a look at the potential fall from grace of outsourcing through how four disruptors (hidden costs, diminished quality, corporate politics, and COVID-19) are driving organizations to backsource.

1.1 Tracing Outsourcing to the Roots of Modern Economics

This initial section gives you a historical overview with a journey that traces the origins of outsourcing. In the last 30 years outsourcing has grown to become a multibillion-dollar industry (Tajdini & Nazari, 2012).

L. A. Mederos, *The Future of Outsourcing*,
Palgrave Studies in Accounting and Finance Practice,
https://doi.org/10.1007/978-3-030-71407-9_1

It is now easier than ever before to conduct business at a global scale and set up international locations to provide services by supplying the initial domestic markets at a lower cost. Outsourcing is widely regarded as a fairly young industry. However, we can trace its essence back to the origins of modern economics and management accounting controls. The first section of this chapter introduces key academic scholars and highlights specific aspects of research and theories that became the foundation supporting outsourcing.

Contrary to popular belief, the essence of outsourcing is not necessarily new, and continuously evolves. We can arguably trace the origins of outsourcing back to Adam Smith who authored *An Inquiry into the Nature and Causes of the Wealth of Nations* (1776). We begin with Adam Smith, who is widely known as the "Father of Capitalism" through his introduction of the Absolute Advantage theory which laid the foundation for the free trade market system. Absolute Advantage theory focuses on the labor productivity aspect of trade, also a competitive benefit of outsourcing. Outsourcing in its purest form may be defined as a strategy used by an organization to source processes or process areas from an external supplier. Adam Smith elevated the business theory practiced at the time called Mercantilism, popular until the eighteenth century and promoted by Thomas Mun, Director of the East India Company, with a heavy focus on exports in lieu of imports (Dong-Sung & Hwy-Chang, 2013). Mercantilism was widely adopted by England which began to tax and limit trade to achieve a favorable balance. Adam Smith was a strong opponent of mercantilism because it promoted the exports of one country over another resulting in a counterbalance or negative impact to the other. Furthermore, Smith believed that mutual trade was beneficial to both countries involved due to the absolute advantage each country may have. His theory was in support of the country **focusing on trading a particular good or service produced at a lower cost with its absolute advantage**.

His work weighed heavily on the efficiency of the market and supports the theory that competition allows for better prices. Purchasing goods or services from an outside vendor would be attained at a lower cost versus producing such goods or services internally. Additionally, he refers to "the invisible hand" driving the economy, which can be referred to in this case as the price point set for a good or service by an outside vendor who specializes in a particular service or product sold at a lower price point than if produced in-house. Hence, although a company may have an absolute advantage over a region, making it harder for other companies to enter, a firm that sells at a lower price point will be in a better position to penetrate that client base (Dixit, 1979).

By 1817, Absolute Advantage eventually evolved into Comparative Advantage when David Ricardo proposed his idea that a country did not specifically need to have an "absolute advantage" over another in order to engage in successful trade. It could simply produce a service or good at a lower cost than if produced by the other country with which they were engaging in trade. Basically, a country competing with another more powerful country should focus on the areas where the stronger country or higher cost country has a disadvantage. Today this practice occurs in countries such as India when it provides information technology to higher cost countries such as the US and/or Switzerland.

1.1.1 The Novel or "Nobel" Step in the Outsourcing Origin Story

The next phase within the outsourcing origin story comes as a gift from Ronald H. Coase. I refer to it as a gift because this 1991 winner of the Nobel Memorial Prize in Economic Sciences did not originally intend to study economics. According to his biography on nobelprize.org, initially he was interested in history and then chemistry, but he wasn't interested in pursuing the math requirements. Hence, his only other alternative was commerce. However, this fascinating coincidence leads to an amazing achievement and does not end there. Early in his life he became a committed socialist and began to study industrial law, essentially setting on a course of study toward a life as a lawyer until he attended Arnold Plant's lectures on business administration. Plant, a professor at the London School of Economics challenged Coase's views on commerce by providing a new perspective. Arnold Plant's influence ultimately led to Coase being awarded the Sir Ernest Cassel Traveling Scholarship which took him to the US.

In the summer of 1932, Coase visited factories in the US and collected the data that would later revolutionize commerce by providing us with the next stop in **the outsourcing origin story**. This evolution occurred when Coase provided us with the basis for the "make-or-buy" decision as part of the transaction cost. In 1937, Ronald H. Coase published, "The Nature of the Firm" which borrowed from the foundation provided by Adam Smith around the practice of fully contracting from the country that can supply a good or product at a lower cost, and later presented with a different elevated perspective by David Ricardo who proposed further specialization of which country to source goods or services from. This specialization took the theory to the next level by helping us assess whether it made sense to contract out instead of producing a product or service in-house by highlighting various costs arising from the transaction itself.

Coase was able to highlight that it was not as simple as having the product or service produced elsewhere but there was a cost associated with contracting out that was not previously being considered. These associated transaction costs of doing business with an outside firm included cost of negotiating a contract, enforcement, and/or acquiring specialized information which was previously only based on price comparison (Coase, 1937). It may appear as we are coming full circle as some of these related transactional costs are being considered "hidden" by some organizations outsourcing today. Coase's impact has rippled down throughout academia and more specifically through one of his own notable Nobel Prize-winning students who he directly influenced. This student was Oliver E. Williamson.

Coase's transactional cost research did not get much attention until Williamson formalized it into a Transactional Cost Economics (TCE) testable theory (Habimana 2016). Williamson is a pioneer and elevated the research by providing a framework to assess organizational failure by applying human and environmental factors. Williamson continued his research within TCE pushing the theory into the mainstream. His 1971 article, "The Vertical Integration of Production: Market Failure Considerations" gave us a more formalized view of the benefits and limits of the internal organization vs. the market, where he challenges antitrust governance of monopolies. This is where we see the next major leap in the outsourcing journey after gaining clarity on transactional cost considerations through highlighting the associated risk, entry barriers, and information processing which would impact the decision to take advantage of market over internal capabilities (Williamson, 1971). One point to consider is if Williamson reached mainstream popularity with his TCE research, then Michael Porter may be referred to as the academic "rock star" of this group.

According to the Harvard Business School website, Michael Porter is the most cited author today in business and economics while simultaneously garnering global praise from both academics and practitioners. In 1979, Porter developed his five forces analysis which empowered firms with a tool to measure if it was profitable to do business in a specific industry. The five forces model was special as it was not just a standalone model. Organizations were able to apply their own secret core competency sauce to enable a firm's specific competitive advantage. The five forces are comprised of the bargaining power of suppliers, threat of new entrants, industry rivalry, threat of substitutes, and buyer bargaining power (Porter, 1979). Soon after in 1985, Porter published a book called *Competitive Advantage: Creating and Sustaining Superior Performance* where he explains Value Chain Analysis. Porter "flipped the accounting script" and focused on a system where customers are central to assessing where the cost and value is realized instead of on the various internal operating departments. Porter essentially provided a mechanism linking where the value was specifically created within an organization. The value chain mainly consisted of both primary and secondary activities. The primary activities are central and have a direct response to production such as sales, marketing and logistics. The second set of activities serve to support the primary areas such as information technology, human resources, and infrastructure related. We may conclude if Smith is the "*father of capitalism*," it may not be a stretch to agree Porter is the "*father of business strategy*." In 1990, Porter authored a book with a similar title, *The Competitive Advantage of Nations* which was revered as a modern equivalent to Smith's revolutionary work (Ryan, 1990). Although Smith's focus was on trade theory, Porter had a unique perspective on competitive theory that led him to author a total of 19 books and over 120 articles. He was honored numerous times including the Adam Smith Award by the National Association of Business Economists, in addition to the Academy of Management's highest award for scholarly contributions to management. This unique perspective gave birth to the Diamond Model which is part of the same competitive advantage theory or "manifesto" and "guiding principle" that served as the foundation for the birth of the outsourcing industry.

1.1.2 The Strategy Model that Helped Birth the Outsourcing Industry

The section below builds upon the outsourcing origin story by making it more tangible by providing an overview of Porter's Diamond Model as it relates to outsourcing. The model helps organizations gauge internal and external competitive factors when doing business in a global environment.

Additionally, this model provides a tool helping organizations visualize the intersection between business strategy and outsourcing. Essentially, outsourcing is part of the strategy to gain a competitive advantage.

The competitive advantage Porter refers to in *The Competitive Advantage of Nations* includes local firms creating processes designed to take advantage of economies of scale to reduce costs through engaging in global strategic partnerships. Porter's Diamond Model allows organizations to analyze their external competitive environment. It also provides a tool to help us understand why a country would have a competitive advantage over another, within a specific industry. The model shows us six factors which begin with Factor Conditions, followed by Firm Strategy, Structure and Rivalry, as well as Demand Conditions, and Related and Supporting Industries, while having Government and chance outside of the diamond but significant to all areas. The Diamond model has been both praised and criticized. Critics of the model such as Rugman (1991) and Dunning (1993), emphasize the model is only applicable to large economies, or Krugman (1994) who argues that a country needs to be successful domestically before it can thrive globally. While some may consider this criticism negative, it explains the foundation for outsourcing for countries or organizations that do not need to achieve a high level of productivity domestically to thrive globally. This is achieved through forming strategic partnerships that provide the country or company with a competitive advantage attained through global outsourcing.

Implementing Porter's Diamond Model allows organizations to apply their national advantage on a global competitive scale. The diamond model is similar to a clock where you have the **Firm Strategy, Structure, and Rivalry** diamond or sections at the 12 o'clock, **Diamond Conditions** at the 3 o'clock, **Related and Supporting Industries** at the 6 o'clock and **Factor Conditions** at the 9 o'clock. Below is an interpretation of the Diamond Model from the book, *The Competitive Advantage of Nations* as applied to global outsourcing.

Firm Strategy, Structure, and Rivalry: This section of the diamond focuses on how a firm is organized and its mission-based structure, including how they are managing their major objectives and dealing with competition. This part of the model takes into consideration the national market barriers of entry as well as the availability of various suppliers and how those suppliers interact with the client's home country leadership seeking to outsource. It allows for regional capabilities both from a technical perspective and motivational factors given that different cultures have different motivational drivers. Additionally, these motivators can lead to management style changes necessary to attaining the highest output from a given country. For example, the difference between using a more inclusive management style in Japan compared to a more authoritative style widely used in Latin America. This strategic approach would allow firms to align home country management structure and multinational host country differences with the overall company strategy. Ultimately, the aim would be to attain a global outsourcing advantage through maximizing global strategic supplier capabilities. Competition is good! Healthy competition gives birth to innovation and sets companies apart. Of course, this is a double edge sword if multiple companies are competing in a specific industry but only one is motivating their workforce to innovate, differentiate themselves, and provide more value to their clients than the rest. This lack of market innovation would lead most clients navigating toward the company making a difference and not the others. On the contrary, a recent example of a healthy rivalry was highlighted when BMW created an advertising titled "retiring is about exploring your wide-open future."

The touching BMW advertisement centered around the last day of Daimler CEO Dr. Dieter Zetsche and shared how highly regarded he was by staff and essentially how he would be missed by employees taking their pictures with him upon his exit. Nothing revolutionary had taken place at this point and the video commercial increasingly showed how Dr. Zetsche would be missed as he was driven to his house. This scene was where ingenuity was on full display when the commercial showed Dr. Zetsche driving out of his driveway in a BMW i8 and suddenly these words were superimposed on the screen, "Thank you, Dieter Zetsche, for so many years of inspiring competition." This is a wonderful example of a company paying respect to their competitor and referring to their healthy competition driving innovation and mutual success.

Demand Condition: Is the overall demand from the home base or domestic market. This occurs when a company seeking to outsource originally built its reputation by having a significant domestic footprint due to dominating their domestic competition. Continuing to build on the BMW and Mercedes commercial storyline, we can conclude this friendly competition's affect was to improve Germany's national engineering standards in such a way it has limited their international strategy to the production of higher end, higher quality vehicles. In addition, Information Technology (IT) advancements have allowed for faster international expansion without the need to build a national empire first. Some examples of web-based sales platforms companies' use to take advantage of online selling provide a global marketplace so other companies can easily set up and globally sell are Alibaba, Amazon, eBay, and fruugo. Through IT advancements, domestic dominance may no longer prove to be as vital for organizations building a global footprint or those setting up to sell to neighboring markets. However, in 1990 during the rise of outsourcing it was a novel way to decide whether to expand internationally.

Related and Supporting Industries: Maximizing opportunities through taking advantage of related and supporting industries. As industries became stronger, they built an expanding labor force while creating ripple effects that positively (or negatively) impact related organizations. For example, a successful US-based IT infrastructure company sets up an offshore location in Warsaw, Poland to offer service support for their European clients and hires hundreds of local university graduates. Their entry into the market results in more Polish students studying IT due to the opportunity of working with an international company that wants to hire Polish workers. This opens the door to hiring locally available and trained labor and attracts additional IT hardware and software development companies who want to take advantage of the available labor surge.

Factor Conditions: These are the overall factors that may or may not be already available in the home or host country. Factors can either be human labor or capital and may either be basic or advanced. For example, basic can be linked to low level skilled resources easily trained more often associated with out-tasking repetitive services from an offshore supplier that could be easily replaced. On the other hand, advanced factors include the high-end niche technical resources that may also serve as outsourcing strategic partners and may assist with the strategic design and implementation of a highly technical solution. Logistics infrastructure of a country may also provide easier transport of goods and services as well as access to natural resources. Furthermore, in addition to the previous example of Related and Supporting IT industry, an advanced Factor Condition would be created in a country such as Poland with a competitive IT industry that shines by producing highly specialized niche resources helping to fuel their overall domestic economy.

Government: The government aspect of the diamond is quite important as it can help build an economy or negatively impact it. An example of positive government impact is when a government invests in their domestic university system to produce top talent that is then available for recruitment by multinational organizations. A similar investment was made by India's domestic government intended to attract global technology companies over the past 20 years. On the other hand, the opposite effect is when governments have repatriated companies and expelled foreign direct investors, as in the example of Cuba in the 1960s, after the communist dictator Fidel Castro took over the presidency by force. Governments can play a significant role in trade by guiding home country companies in the selection of countries to outsource goods or services to through tariff manipulation. More recently, the US and China have been going through a trade war ever since President Trump was elected president and became focused on trade balance (Mutikani, 2019). Since January 22, 2018, both countries have been raising tariffs on each other's imports when Trump announced China would be fined over intellectual property theft (Mutikani, 2019). In 2018, the BBC also released a documentary called, *China vs. USA, Empires at War* where intellectual property theft was highlighted and described the US' efforts to increase tariffs on China to drive the domestic US economy while reducing offshore outsourcing.

Chance: The unknown possibility of what could happen given the right situation. During my conversation with a friend who is a star software sales leader at a global up and coming company, I asked her, "what makes you so globally successful?" Her response was quick and simple, "territory, timing and talent!" The three Ts of sales performance. I loved her response because it was focused around trying to control "chance" itself by being prepared to take chances whenever they emerged. These three Ts also describe being in the right place, at the right time, and prepared to meet the challenge. Immediately, I was intrigued and when broken down I realized this was a widely used sales strategy of controlling chance. The way she owned the three Ts was to create the chances that differentiated her from her peers, or in the sales world, her competition! She further explained how she was trained to create opportunities out of chance given various potential sales scenarios that resulted in her successful career. Additionally, chance can be a differentiating success factor when companies are considering international markets. A new company considering international expansion can begin to control their chances of success through working with regional offshore suppliers from the start. For example, a Latin America-based small- to medium-sized business with the sole goal of selling to the US market could bypass local opportunities.

Although chance occurs when least expected, it can impact any of the five sections of the diamond model at any time.

The overall impact of the diamond model on an organization is to provide a way to be more globally competitive. One of the major objectives of implementing the diamond model is to use a tool that helps organizations perform better than their competition by increasing profits and reducing financial losses. One of the major goals for implementing an outsourcing strategy is to have a favorable impact on the Profit & Loss (P&L) statement. The next section covers the evolution of managerial accounting and its growth from the initial stage to understanding the advantage one business has over another, up to the mature stage including ways to create measurable value. While the diamond model helps organizations understand their competitive advantage, managerial accounting could have an effect on the entire management system that measures and evaluates ongoing success.

1.2 The Rise of Outsourcing Through the Evolution of Accounting

The first part of this chapter shined a light on the building blocks that when put together begin to tell the story of how outsourcing came to be. Tracing the roots of outsourcing further covers the historic origins through understanding the "**what**" happened as a part of academic theory. The section covered the "**how**" a firm can have a specific competitive advantage with a review of Porter's Diamond Model, linking strategy and outsourcing. Now the text will cover the "**so what**" aspect by understanding the impact managerial accounting has on an organization's competitive landscape. The bridge between strategy, outsourcing and management accounting can be leveraged along with the business' objective to refine a competitive advantage so the business can be more profitable and thrive. This section begins by highlighting the importance of the inclusion of strategic competition as a part of the evolution of managerial accounting and includes the four distinct evolutionary stages of managerial accounting as described by the International Federation of Accountants. The overall accounting discipline is comprised of two major fields, financial accounting and managerial accounting. One of the major allures for engaging in an outsourcing relationship is the ability to impact both areas relatively quickly. For example, a large airline company may engage with a global outsourcing company to outsource their entire

IT capabilities. This type of outsourcing engagement allows the airline company to stop financially accounting for costs associated with owning their IT infrastructure since it would be owned by the service provider. Equally significant is management accounting, as it provides structure to plan and manage toward specific company goals. The below describes both in greater detail.

1.2.1 *The Birth of Outsourcing Through Financial Accounting*

Financial accounting is a process that records precise economic actions taken by the organization for its external stakeholders, lenders, and/or regulators. Financial reporting is mandatory for publicly traded companies within the US dating back to the initial Securities Act of 1933, passed by former President Franklin D. Roosevelt and frequently enhanced to protect investors from fraud. Publicly traded companies in the US also need to follow Generally Accepted Accounting Principles (GAAP) when creating their financial accounting reports in order to maintain a common structure of methods and practices to help anyone outside of the company understand their financials across industries. However, countries outside of the US also have accounting standards such as the International Financial Reporting Standards (IFRS) which is used by a large portion of the world. Although they are two different accounting standards, they are both meant to unify rules and allow for common interpretation of financials by their respective users. Ultimately, financial accounting is controlled and must provide a precise view of past transactions to external stakeholders in a way that everyone can understand such transactions by following a common set of rules from either the GAAP or IFRS structure.

The advancements in technology and management accounting in the 1980s and 1990s empowered organizations with the newly found ability to engage in global business while understanding where costs originated and recorded in the P&L with greater detail than ever before. This was also the time when **subcontracting evolved into outsourcing by adding the strategic partnership element** to the engagement as well as the transfer of process ownership to the company performing the contracted services. Hence, **outsourcing is defined as a strategic relationship where an external organization brings value to another by taking contractual ownership of another's internal processes for a given time**. The first engagement that received the honor of kick starting the outsourcing industry was the iconic IBM and Kodak 1989 deal (Loh

& Venkatraman, 1992) and (Fjermestad & Saitta, 2005). Outsourcing is a relatively young field that has grown to become a multibillion-dollar industry mainly due to one thing—it helps companies achieve their strategic objectives!

Through outsourcing, an organization may rapidly build a workforce using local resources and not necessarily hire and incorporate more staff internally. Outsourcing would allow the organization to ramp up or also ramp down according to demand, independent of local labor laws. Outsourcing further provides business with the flexibility to quickly augment their staff by having a provider take on additional work shifts. Depending on the service level agreement (SLA), the provider could be responsible for just supplying the headcount or could go as far as owning the entire supply chain around the product it is creating. Outsourcing also plays a key role in logistics since many organizations don't maintain a logistics network to globally deliver products. In response, organizations can create a relationship with a key logistics supplier to either have a local warehouse presence, local distribution, or even local manufacturing.

Outsourcing providers seek opportunities to deliver services at lower operating costs to countries which are commonly known for having higher wage and labor costs. As a direct outcome of outsourcing, countries normally associated with higher labor costs, such as Switzerland, may have the opportunity to obtain services from a lower cost country. The commonly known lower cost countries are usually emerging markets with thriving technology or specific industry expertise. The status of lower cost countries may progressively shift from very low cost to medium cost and up according to the maturity and skills of their workforce. Another reason some of the lower cost economies may begin to see increasing cost to doing business may be related to competition. Many multinational companies may compete for the same pool of talented individuals driving salaries upward and at the same time diminishing supply.

1.2.2 The Birth of Outsourcing Through Management Accounting

Managerial accounting is meant to provide internal stakeholders with an unregulated view of what is currently taking place and how the future may look within an organization. The industrial revolution paved the way for **bookkeeping to evolve into management accounting**. This initial leap allowed businesses to make key decisions by tracking their product's profitability with more cost sharing available between product lines.

The **first phase of management accounting** significantly helped organizations understand where their cost was originated. The **second phase provided** a way to categorize and assign such costs which then facilitated enhanced planning. The natural progression took place and after phase one and two were completed, associated costs could be analyzed and reduced. Cost reduction techniques became the gold standard and companies such as Motorola, GE, and Allied Signal were among the leaders in their field by implementing total production programs which gained popularity that shortly after American Express, IBM, and globally many more started taking advantage of this methodology (Yang & Yeh, 2007). The **third phase** was vital to the evolution of outsourcing as it was during this stage when outsourcing began to thrive. Organizations finally were able to structure their processes in a way to be improved by reducing production costs and simultaneously increasing quality output through **Lean Six Sigma (LSS)**. LSS provides organizations with a competitive advantage through focusing on overall defect reductions while reducing costs. Organizations eventually maximized their cost reductions internally and also began working with their suppliers to improve processes across industries. For example, Toyota and Ford, which both survived the 2008 global economic crisis (Beelaerts van Blokland, van de Koppel, Lodewijks, & Breen, 2019). This cross-industry effort became part of the outsourcing evolution, as automotive makers realized an outcome of a successful process improvement effort was a fully documented process. Interestingly, this fully documented process would later be one of the key requirements to perform a successful outsourcing engagement (Mederos, 2018).

Fully documenting and structuring processes provided organizations with the capability to immediately take entire processes out of their financial statements and hand them over to an external service provider to perform those formerly in-house responsibilities. This quick way to reduce costs helped start the wave of the 1980s' automotive outsourcing. However, this ongoing focus on reducing cost from the financial statements has its limitations as there is ultimately an opportunity cost to the client due to over outsourcing and losing control of quality and value.

The **fourth phase** was quite different from the previous three as the focus changed from supply to demand. However, one of the key foundational benefits of management accounting is the ability to help managers make better decisions. The fourth phase focused on the past and what could be done differently in the future, but still lacked the ability to use the past to make better and timely decisions in the future. Although the fourth phase still took advantage of reporting by looking back at what had taken place.

Planning, Controlling, and Decision-Making

Management accounting has served as the foundation for outsourcing's success through the **Planning**, **Controlling**, and **Decision-Making** pillars. These three foundational pillars have served as the success controls that have assisted leaders in achieving their goals while creating management accountability.

Planning is the infrastructure glue that binds effort and success. Kaplan and Norton's (2008) The Execution Premium emphasizes most organizations do not have a formal mechanism linking strategy and operations. Without planning there is no mechanism or path to achieve the goals they strive for. Planning is crucial throughout the entire value chain and is critical to the success of an organization's major objectives. For example, an organization's strategy may include a reduction in labor cost while internationally expanding to a new market. This organization may plan to engage with multiple outsourcing providers to achieve their objectives. The plan would include specific performance goals and measures linked to the overall cost-cutting and expansion strategy. Additionally, the planning pillar includes budgeting. **Budgets** are financial plans that help organizations achieve and manage future goals. Budgets include the expected target of the expected cost for running the business and the financial gains the company is expecting, within a set time frame. Budgets also set a structure so individual departments are provided with financial means to maintain current operations, hire new staff, procure services, and communicate up the hierarchy how well their specific area is financially managed. The common goal is to remain within the original budget's expected inflows and outflows. Organizations seek to minimize the risk of having misaligned targets from results and implement multiple controlling tools to limit this risk.

Controlling is the second pillar and it encompasses activities and tools that help leaders control the path from plan to actual results with the least possible amount of variance. Balanced Score Cards (BSC) play a key role within this pillar as it helps organizations control their outsourcing objectives. For example, financial targets can be tracked and monitored such as matching the outsourced engagement by meeting the promised labor cost reductions. The BSC may also serve to track the nonfinancial strategic objectives of the engagements, such as the number of process improvements realized through the outsourced engagements and access gains to new technological innovations from the outsourcing provider's specialized expertise. And organizations have traditionally consolidated the controlling efforts of large outsourcing deals by having one major supplier perform most of the outsourced services. This large transfer of process ownership to a main supplier helps to limit and funnel the quantity of decisions needed to be made to assure outsourced services remained as originally agreed.

The third pillar is **decision-making** and this capability stems from the entire value chain beginning with the initial decision to initiate operations, followed by the make or buy decision, to even answering the dreaded question of "does it makes sense to stay in business?" A foundational benefit of management accounting is providing leaders with accountability. However, leaders need data, tools, and process outcomes to be held accountable and make the best decisions. Managers create a plan to achieve a specific goal and receive performance reports to help them understand any deviations from the goal which improves their ability to make more well-informed decisions. In addition, key reports are used to gauge performance of financial and nonfinancial objectives. The reports make performance data available to provide leaders with decision-making tools to thrive.

1.2.3 The Rise of Outsourcing Through the Evolution of Management Accounting

Over the last few decades management accounting has significantly evolved from solely providing cost information to interpreting data, while taking into consideration external competitive forces supporting the increasingly needed alignment with business strategy (Hoffjan & Wömpener, 2006). Simmonds (1981) is further credited with appointing the term Strategic Management Accounting (SMA) as he highlights the importance of competition and the need to elevate management accounting to focus on strategic alternatives. Additionally, authors have built upon Porter's Value Chain Analysis such as Bromwich and Bhimani (1994) who elevated it through applying product attributes to allocate costs. The 1980s was a time when practitioners were craving new applied accounting methods and received guidance by using Porter's Value Chain Analysis as well as Bromwich and Bhimani's applications. Furthermore, the overall evolution of management accounting has four documented and widely accepted stages.

According to the International Federation of Accountants, IFAC (1998) managerial accounting has had four distinct evolutionary stages as follows:

Stage 1: Cost Determination and Financial Control (prior to 1950).
Stage 2: Information for Management Planning and Control (1950s–1960s).
Stage 3: Reduction of Waste of Resources in Business Processes (1980s).
Stage 4: Creation of Value through Effective Resource Use (1990s).

The first stage focused on determining product costs with little regard to price or quality permitting management to mainly focus on capacity (Abdel-Kader & Luther, 2006). Understanding product cost is vital in the decision to make or buy a product. The second stage was indeed an evolution as it **provided information for planning and controlling including decision analysis** and responsibility accounting. However, this activity was not yet strategic and mainly focused on internal administration. This stage essentially empowered managers to develop performance measures to help them understand the areas of the business that were performing better than others. While the first and second stages set the foundation for the capability to outsource, one can argue the third and fourth stages facilitated the official birth of outsourcing.

The **third stage** was the first evolutionary jump in response to external competitive factors. This stage reflects the first time that **quality was valued central to a company's success**. Additional focus around operational improvements leading to cost reductions provided organizations with immediate competitive ammunition by having internal controllable measures of success independent of industry and fully applicable to any company's internal processes. Lean and six sigma methodologies provided organizations with a guidebook on how to implement waste reduction controls. Along with recognizing the founding father's perspective, we can conclude that William Edwards Deming is the "*Father of Total Quality Controls*." In 1928, Deming attained his PhD from Yale in the field of Theoretical Physics and spent his early career working at the US Department of Agriculture (USDA). Luckily for those of us working in the world of statistics and the continuous improvements community, he retired from the USDA after a decade of service. Soon after, he began consulting and lecturing at Stanford on statistical quality improvements, but his message did not impact any change in US production. After the war ended, he received an invitation to help revive the Japanese economy and accepted with one major condition. This condition was the leaders had to participate in order to realize a turnaround within five years. It appears that Deming took his own advice and learned from previous mistakes while continuously improving and applying his learning to his own business endeavors by including support of leadership as key to the outcome of the initiative. The Japanese labor union Keidanren accepted his conditions, resulting in improved quality and productivity within only four years! Soon after his work was widely adopted in the US and pivotal in the creation of quality and process improvement methodologies. The process improvement methodologies packaged processes ready for outsourcing by having them well-documented, improved, and controlled. This controlling package now serves as the basic foundational requirement for beginning to successfully outsource.

The **fourth stage** evolved into a customer value-driven competitive environment. Advancements in technology, such as the internet, reduced global distances between key human resources as well as **helping to transform data itself into a coveted information resource advantage**. At this point, organizations were able to take advantage of Porter's Value Chain Analysis and Diamond Model, by combining them with key evolutionary objectives from the previous three management accounting stages. These steps drove a sourcing revolution that assisted in the birth of outsourcing. The fourth stage of management accounting helped business see value as more than just financially **driven objectives by focusing on the client-specific perspective**. We witnessed this industry change when organizations began to implement both strategic financial and nonfinancial controls such as the Balanced Scorecards and Activity-Based Costing (ABC). The introduction of ABC within this stage may have further fueled the cost reduction hysteria by providing leaders with visibility into where such value and cost were born.

The balanced scorecard was created by Robert Kaplan and David Norton with the goal to provide business with a framework to measure **financial and nonfinancial business performance**. Its framework is made up of four major perspectives including Financial, Internal Business Process, Innovation and Learning, and Customer. These four major areas must be aligned to the corporate strategy and are further expanded into two major pillars including specific goals and key performance indicators (KPIs). A clear leap from the previous stage while it also includes internal business process improvements, it also fosters innovation to successfully compete. The advancements in technology brought more access to information and data which supported the capability to break down costs further and allowed us to jump from traditional costing to Activity-Based Costing (ABC). Traditional costing provides a straightforward approach to externally communicating costs by computing the overhead rate for an entire location. This overhead rate is computed by dividing the total location overhead costs by the overall labor hours at that location.

Robert S. Kaplan and W. Bruns provided us with the first clear detailed overview of ABC in their 1987 book *Accounting and Management: A Field Study Perspective.* ABC extends the impact of traditional costing by going beyond direct labor and provides an enhanced view of non-direct costs by having multiple cost pools or activities which generated costs. The activities selected to assess costs are subject to individual companies attempting to gauge the specific product or line cost. These costs would entail allocating specific activities within cost pools that make up the overall product in question. These cost pools could be related to manufacturing or even the customer service support of specific products. Organizations are still required to run traditional reporting for external reporting, but the enhanced ABC detailed view provides internal leaders with greater clarity into controlling the specific performance of specific products.

The management accounting controls reviewed through this section have helped outsourcing grow into the thriving industry that it is today. The key success controls that allowed outsourcing to thrive are planning, controlling and decision-making. We also covered the phases of management accounting as they also provided additional building blocks through cost structure, ability to handle and work with data, and reduce waste while ultimately focusing on value creation through affective use of resources. However, outsourcing controls are beginning to be challenged through the backsourcing phenomenon which may potentially be the fall of outsourcing.

1.3 The Potential Fall of Outsourcing and Need for Further Evolution

Backsourcing is defined by repatriating the processes that were once outsourced. Repatriation in this sense refers to a company and not necessarily a country. For example, a global company based in the US could stop engaging in an outsourcing arrangement with a service provider out of China and then mobilize their own internal operations in Southeast Asia to fully take over the processes. Some authors have interchangeably used backsourcing and insourcing since this is a young field with much of the terminology is still to be settled. However, they are significantly different terms. Insourcing is simply sourcing from within. Please allow me to expand upon the term insourcing, this could exist in a company supplying goods or services to same or other business units within the company itself. However, backsourcing is bringing back certain processes (goods and/or services) that were previously outsourced. This phenomenon has now grown into a trend as seen by GM hiring around 3000 Hewlett-Packard (HP) employees already staffed at GM's IT operations (Maxey, 2014). As well as Apple beginning to produce US manufactured MAC computers (Minahan, 2013; Denning, 2013). Also, MediaCorp and Kellwood fully backsourced their IT operations within the last decade in Europe (Kotlarsky & Bognar, 2012). Another well-publicized outsourcing "break-up" took place between IBM and JPMorgan after the latter's merger with Bank One. In 2004, this seven-year $5 Billion deal was estimated at the time, as the largest ever however it resulted in backsourcing within only three years (Veltri, Saunders, & Kavan, 2008). The backsourcing phenomenon was growing and as cases became more frequent so was the ambiguity of exactly why organizations were beginning to backsource.

In order to further define this ambiguity and fully explore backsourcing phenomena, I conducted qualitative research by interviewing arguably some of the leading outsourcing minds of the twenty-first century. The data was attained by asking open-ended questions to 26 participants that were all part of multinational organizations with significant outsourcing experience. The participants were made up of executives and multi-year experienced professionals based out of North America and Europe. The research participants included both sides of the outsourcing story by including service providers as well as clients purchasing outsourcing services. This unique dual perspective allows us to see beyond the outsourcing veil to truly understand why organizations were beginning to backsource. Additionally, this research was performed using the Charmaz (2006) constructivist approach using grounded theory which allowed us to see three main pillars where the intersection between management accounting and outsourcing lies. The first of these pillars is the growing perception that hidden costs are present and growing as part of an outsourcing relationship. The second is the reduction in quality of supplied processes due to continuous focus on cost reduction, while the third main pillar supporting the intersection with management accounting is the uncontrolled corporate politics that may negatively impact the overall outsourcing relationship. These three pillars should be controlled and serve as a foundational support to this highway. These pillars are currently uncontrolled and limit the success of outsourcing engagements and are some of the leading reasons for organizations to begin considering a backsourcing strategy. The research highlighted in this section sheds light on current outsourcing fundamental failing controls labeled as "curses" due to their severity in negatively impacting the entire outsourcing engagement relationship.

1.3.1 *The Curse of Perceived Hidden Cost*

The overall reduction of an organization's costs is widely accepted as one of the main benefits of outsourcing. However, many research participants highlighted that they actually found additional costs when outsourcing which included associated costs for services taking much longer to complete than expected. A participant conveyed a clear description of the cost problems he had faced when he stated it was not a one-to-one service trade-off when starting to outsource. He stated that it would take him up to six days to complete a task that would have usually only taken two days with onshore resources. Also, the cost calculated when the initial deal was drafted did not include associated rework due to language barriers. However, his main stakeholders expected the same output results from the offshore team while not budgeting for the new challenges having offshore resources presented to them. This increased cost of doing business was viewed as hidden since it had not been included in the original contract. This additional unplanned and unbudgeted cost ultimately led to diminished supplier satisfaction. An additional variant of having unbudgeted hidden costs included products bring sold unbundled from their implementation labor costs.

A key illustration of this variant came to light when an executive purchased an Enterprise Resource Planning (ERP) solution used to integrate business processes but did not include the necessary Point of Sale associated services, so the overall solution was incomplete. However, there are two sides to this illustration. The first is the client's point of view who may have understandably felt deceived by this perceived hidden cost as he budgeted for and purchased half of a solution. While the other side of the illustration shows the servicer provider's point of view who sells modular solutions based on client requests. The seller's perspective in this case was that they sell portions of solutions for the ability to upsell additional services as variable costs to the client. This complete view of the ERP's limited effect came to light after both sides of the outsourcing story participated in this research. Suppliers also associated the increase in variable cost as ad hoc services. However, the overall sentiment toward ad hoc services was that their associated cost was increasing in large part due to increasing labor costs at previously described low-cost locations such as India.

Outsourcing clients who were doing business with a well-known provider of a specific in-demand technology, frequently were under the impression their overall contract would also provide them with access to such technology. This misalignment service expectation was viewed as a hidden cost by the service clients who perceived such access to the technology as a significant reason for doing business with the well-known outsourcing technology provider. This perceived hidden cost was also proven to be frustrating to the service provider who had to regularly educate the client(s) that it was not part of the original agreement and clients would have to pay the premium for the requested additional noncontracted services.

1.3.2 The Curse of Diminished Quality Impacting Engagement Satisfaction

Quality was shown to be a significant factor of why organizations were beginning to backsource. Participants further stated there was a decrease in the perceived quality of processes provided by outsourcing suppliers. In addition, participants stated the quality of outsourced processes was increasingly getting worse year over year, while contracts often pushed for a reduction in price for services provided during the same time. Prices were decreasing but also simultaneously bringing down quality. In addition, there was a link in regard to lowering the quality by increasing rework costs by as much as three times their onshore estimates to complete outsourced process. As could be expected, reduced quality led to an increase in cost and ultimately dissatisfied customers. Although there appears to be an almost blanket sentiment toward a decrease in quality, some participants said they would prefer to pay a price premium to assure the expected quality remained.

Decreasing quality was shown to be a key contributor in decreased outsourcing satisfaction. With the result that organizations are either demanding higher quality from their outsourcing providers or beginning to think of ways to own the outsourcing processes through backsourcing. By itself, missing quality measures may be seen as straightforward, but it actually drives the demand for organizations to rethink their sourcing options. This has further driven the outsourcing evolution by helping organizations realize they needed to either demand more from their suppliers or to change their sourcing models. With the maturity of outsourcing and the ever-changing business environment, it explains why organizations are changing their sourcing models in response to the current outsourcing environment.

1.3.3 The Curse of Corporate Politics

The impact of the relationship as a part of corporate politics was multifaceted. Some participants mentioned they had seen a breakdown in the relationship negatively impacted an outsourcing engagement when otherwise the core technical processes were working well. Also, some participants of this research highlighted how some executives within their organizations used outsourcing to cut through their own organizations' red tape in order to achieve an objective they would otherwise not be able to internally drive. This avoidance by executives coincides with participants affirming the higher they climbed in the organization so did the amount of politics.

The research revealed that the person managing the relationship should be able to also manage the political landscape. This skill proved to be vital in successfully driving outsourcing engagements. However, a participant also observed that by adding an outsource provider to the communication hierarchy was also used to impede decision-making and diminished the overall outsourcing relationship. For example, an organization purposefully inserted a communication layer between the executive decision-makers and the operations staff seeking guidance to run the business. They added "red tape" by using corporate politics as a buffer against being held accountable when key decisions had to be made. The managers were gaming the system while destroying the value sought (Jensen, 2003).

The political implications associated with outsourcing can also be as simple as new leadership coming in with a different vision. It is often the case that new leaders may wish to make large-scale earth-shaking moves in order to set their mark on the organization. For example, one can argue the famous IBM and JPMorgan outsourcing breakup we discussed earlier in the chapter would not have taken place if Bank One had not merged with JPMorgan. Leadership changes do impact a decision to change suppliers or even to backsource. In addition, when new leadership makes changes it can be for altruistic reasons or most likely with the goal to change the organization's direction toward a more financially successful path. Conversely making changes could be construed as simply a new leader trying to gain power and control. Often new leaders are incentivized with a bonus tied to their budget goals which also leads to increased politics (Jensen, 2001). Regardless of the reason, leadership changes are additional corporate political curses that outsourcing providers should hedge and manage against.

1.3.4 The Curse of COVID-19 Disrupting Outsourcing with RPA's Help

Backsourcing is currently taking place due to misalignment of outsourcing controls that spawned the evolution of the outsourcing industry. Organizations are bringing back control of certain key previously outsourced processes to maximize their overall outsourcing relationships. And backsourcing has become part of the overall evolution of outsourcing. Backsourcing key elements such as the control of critical success factors to limit the risks associated with politics and hidden costs provides impetus to the success of the overall outsourcing strategy. Pharmaceutical companies such as Vertex listed significant risks in their 2019 annual report related to dependence on outsourcing providers, including those based in China, that could lead to supply chain disruptions, which could significantly impact their patients and the company's overall sovereignty(Vertex,

2020). However, it may take the impact of a global seismic event in combination with existing technological advancements for backsourcing to fully blossom. This global shifting or seismic event could be the current global Coronavirus (COVID-19) pandemic. According to CDC.gov, the Coronavirus is a highly contagious virus that has killed over 67,000 people in the US alone as of May 2020. The virus which originated in China has already resulted in over 30 million people seeking unemployment in the US by April 2020 and economies such as Canada, France, Germany, Italy, Japan, and the UK are expected to enter into a recession this year (Jones et al., 2020).

This global shift could help drive the future of backsourcing to have more of an impact on the evolution of the outsourcing industry. The effects of the Coronavirus have been felt globally and multiple countries have stepped in and supported backsourcing more than ever before. Japan has allocated $2 billion to help their organizations exit China and backsource, and the White House National Economic Council Director, Larry Kudlow recommended that the US suggest their companies also backsource out of China (Rapoza, 2020). And according to WHO in a news release on March 3, 2020, the overall shortages of Personal Protective Equipment (PPE) were endangering health workers worldwide. CNBC reporter Adam Jeffrey said on April 18, 2020 that US healthcare workers were protesting due to lack of PPE which lead to Federal and State Governments working together to source protective gear. The lack of PPE availability fueled the global sentiment toward backsourcing. The lack of PPE availability further fueled the global sentiment towards backsourcing. As a response, the World Customs Organization Commission Council and countries such as Argentina, Brazil, India, Russia, Switzerland, the US, and the European Union adopted temporary export restrictions on medical supplies in March 2020 (wcoomd.org).

Due to this seismic event, backsourcing may finally have the potential to become an industry on its own. The model below captures the potential ecosystem where backsourcing could thrive. However, this forecast is difficult to quantify as we currently go through this global Coronavirus pandemic and we would need to do more research and see what the future has in store for backsourcing (Fig. 1.1).

As mentioned earlier in this chapter, outsourcing is a thriving multibillion-dollar industry built on the logic that greater expertise may be retained at lower cost. This multi-decade corporate behavior may not be permanently forgotten solely due to the Coronavirus pandemic. The

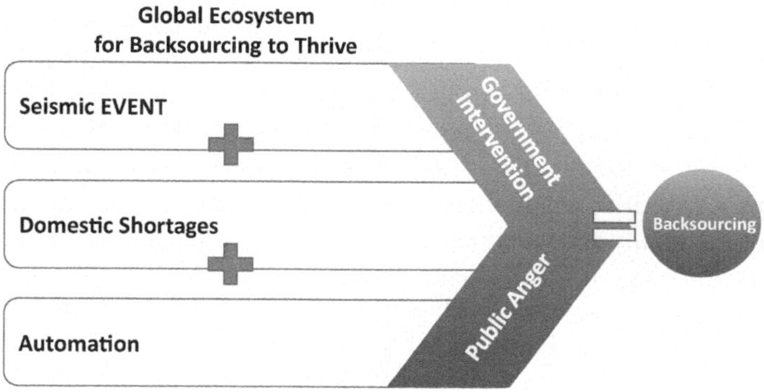

Fig. 1.1 Global ecosystem for backsourcing to thrive

reason for this is that organizations as well as consumers have grown accustomed to lower prices. We humans have historically short memories and tend to switch brands and products when we see a price increase (Van Tripj et al., 1996). Backsourcing needs a responsive ecosystem to grow. Usually this ecosystem is formed after a public outcry or public anger due to a seismic event that prompts the government to step in and assist. The COVID-19 is this current seismic event where the government needed to step in and help with domestic shortages such as PPEs. Backsourcing is currently on the news through national shortages and governments proposing funding opportunities due to losing their sovereignty to offshoring. An example is France where the public vociferously demonstrates against potentially of losing their health sovereignty. Unfortunately, France has reported close to 30,000 COVID-19-related deaths and Sanofi, the French pharmaceutical company promised to make the US their first priority for their vaccine, in which they invested over $600 million in research (Beardsley, 2020). The unified anger expressed in France against Sanofi was so strong it led the Chairman of the Board speaking on national television to reverse the company's comments and reassure people the vaccine will be widely available (Bostock, 2020). This example illustrates France's response to the threat of losing access to its homegrown pharmaceutical capabilities, but also that a culture standing together can strengthen its foundation and affect the direction of their national products and safety. Another recent development that is driving backsourcing has come through the form of Robotics Process Automation (RPA).

RPA is a software program or platform created to automate repetitive processes which are often referred to as "bots" in shortened version (Cooper et al., 2019). These bots are designed to mimic human behavior regardless of the human's geographic location. This disruptive technology could be optimal for creating a bot in workplaces where a human performs a repetitive manual task as part of an outsourcing engagement. For example, many accounting processes may be automated to reduce the cost of production such as Activity-Based Costing and flow through stage cost. Hence, organizations seeking to backsource may now have a bonus to consider doing so. Through RPA, organizations can fully bring back control of their process as well as reduce the cost of production through automation. Although RPA is a young field, research has already proven many benefits in the manufacturing industry by reducing human-made errors, reducing processing time, increasing productivity as well as data accuracy (Radke et al., 2020). Given this global pandemic is so novel, future researchers may want to study the effects of RPA on current global outsourcing engagements that include manual repetitive labor. It would be interesting to research the pandemic's lasting effects and how it may lead to the faster adoption of the available disruptive technologies within outsourcing, such as RPA.

1.4 Conclusion

This chapter reaches back to the origins of modern commerce to highlight the essence of outsourcing as it relates to key evolutionary stages within the economic theory that laid the foundation for outsourcing. Tracing the evolutionary journey, we were able to see how respected academics and economists such as Adam Smith, David Ricardo, Ronald H. Coase and Michael Porter helped set the foundation for what we now know as outsourcing. The chapter then continued on the evolutionary trajectory moving into management accounting and how the evolution of management accounting ultimately provided outsourcing with the success controls it needed to thrive. These controls are planning, controlling and decision-making.

Management accounting has had four major evolutionary stages starting with cost determination and financial control which set the foundation for what is the actual product price and cost but left much to be desired as it did not focus on quality. The second stage was indeed an evolution as it provided planning, controlling and decision analysis essential for any business. This third stage was key as quality was now being viewed as a strategic controllable factor and central to a company's success. This third stage solidifies the foundation for the birth of outsourcing as it promoted standard processes for improvements while essentially preparing them for potential outsourcing readiness. The fourth stage takes that preparedness to the next level as it allows the creation of value through effective resource use. This last stage maximized the value of outsourcing itself. The evolution of management accounting is essentially a lane on the global business highway, while outsourcing is another lane guiding businesses to reach a mutually agreed-upon destination. However, both of these roads lead to an intersection called backsourcing, which provides an exit from the standard outsourcing practices we have come to know.

The backsourcing exit has become increasingly popular in recent years due to companies experiencing increases in costs associated with outsourcing, decreased quality of outsourced processes, and increased political red tape. Furthermore, we are now facing one of the largest external seismic events in recent history through the global impact of COVID-19. The entire world has been impacted due to this virus and although we may move forward as economies begin to open, we may be moving on to a potential new reality. The long-lasting effects of COVID-19 may have changed the entire outsourcing industry in such a way that backsourcing may not only become a part of the evolution of outsourcing but an industry on its own.

Bibliography

Abdel-Kader, M., & Luther, R. (2006). IFAC's Conception of the Evolution of Management. *Advances in Management Accounting, 15*, 229–247.

Beardsley, E (2020). *French Drug Giant Sanofi Takes Heat After Suggesting U.S. May Get 1st Vaccine Access*. Retrieved from https://www.npr.org/2020/05/15/856293764/french-drug-giant-sanofi-takes-heat-after-suggesting-u-s-may-get-1st-vaccine-acc.

Beelaerts van Blokland, W., van de Koppel, S., Lodewijks, G., & Breen, W. (2019). Method for performance measurement of car companies from a stability-value leverage perspective: The balancing act between investment in R&D, supply chain configuration and value creation. *International Journal of Lean Six Sigma, 10*(1), 411–434.

Bostock, B. (2020). *Sanofi walked back a promise to give the US priority access to its coronavirus vaccine after outrage from the French government*. Retrieved

from https://www.businessinsider.com/coronavirus-vaccine-sanofi-scraps-us-priority-france-outrage-macron-2020-5.
Bromwich, M., & Bhimani, A. (1994). *Management accounting: Pathways to progress*. Chartered Institute of Management Accountants.
Charmaz, K. (2006). *Constructing grounded theory: A practical guide through qualitative analysis*. London: Sage.
Coase, R. H. (1937). The nature of the firm. *Economica, 4*(16), 386. https://doi.org/10.2307/2626876.
Cooper, L. A., Holderness, D. K., Sorensen, T. L., & Wood, D. A. (2019). Robotic process automation in public accounting. *Accounting Horizons, 33*(4), 15.
Denning, S. (2013). What went wrong at Boeing. *Strategy & Leadership, 41*(3), 36–41. https://doi.org/10.1108/10878571311323208.
Dixit, Avinash. (1979). A model of Duopoly suggesting a theory of entry barriers. *The Bell Journal of Economics, 10*(1), 20. https://doi.org/10.2307/3003317.
Dong-Sung, C., & Hwy-Chang, M. (2013). *From Adam Smith to Michael Porter: Evolution of competitiveness theory* (Vol. 7, extended edition). Singapore: World Scientific.
Dufour, A. (Director). (2007). *China vs. USA: Empires at war* [Video file]. Ampersand. Retrieved from Alexander Street database.
Dunning, J. H. (1993). Internationalizing Porter's diamond. *Management International Review, 33*(2), 7–15.
Fjermestad, J., & Saitta, J. A. (2005). A strategic management framework for IT outsourcing: A review of the literature and the development of a success factors model. *Journal of Information Technology Case and Application Research, 7*(3), 42–60.
Habimana, O. (2016). From Coase to Williamson: Evolution, formalization and empirics of transaction cost economics. *Journal of Social Economics, Research Academy of Social Sciences, 3*(1), 36–42.
Hoffjan, A., & Wömpener, A. (2006). Comparative analysis of strategic management accounting in German- and English-language general management accounting textbooks. *Schmalenbach Business Review (SBR), 58*(3), 234–258. https://doi.org/10.1007/BF03396733.
International Federation of Accountants (IFAC). (1998). International Management Practice Statement Accounting Concepts, New York.
Jensen, M. (2003). Paying people to lie: The truth about the budgeting process. *European Financial Management, 9*(3), 379–406.
Jensen, M. C. (2001). Corporate budgeting is broken, let's fix it. *Harvard Business Review, 79,* 94–101.

Jones, L., Palumbo, D., & Brown, D. (2020, April 30). *Coronavirus: A visual guide to the economic impact*. BBC News. https://www.bbc.com/news/business-51706225.

Kaplan, R. S., & Bruns, W. (1987). *Accounting and management: Field study perspectives*. Boston, MA: Harvard Business School Press.

Kaplan, R. S., & Norton, D. P. (2008). *The execution premium: Linking strategy to operations for competitive advantage*. Boston, MA: Harvard Business Press.

Krugman, P. (1994). Competitiveness: A dangerous obsession. *Foreign Affairs, 73*(2), 28–44.

Loh, L., & Venkatraman, N. (1992). Diffusion of information technology outsourcing: Influence sources and the Kodak effect. *Information Systems Research, 3*(4), 334–358. https://doi.org/10.1287/isre.3.4.334.

Maxey, K. (2014). *GM pursues IT insourcing for better alignment and economics*. Engineering.com. Retrieved January 18, 2015, from http://www.engineering.com/Blogs/tabid/3207/ArticleID/7469/GM-Pursues-IT-Insourcing-for-Better-Alignment-and-Economics.aspx.

Mederos, L. A. (2018). *Why are companies beginning to backsource? A look into the evolution of the outsourcing industry*. DBA thesis, Grenoble École de Management.

Minahan, T. (2013). *Is the U.S. the next low-cost region: Redux?* Forbes.com. Retrieved April 26, 2020, from http://www.forbes.com/sites/sap/2013/01/18/is-the-u-s-the-next-low-cost-region-redux.

Mutikani, L. (2019, September 4). *U.S. trade deficit shrinks, gap with China remains elevated*. Retrieved from https://www.reuters.com/article/us-usa-economy-trade/u-s-trade-deficit-shrinks-gap-with-china-remains-elevated-idUSKCN1VP1NT.

Porter, M. E. (1979). How competitive forces shape strategy. *Harvard Business Review, 57*(2), 137.

Porter, M. E. (1985). *Competitive advantage: Creating and sustaining superior performance*. New York: The Free Press.

Porter, M. E. (1990). *The competitive advantage of nations*. New York: Free Press.

Radke, A. M., Dang, Minh Trang, & Tan, A. (2020). Using robotic process automation (Rpa) to enhance item master data maintenance process. *LogForum, 16*(1), 129.

Rapoza, K. (2020). Kudlow: *Kudlow: 'Pay The Moving Costs' Of American Companies Leaving China*. Retrieved from https://www.forbes.com/sites/kenrapoza/2020/04/10/kudlow-pay-the-moving-costs-of-american-companies-leaving-china/.

Ricardo, D. (1971 [1817]). *The principles of political economy and taxation*. Baltimore: Penguin.

Rugman, A. M. (1991). Diamond in the rough. *Business Quarterly, 55*(Winter), 61–64.
Ryan, R. (1990, July 9). A grand disunity. *National Review*, pp. 46–47.
Simmonds, K. (1981, April). Strategic management accounting. *Management Accounting (UK), 59,* 26–29.
Smith, A. (1937 [1776]). An inquiry into the nature and causes of the wealth nations. In C. W. Eliot (Ed.), *The Harvard Classics*. New York: P. Collier & Son Corporation.
Tajdini, S., & Nazari, M. (2012). IS outsourcing decision: A quantitative approach. *International Journal of Business and Management, 7*(2), 113–129. Retrieved from http://search.proquest.com/docview/928758847?accountid=42864.
Van Tripj, H. C. M., Hoyer, W. D., & Inman, J. J. (1996). Why switch? Product category-level explanations for true variety-seeking behavior. *Journal of Marketing Research (JMR), 33*(3), 281–292. https://doi.org/10.2307/3152125.
Veltri, N. F., Saunders, C. S., & Kavan, C. B. (2008). Information systems backsourcing: Correcting problems and responding to opportunities. *California Management Review, 51*(1), 50–76. https://doi.org/10.2307/41166468.
Vertex. (2020). *Form 10-K 2019.* Retrieved from https://investors.vrtx.com/static-files/d367879f-24ad-4036-942b-7d85359e919e.
Williamson, O. (1971). The vertical integration of production: Market failure considerations. *The American Economic Review, 61*(2), 112.
World Customs Organization. (2020, May 25). World Customs Organization. Retrieved from http://www.wcoomd.org/en/topics/facilitation/activities-and-programmes/natural-disaster/list-of-countries-coronavirus.aspx.
World Health Organization: WHO. (2020, March 3). *Shortage of personal protective equipment endangering health workers worldwide.* Retrieved from https://www.who.int/news-room/detail/03-03-2020-shortage-of-personal-protective-equipment-endangering-health-workers-worldwide.
Yang, C.-C., & Yeh, T.-M. (2007). An Integrated Model of Hoshin Management and Six Sigma in High-Tech Firms. *Total Quality Management & Business Excellence, 18*(6), 653–665. https://doi.org/10.1080/14783360701349476.
Zheng, S., & Wang, Q. (2017). Mitigating hidden costs in service offshoring: A strategic management perspective. *Industrial Management & Data Systems, 117*(6), 1058–1076. https://doi.org/10.1108/IMDS-05-2016-0187.

CHAPTER 2

Theorizing Backsourcing: At the Intersection of Strategy, Operations, and Control

This chapter is broken into two major sections. The first section begins with an overview of the strategic advantages that organizations can attain through an outsourcing relationship. The second section is comprised of four additional sections beginning with a discussion on the current disconnect within the outsourcing and backsourcing communities due to the lack of an agreed-upon definition of the process. Then we explore key strategic factors that should be taken into consideration to avoid the potential for backsourcing. These key factors are controlling costs, aligning global service agreements, and assessing potential partnerships to determine if there is a potential risk for training the future competition.

The second section of the chapter is an attempt to begin creating the specific body of knowledge of backsourcing. We do have to borrow from the outsourcing body of knowledge due to backsourcing being at such an early stage. The three main academic communities we borrow from are Critical Success Factor, Risk Management, and Outsourcing Strategy. The reason the selection of these three communities of knowledge is due to the strict sense of understanding if either of these areas fails, then the outsourcing engagement has the significant potential to transform into backsourcing. This growing movement was birthed from outsourcing failures and faces similar challenges as previously mentioned, agreeing upon a

L. A. Mederos, *The Future of Outsourcing*,
Palgrave Studies in Accounting and Finance Practice,
https://doi.org/10.1007/978-3-030-71407-9_2

definition of backsourcing. Ultimately, the backsourcing industry is taking shape and has not yet developed a solid body of knowledge.

2.1 Access to a Strategic Advantage

Outsourcing has quickly grown to become a significant part of conducting business worldwide. However, as important as it may be, it is still a relatively young industry. Albeit one that has grown to become a multibillion-dollar industry, with a strong focus on technology-related services, including 30% just within the IT sector (Tajdini & Nazari, 2012). This rapid growth has been widely credited to the strategic advantage that outsourcing provides.

An organization may gain a strategic advantage by rapidly building a workforce using local resources through outsourcing which it would not have to necessarily hire and/or incorporate internally. Outsourcing allows organizations to ramp up or down according to demand, independent of local labor laws. Outsourcing plays a key role in logistics as not many organizations maintain a robust logistics network to deliver products globally. In response, organizations are able to create a relationship with a logistics supplier to have a local warehouse presence, local distribution, or even local manufacturing. Outsourcing has proven to clearly provide companies with a competitive advantage.

A service provider's financial possibilities also exponentially grow through contract extensions or renewals due to the investment already made as part of setting up the service infrastructure. Similar to the benefits the service provider would gain, the outsource client would also have the possibility to lead in the market by decreasing their **operating costs** through an outsourcing relationship. Outsourcing by design is meant to be an **inter-organizational** relationship **to benefit** both the service provider and client. This inter-organization relationship should lead to the creation of additional benefits through outsourcing (Letica, 2016).

Aman et al. (2012) suggests setting aside the global benefits of outsourcing technology and focus on cost reduction. Instead, organizations could focus on targeted transaction cost levels to attain service satisfaction through price (Aman et al., 2012). Additionally, organizations can gain a competitive advantage through strategic cost-focused supplier partnerships resulting in mutually beneficial relationships (Cleary & McLarney, 2019). Outsourcing gained popularity from the original cost cutting objectives, however, the industry is maturing, and organizations are shifting requirements to attain additional technology capabilities and service improvements (Garg & Jain, 2019).

Fjermestad and Saitta (2005) and Murray et al. (2009) further suggest that outsourcing goes **beyond a cost advantage** strategy to provide businesses with an increased goods or delivery supply base, increased technical expertise due to an extended reach of specialized locations, and increased geographic proximity to consumers.

Outsourcing further provides business with the strategic advantage of quickly **augmenting staff** by having a provider take on additional shifts. Depending on the service level agreement (SLA), the outsourcing company could be responsible for solely providing the additional headcount similar to a subcontracting arrangement or could go as far as **owning the entire supply chain** of the product it is supplying. Outsourcing further allows organizations access to talented individuals which they would otherwise not have exposure to utilize. The talent available by outsourcing can range anywhere from low skill levels to perform repetitive tasks to highly sought-after specialized niche skills. Through technology, organizations now have more access to **global talent** than ever before. It is now easier to conduct business on a global scale and to set up international locations to provide international services strategically targeting domestic markets. Additionally, building on Jensen and Pedersen (2012), the ability to use a global workforce to tap into the globally dispersed talent and attain the best subject matter experts (SMEs) in a given field is now easier than ever before.

2.1.1 *One Language, Many Definitions*

Subcontracting evolved into outsourcing when the strategic partnership element was added along with ownership of processes. The widely accepted landmark deal that officially created the "outsourcing" industry was the famous 1989 IBM and Kodak deal when IBM became responsible for Kodak's Information Technology (IT) infrastructure. Due to their revolutionary arrangement, the term subcontracting was replaced by outsourcing (Applegate & Montealegre, 1991). The key factor in common was both organizations had a problem-solving objective that led to a more strategic partnership than with a typical subcontractor. **Variations on the definition of outsourcing** are still occurring but, in general focus less on business outcomes and more on transactional aspects of the activity. As with any "new" or recently developed field, researchers do not homogeneously agree on the specific definition of outsourcing (Tajdini & Nazari, 2012; Soils et al., 2013). For example, Banerjee and Williams (2009) studied outsourcing as a fee-based transaction service, pointing out conventional definitions illogically limit outsourcing to only a task-oriented exercise. They did attempt to include value creation in their definition but were limited from the start by their focus on out-tasking, such as fast delivery of non-critical services from the outsourcer's perspective. **Out-tasking** is related to repetitive low-value activities that organizations prefer their key resources not spend time on. Out-tasked activities can range from running a manual script, racking servers on a data center rack and/or providing a specific service on a project. These activities may bring value to an organization and truly be part of their strategic roadmap but may not qualify as strategic activities. For example, it may be part of an outsourcing strategy to use low-cost vendors who are available to perform tasks within a given time frame, however, the task itself is not part of the actual corporate strategy.

Soils et al. (2013) have a slightly different take on the definition as they highlight and refer to outsourcing from the perspective of the "make or buy" decision. In addition, from the operational perspective, outsourcing is seen as more than just a make or buy decision associated with cost reductions. Banerjee and Williams (2009) also focus on cost reduction as their central research concentration and their findings would generally align with Soils et al. (2013) in regard to cost importance as a bridging driver of the engagement's negotiation.

However, Fjermestad and Saitta (2005) take a different approach. They focus on outsourcing as not simply a make or buy decision to reduce cost. They view outsourcing as a strategic competitive advantage. Therefore, an organization may be able to position itself stronger in a new market or region. It may also provide services in a collapsed time frame than if it built its workforce through hiring, training, and development to meet the specific market demands. **The difference between subcontracting and outsourcing is the strategic aspect that outsourcing provides. Outsourcing** refers to the partnership with an outside service provider seeking a strategic competitive advantage through a mutually beneficial relationship.

The definition becomes more complex when we add the offshoring aspect. **Offshoring** refers to when an organization procures services or products from a firm located beyond their national borders (Murray et al.,

2009; Peslak, 2012). This terminology has been forming since the 1990s as well as the prioritization of preferred countries where to do business, such as China which has become the global go-to for production, and India for services (Erber & Sayed-Ahmed, 2005). **We will refer to offshoring as the business practice of an organization that sets up processes or operations outside of their base country**. It depends on the specific company's sourcing strategy and how they decide whether to offshore internally (through internal offshoring) or using a service provider. **Internal Offshoring means** the company seeks to offshore their operations outside the home country borders by setting up a supply chain to their home country and/or to other specifically targeted markets. They would essentially be buying services from themselves.

Internal offshoring provides organizations with an added capability to supply company demand that may lead to internal or external client deliverables. The major difference between outsourcing and offshoring is that offshoring is a task-based activity performed outside a country's borders and more focus on global strategy linked to seeking a productivity advantage (Jensen & Pedersen, 2012). Jensen and Pedersen (2012) focus on efficiency as a key indicator to prevent backsourcing from taking place. Jensen and Pedersen (2012) highlights that due to a range of evolutionary drivers such as trade liberalization, economic reforms, opening previously untapped markets, and increased information technology, companies who have global operations can now offshore services within their company.

An alternative offshoring option is to offshore within an outsourced environment. **Offshore-Outsourcing** occurs when the company looking to expand their market penetration or sourcing options in a specific country, dictates the environment to provide goods or services using an offshore service provider in the preferred country. In this scenario, the company looking to outsource would step into the engagement as they would any other outsourcing strategy, but with the goal to offshore. Conversely, an alternative offshoring scenario is outsourcing in an offshore environment. **Outsourcing-Offshore** is when a company chooses to outsource a process with the actual location strategy as a secondary consideration. This option may be associated with traditional outsourcing cost-saving techniques where the purpose is to outsource, regardless of where the services are provided.

Variations in the definition of backsourcing can also be found today. We established that outsourcing is a relatively young field. However, backsourcing is even younger, and agreeing upon the terminology is still in its formative stage. The recent literature on backsourcing has not fully adopted a common definition. For the purposes of our discussion, we will refer to **Backsourcing as meaning** the repatriation of processes previously outsourced.

Some authors, such as Hodosi and Rusu (2013) and Denning (2012, 2013) prefer the term "insourcing," while others such as Walterbusch et al. (2013) and Solli-Sæther and Gottschalk (2015) promote the terminology "backsourcing". I struggle with understanding why "insourcing" could gain popularity and be adopted to mean the ownership of previous outsourcing processes. If the word itself means to create inhouse it could become known as "inside-sourcing." Insourcing should be used when companies source from within. However, the action of bringing back processes should be referred to as "backsourcing." As in its simplest form, the word's literal meaning is to bring "back-sourcing" capabilities or "bringing sourcing back," home.

Thakur-Wernz (2019) elegantly and simply describes backsourcing as the "re-internalization" of an area that was earlier outsourced. Similarly, according to Solli-Sæther and Gottschalk (2015), backsourcing is the "reverse from outsourcing or offshoring." Keeping in mind there is a slight difference between outsourcing and offshoring, with outsourcing always deployed externally but not necessarily overseas. While offshoring could be deployed internally; some of the early-stage research reefer to using an exact understanding of backsourcing, which is a business practice that occurs when a contract ends and an organization brings their services back to their home country. Moving forward, whenever we refer to backsourcing, we will refer to the actions taken after the termination of an outsourcing contract. Referring to backsourcing after the termination of a contract provides a clear break between having services performed in-house and outside, as an outcome of a sourcing decision change.

2.1.2 Controlling Costs in Search of Outsourcing Success

Country selection is vital in an outsourcing relationship even if there is no client market associated with the country where the services are provided. For example, an American company may engage with an Indian firm to provide IT services to their Western European clients. In this scenario, the American company may seek a specific cost point correlating to desired skillset and the country's provider capabilities. Outsourcing service providers seek opportunities to supply services at lower operating costs to organizations in countries that have a reputation for paying higher wage and labor costs. This is the **cost country paradigm** which is focused on achieving a lower cost than available in the business' home country. As a direct outcome of outsourcing, countries normally associated with higher labor costs, such as Switzerland, may have the opportunity to obtain services from a lower cost country.

The commonly known lower cost countries are usually emerging markets with a thriving technology or specific industry supply. The lower cost countries may shift from low cost to medium cost countries and so on according to the maturity of their workforce. Another reason some of the lower cost economies may show increasing costs of doing business could be related to competition. Various multinational organizations may compete for the same pool of talented individuals driving salaries upwards and at the same time diminishing supply. The Fig. 2.1 shows a high-level salary to cost depicting of country cost classifications.

Making a vendor selection decision arguably could be the most crucial aspect of any outsourcing relationship. An organization may have all the processes in place, trained resources, and best intentions of engaging with an outsourcing provider, but will not be able to accomplish their desired

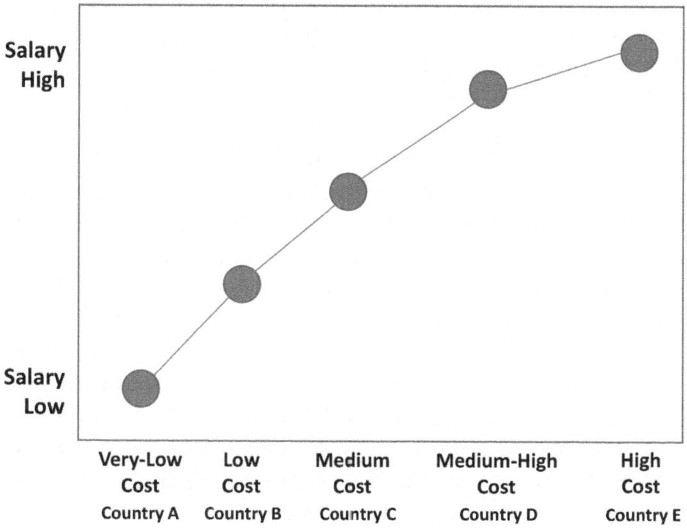

Fig. 2.1 High-level country cost classification

objectives if the vendor is neither willing, nor able to successfully work together. Organizations should review the value each potential vendor may add to their operating model. Some of the vetting criteria should entail **response time, warranty, price, provider financial stability and switching cost**.

Response time can be critical to customer satisfaction and selecting a provider within the same **global proximity can automatically reduce the perceived response time**. For example, when it comes to IT infrastructure such as server uptime, a minute of downtime can destroy potential SLAs and lead to hefty financial penalties. However, there are other non-financially burdensome activities that can have a negative impact on overall client satisfaction. For example, when conducting business in a global environment and working with multiple countries with lags in time zones. It is also especially important that both **the client and the service provider have the same understanding of expected response time**. Response time is the lead time it takes to act on a request including the accumulated wait time. For example, an outsource client places a call to a service provider and opens a service ticket to have an address changed in the system at 8:00 PM Central European Time (CET). However, the call center resources working on that specific ticket could be in Argentina working on Argentina Time (ART). In this example, the Argentina resources would begin their operating hours much later in the CET zone's day due to different time zones.

The lead time delays could be compounded by not having a prioritization system of tickets and a specific address change ticket may not have been worked on first thing the following day. As an outcome of this misaligned expectation, the outsourcing client could perceive that it takes two full days to change an address even though the service provider records it as being completed within one full business day. Having a mutual understanding and definition of response time would be critical to draft at the beginning of any relationship and contract.

Another key area that outsourcing clients could take into consideration, as a service provider differentiator, is the **provision of warranty**. The handling of warranty claims can help determine the overall trust in the relationship by how quickly a problem is fixed and the overall number of times that warranties need to be used. Including warranty as part of the agreement normally shows good intention specifically if the service provider covers transport and manufacturing rework. Additionally, this type of warranty would be a beneficial differentiator if the products were not accepted by the end user or failed to meet pre-agreed standards. There is frequently a trade-off between price and quality that organizations must consider. An organization may focus on price reductions but fail to secure the warranty requirements needed to conduct business. For this reason, it is critical for organizations to assess their complete outsourcing requirements and compare them with the proposed pricing and their own cost sensitivity.

Cost sensitivity is essentially the client's way to include price elasticity within outsourcing and is pushed to the forefront when considering the impact that originally accepted prices have on the engagement's overall satisfaction. Independent of quality of service, the **price structure** of an outsourcing deal may lead to the overall demise of the relationship. There are various pricing models which vendors can offer ranging from low initial 'bare bones' cost with a piecemeal approach, to the polar opposite all-inclusive **Global Service Agreement** (GSA). GSAs provide a pre-negotiated overall agreement of services and prices to be found within the outsourcing relationship. Most mature outsourcing organizations focus on negotiating prices lower than the cost of owning such processes themselves. Each year, global service agreements may include a price percentage reduction in response to having the overall infrastructure investment in place due to cost of servicing the client decreasing year over year. The price percentage decrease agreed upon is usually a percentage decrease from the previous year. However, if we were in the fifth year of a five-year deal, the cost reductions could be exponential due to the potential for contract renewal.

I remember working on a global IT infrastructure engagement where the first two years were a complete loss to the outsourcer. Although, we knew we were running at a loss, we were still hopeful as we had forecasted the third, fourth, and fifth year to be significantly more profitable, warranting the initial investment. The ideal scenario would be if the client would sign the contract renewal after the fifth year due to the heavily weighted costs incurred early on. Multiyear price reductions usually differentiate vendors during the selection criteria, and a financially stable vendor must be required when selecting an outsourcing partner.

The **financial stability** of an outsourcing provider should be taken into consideration before entering an outsourcing relationship. For example, an organization seeking to outsource their IT environment must feel comfortable the service provider has the finances to place staff, acquire hardware, license software, travel, cover associated costs for transitioning, build the infrastructure, and maintain the environment. Therefore, it is important to contract with a financially stable service provider who may not go out of business before approaching a key deliverable or deadline for which the outsourcing client is legally liable. Service providers should be financially stable and able to cover overhead to continue running the business through any potential payment disputes with a specific client. Preferably, or at a bare minimum, the service provider should not run its operations with just enough funds to cover its payroll month over month. Also, financial stability is quite important given any global outsourcing contract where the financial exchange reaches across multiple countries, exchange rates and complexity of **third-party associated costs**. Third Party vendors add complexity to any outsourcing deal as they may be responsible for providing key services or goods to a vendor who is then providing those goods or services to the main client. GSAs can include provisions to limit third-party suppliers and even restrict regions from which service is not desirable by the contracting client. Using third party suppliers may add more complexity to an outsourcing deal leading to increased switching costs.

Switching costs is another deterrent for a company to either back-source or change suppliers. Depending on the outsourcing relationship, it can prove costly to change suppliers. Some relationships can be so intertwined the supplier may even own the processes which are integral to the client's business operational success. The more intertwined the relationship is, the harder it may be to sever. Most service providers' dream is to have their processes deeply embedded with a client to increase the client's dependency on the supplier to provide services to the end user or even the client of the client. In that case, the outsourcing service provider would be in a strong position to negotiate for their existence and value. However, if the service client decides to look for an alternate supplier, it must take into consideration the cost of switching.

The switching costs may include having to buy back processes, standard operating procedures, hardware, software licenses, or anything else integral to the operations, which at that point could be owned by the supplier itself. The cost of switching providers may prove to be a deterrent for any outsourcing client to change suppliers and, as such, must be well managed, not only at the beginning of the relationship but throughout the contract life cycle. Suppliers may find it beneficial to add services to their original contract. As such, the value of the existing contract continues to grow while further embedding the supplier into the customer's operations. As more services are added to the original contract, the greater the possible service value provided. As the relationship grows the harder it becomes to sever the relationship. It should be noted, with the increasing value, the costs associated also increase. However, some of the increasing costs are sometimes labeled as "hidden" due to their lack of visibility in the original service agreement.

Hidden costs may not be obvious but can be associated with outsourcing costs either not budgeted or not clearly indicated as part of the original agreement or the GSA. The increase of hidden costs may also negatively impact the overall relationship satisfaction (Larsen et al., 2013). Hidden costs could range from refreshing a server that had reached the end of its life cycle, to the cost of transitioning from providing services in-house. The perceived hidden costs can include any type of cost the client had not foreseen or included in the budget. Some contracts may include a specific software but not the software implementation or maintenance. Some clients may perceive the lack of full-service implementation to be associated with hidden costs, while the service provider may label the additional costs as upsell opportunities.

A more detailed example of perceived hidden costs may be reflected in a contract that does not clearly state the servers hosting key databases needed to be migrated to a new server after a duration of time in their life cycle. This can be found within the pharmaceutical industry where it is the norm to refresh servers in order to secure information and increase speed. However, a pharmaceutical client may be in a situation where they must contractually pay for the migration of the design, development, testing, and possibly the new server itself, for example. Given such a scenario, the client may be in a situation where either they pay for the overall service or have to accept certain risk and liability associated with not refreshing their servers. As one can imagine, this cost would not be desirable to the client, if not previously budgeted. On the other hand, the service provider may not perceive these costs to be hidden but more in line with generally accepted costs of doing business and complying with possible regulatory standards. Another cost which may be hidden is the transition cost associated with entering an outsourcing relationship.

Outsourcing clients also have responsibilities to facilitate the outsourcing engagement. Both the client and service provider are mutually responsible for their success during their transition of responsibilities. Depending on the outsourcing matrix of responsibilities, certain processes may remain in-house which feed into other processes owned by the outsource service provider. In addition to supporting processes that feed into others, there may still be company-specific knowledge transfer and internal processes delineated by the client to the service providers which are integral to the overall success of the relationship. For example, as a part of an IT outsourcing contract, the knowledge transfer should be well documented and conducted during the transition stage. As in traditional business models, the **transition stage** is the time frame in which the initial change of ownership of processes from the client to the service provider occurs.

The transition stage is integral to the overall success of an outsourcing deal, as quality levels are set and the overall structure and performance expectations of the engagement. This stage also takes into consideration the transfer of resources, creation of processes, and the scope is further defined. Depending on how the contract is structured, the **transition costs** may include the cost of laying-off staff which may be redundant after the contract is in place, training the outsourced staff, having temporary staff in place who manage the transition from providing services in-house to having an outside vendor provide same services. Transition costs can further include having to create processes and standard operating procedures which may have never been created nor documented through simply being performed as part of the client's **Business as Usual** (BAU) practices. BAU is the generally accepted acronym referring to the usual business practices performed to accomplish daily activities and tasks that help to achieve overall operational goals.

2.1.3 Avoiding Operational Failure Through Service Agreements

Offshoring may ultimately increase the overall costs and negatively impact business-critical processes affecting the overall existence of an organization (Denning, 2013). Engaging in outsourcing may entail a multimillion-dollar investment with key valuable resources handing over their keys to the business and proprietary skills to service providers. Therefore, companies should understand, manage and be able to deal with not only the benefits but also risks associated with outsourcing. There have been a number of large multi-billion dollar outsourcing deals that have resulted in backsourcing such as Cable and Wireless, UK and IBM, Continental Airlines and EDS, as well as Sears Holding Corp and CSC which has recently merged with Hewlett Packard Enterprises (Veltri et al., 2008). The companies mentioned above are large organizations with the capability to engage in billion-dollar outsourcing deals. These large organizations chose to engage in outsourcing independent of their own capabilities to provide such services from within. One can argue their decision to outsource would be simple by taking advantage of their purchasing power as a means to negotiate an outstanding deal.

Despite this initial insourcing capability (yes, that would be insourcing as we are talking about services before they were outsourced), they decided to engage in an outsourcing relationship. However, something happened which made them change their sourcing strategy from outsourcing to taking back ownership of previously outsourced processes. In other words, they backsourced. The documented backsourcing trend has served multiple industries and is proof it is not specific only to the manufacturing, airline, or telecommunication industries.

Organizations would benefit from hedging against some of the challenges that are not overt. For example, one way of hedging against potential service provider challenges would be to implement **Service Level Agreements** (SLAs). A Service Level Agreement is the written agreement between the company performing the outsourcing services and the client. The service level agreements generally set the "level" and standards of responsibility for both parties involved and can include expectations of service related to quality and lead time and scope of service provided by each party. An SLA can include a statement defining the percentage of server uptime and lead time expected when responding to a service request.

Some organizations may impose financial penalties if SLAs are not met. These penalties are meant to serve as a **commitment guaranty**. For example, organizations working with global suppliers may face challenges if they are not designated as a **supplier's preferred customer** and may have to require supply chain adjustments to have products ready to ship and meet delivery lead times (Steinle & Schiele, 2008). There are multiple challenges when dealing with suppliers, such as that faced by not being a preferred customer. This specific challenge is quite real and not quickly noticed. As such, companies may not be aware their goods are taking longer to reach their intended customer base than needed because the supplier may have prioritized another customer. This logistics model may be an acceptable practice if it still meets the required SLA, and the organization is not being out prioritized by a competitor supplying the same region. In such a case, the company purchasing the services, or the "client" should evaluate the relationship and available opportunities. If the client continues to remain in that situation, they may lose customers due to time to market delays and ability to cover demand. Having agreed to SLAs with associated penalties in advance, may assist if the supplier hasn't designated preferred customer status to the contracting company.

Another point of caution in regard to SLAs is to carefully gauge the penalty amount with the service expectation to be provided. I worked with IBM assisting a global client to finish a large transition. It was late November, and the entire IBM and client teams were working day and night to assure the IT infrastructure environment was set and ready to be deployed prior to the end of year holiday break. Although we were two separate companies, it felt like one team helping each other achieve the overall IT readiness goal. This time of the year was incredibly special because most international consultants went to their respective homes to be with family and the local resources understandably also wanted to spend time with their loved ones during the December festivities. It became somewhat of an unspoken rule that we should all work much harder in November to spend time with our respective families back home. After working nonstop for seven days straight with only naps in between days, we decided to take a walk to a local restaurant and grab some fresh air and a quick dinner before going back to the office.

To my surprise I ran into an old acquaintance that worked for a similar company. He seemed fresh and full of energy in comparison to the walking zombie that I must have resembled. He was well respected within the industry, client circles, and honestly, I also thought he was brilliant. I was impressed with how sharp and rested he looked, so I had to learn his secret. I shook his hand with fear in my voice for not knowing the secret of his success, as if I was a junior consultant about to meet the company's CEO on my second day at work. I quietly asked him in an almost whisper level with what I can imagine was a cracking voice, the somewhat rhetoric question of "how are you dealing with the year-end madness"? To my surprise, he laughed and quickly responded, "what madness, I am loving it"! I was shocked! At this point, the thought crossed my mind that he was going mad! As I was starting to wonder about his mental health, he grabbed my shoulder and pulled me closer. Then he put his face right next to my ear and whispered, "it's more profitable for us to pay the penalties than to meet the SLAs". As you can imagine, my heart dropped!

I was immediately disappointed in him and his leadership when I learned that they had not communicated prior to missing the SLA, nor put a critical situation action plan in place to remediate the situation. That experience did teach me a couple of lessons that I still hold dear to this day. The first lesson was to never lower my own high-quality standards and provide lesser than previously commitment. This lesson is not as simple as continuously performing at a high level because there are senior executives that are also balancing out the cost of associated penalties against labor and operations at a client's site. This political conundrum must be navigated with extreme care. The goal is not to get fired for insubordination but fulfill the agreed commitments written in the SLAs. If there are commitments in the SLAs that are not attainable, then both companies should discuss the issues and agree on a remediation plan and settle on potential penalties before missing the deadline in the specific SLA. This way, both companies understand there was a problem and reset expectations. The second lesson I learned was that sales organizations must fully align with the delivery teams to draft relevant SLA to encourage both parties to comply and not severely damage the other, in order to meet the SLA. Although companies may hedge risks and find ways of adapting to suppliers' distribution channels, there still may be a quality discrepancy between performance and expectation of service (Malhotra, 2014; Soils et al., 2013). Even after drafting solid service level agreements, there can always be a subjective difference between what the customer has in their mind and what the provider delivers within the outsourcing relationship.

Furthermore, expected quality of a product or service can be subjective to either party's interpretation. The ultimate standards supplied often depend on the end client's purchasing power. Some clients may be extremely price-sensitive but not require such a high level of quality, while others may not be price-sensitive but may require a high-quality product or service to be provided. This is another reason why setting and documenting expectation is vital to the operational success of an outsourcing engagement. The **expected quality of service** is also a challenge that should be managed. **Quality is subjective unless it can be measured**. Quality is associated with the level and expectation of services provided by the outsourcing organization. Unless mutually agreed upon, the client's expected quality could range widely if all parties have not agreed to what success would look like at SLA creation. Independent of pricing, two different clients could have different levels of expectation around what they perceive as high-quality services. Examples could range from a client expecting to meet a specific SLA around solely dispatching a printer paper refill ticket by an onsite outsourced support staff, to something more comprehensive as a client expecting technical resources who already understand specific industry solutions and can help transition the printer capabilities to the cloud. Although, it is commonly accepted that lower quality service is normally associated with more inexperienced staff who are not able to address most client concerns and may even need coaching from the client themselves. Additional lower quality level concerns could be associated with having temporary solutions that are not sustainable or fully address the root cause of a problem. The importance of initial client and service provider alignment with the understanding of what "quality" means to each other and how to measure it should ultimately lead to a successful outsourcing engagement.

2.1.4 *Friends, Enemies, and Training the Competition*

There is evidence of the increasing trend of some companies simultaneously outsourcing and going offshore while others do the opposite. Google is a prime example of a company removing business formerly offshored. In 2010, Google decided to fully withdraw from mainland China due to factors ranging from human rights violations and cybersecurity issues to intellectual property infringements (Tan, 2018). Although not all backsourcing strategy changes are as extreme as Google's reaction to China's obstructive government actions. In fact, some research on internationalization suggests organizations may put their competitive advantage at risk and potentially lose valuable knowledge by outsourcing (Hodosi & Rusu, 2013). If this occurs, the organization inevitably faces the liability of foreignness.

Liability of foreignness is the cost that organizations face when doing business internationally compared to other local firms. The local firm has the home-field advantage. This is a significant advantage and extends to having access to local politicians, an understanding of the local culture and geographical norms. Multinational organizations aware of the threat and liability of foreignness have the option to develop strategies to counteract such risks. Some of the strategies that global firms deploy to fight liability of foreignness is empowering their local management with higher than average decision-making power that results in an autonomous environment where they can interact locally in a timely manner. Outsourcing to a local firm may also help reduce the liability of foreignness by partnering with a local trusted firm who is responsible for service output. Given all possible options, local firms should have the flexibility to work as the market demands, following local laws and **corporate ethical standards** provided by the outsourcing client.

An organization may find itself in a situation that may not be clearly legal or ethical in the home country. Hence, organizations seeking to do business in an international environment should write their ethical parameters before engaging in international business. It is important all firms conduct business within the legal framework of both parent and host country. However, organizations could find themselves in an adverse environment unless their ethical standards, values, and norms are fully written and communicated internally and externally. It is important to communicate internally to train staff and set expectations. However, it is also important to have ethical standards communicated to business partners and service providers to set the rules of ethical business practices.

This chapter does not detail the legal aspects of doing business internationally, it encourages all to follow the laws of wherever market they do business. Laws will differ from country to country and it is essential all laws from both home and host country are followed. On the question of whether to go ahead or avoid a grey area in business dealings; it is recommended to consult with the organization's legal team to avoid the potential for misconduct. Furthermore, most international corporations also have written corporate ethics which state their values. A corporation's ethics will also clearly convey the type of international business practices related to hiring and paying for labor they may or may not accept.

Global organizations seeking to partner with local suppliers for specific market penetration can and often develop mutually beneficial partnerships. However, these **partnerships can turn into competition** as the local suppliers grow powerful. Outsourcing organizations may become vulnerable after transferring critical and vital processes to their suppliers (Agrawal & Haleem, 2011). Unfortunately, local suppliers can also become direct competitors and provide the previously outsourced capabilities to the desired markets (Prahalad & Hamel, 1990). Competition is healthy and should be common to doing business. However, external competition from previously contracted direct suppliers may prove detrimental to doing business in a specific region. Competition from a previous supplier becomes more sensitive when it occurs in a country where the outsourcing client initially used the same provider to penetrate that local target market. The supplier may have the resources and local knowledge, but not the product or service delivery knowledge. However, the supplier may have attained their newfound expertise while providing services to the previous outsourcing client. So now the supplier could provide the same product or service at the same level of quality at a potentially lower price than the original company. This creates a competitor who knows the local market, the processes, and their internal business operations all from the original outsource client For example, automakers like GM, Toyota and Volkswagen have earned only a fraction of their potential revenue in China due to having to work with local suppliers who later develop their own cars, eerily resembling the European and American car designs (Shane, 2018). Therefore, the vendor and country selection process are crucial, and suppliers should be fully vetted before the start of any relationship.

2.2 Building the Backsourcing Body of Knowledge

The following section will begin to build the backsourcing body of knowledge. As backsourcing is born out of outsourcing, so are the community and the three major areas that support the creation of backsourcing. These areas cover the metamorphosis of Critical Success Factors, Risk Management and Outsourcing Strategy from outsourcing to the new backsourcing body of knowledge. The section begins with an introduction of the three areas as well as justification for borrowing from outsourcing and how their performance impacts the overall reasons to backsource. We then go into more detail and cover each area to understand its impact and how they are vital to the creation of the backsourcing body of knowledge.

2.2.1 First Steps Towards Building a New Body of Knowledge

The process of developing backsourcing's body of knowledge as a practice is still in its early stages. As of January 28, 2018, ProQuest research has only 49 peer-reviewed articles from scholarly journals dating back to 2003, with the majority of articles published in the last few years. This reflects an increased awareness of backsourcing. In order to begin building a BOK for backsourcing, I have pulled from well-established overlapping outsourcing communities or fields of study which include **Critical Success Factors**, **Risk Management** and **Outsourcing Strategy**. The largest amount of research has been conducted or recorded in these three major communities. However, there is rarely a debate about which community is the greatest outsourcing culprit leading to backsourcing. These communities mainly work independently where most research is focused on the specific silo and not cross-over as reasons for backsourcing.

Selecting these three communities provides a comprehensive cross reference for a successful outsourcing engagement. With the understanding that if the activities which are a part of these three communities are performed well, then backsourcing should be limited. However, the inverse is true if performing these activities at a sub-par level then the potential for backsourcing exists. The idea is that the available BOK has the ability to bring value to an outsourcing relationship if activities are performed well. However, if we follow this logic, then the inverse can also be true in that backsourcing would exist if the activities are not performed well.

Figure 2.2 shows the three bodies of knowledge with the cross foundational requirement being performance. As this work is aimed at starting to build a backsourcing body of knowledge, it borrows from outsourcing and assumes that if a specific area is not being performed well and adds no value, then the client would backsource. However, if an area is performing well and adding value, then that specific area is not contributing to backsourcing and the organization will continue to

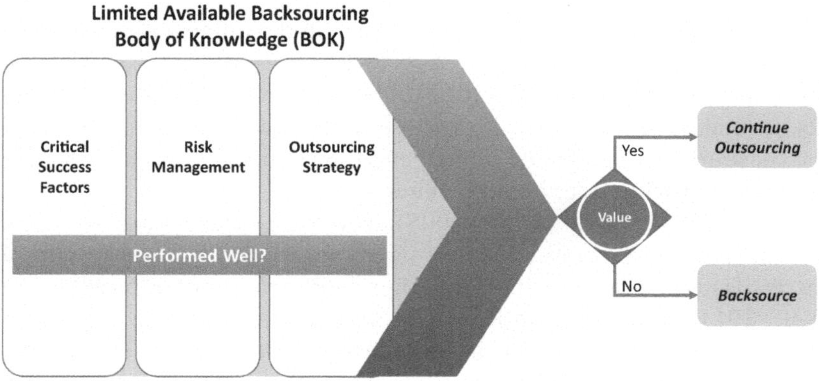

Fig. 2.2 Bodies of knowledge reviewed as part of the literature review

outsource. All areas are independent of each other since we are currently building the backsourcing academic community.

2.2.2 *Backsourcing Metamorphosis: Critical Success Factors*

The outsourcing critical success factors section is structured by beginning with a clear definition, followed by current business models including the application of available research, benefits, impact on backsourcing, and finishes with recently identified areas for improvement. Ultimately throughout this section, the focus is on the cross impact leading to a company's decision to backsource.

Within an organization, the **critical success factors** (CSFs) are the key elements necessary in achieving success and attaining its strategic objectives (Saraeenia & Monfared, 2015). Researchers such as Hodosi and Rusu (2013) have studied and made contributions to the outsourcing critical success factors body of knowledge through the benefits of continuous improvements. Hodosi and Rusu (2013) explained how key critical success factors could be detrimental to an outsourcing engagement if not achieved. There are multiple subcommunities within the critical success factor of outsourcing which heavily focus on a specific research area such as Ali et al.'s (2011) research on knowledge transfer between client and supplier impacting project success. In turn, we can take that view and turn it around to show the possibility for the opposite being true, where lack of proper knowledge transfer could lead to backsourcing. Another subcommunity focuses on maintaining a cap on the number of outsourced processes that would limit the need to backsource with process limitation research by Gulla and Gupta (2012). Their research highlights the benefits of limiting the quantity of processes outsourced and their effects. If the outsourced processes are limited and the relationship maintained, the potential to backsource should be limited.

Gottschalk and Solli-Sæther (2005) provide an excellent assessment of eleven academic theories and their significance when it came to critical success factors of outsourcing. Although their work is not as recent as Ali et al. (2011) or Hodosi and Rusu (2013) it provides a strong foundation on which to build upon. Their research was based on case studies and surveys that included IBM, CSC, and EDS, three of the largest global outsourcing providers. Their research was special through their originality as it supported the combination of success factors and academic theory into practice. Additionally, the data collection included exit strategies which can eventually lead to backsourcing decisions. Ultimately, the paper ranked the core competency and stakeholder theory as the two most critical factors of an outsourcing relationship.

The amount of research focusing on critical success factors of outsourcing around benefits attained and disadvantages is quite thorough. Iqbal and Aasim (2013) detailed this subcommunity and went as far as linking key advantages and disadvantages with key community contributors. They essentially created tables linking key areas of impact within the subcommunity and suggested authors to further review. Their study and applicability of CSFs shares the advantages and decreases the potential to backsource within an outsourcing relationship.

2.2.3 Backsourcing Metamorphosis: Risk Management

Risk management is defined as dealing with or controlling events, situations, or activities which may lead to potential losses (Qin et al., 2012). Risk management does not necessarily mean the potential for risk will or will not lead to the actual outcome. It is the process of managing and controlling the possibilities that an event will lead to unfavorable outcomes. Although the body of knowledge regarding risk management is quite extensive, there have been few studies on backsourcing decisions made based on risk management experience (Gorla & Lau, 2010). Risk needs to be minimized, as the potential exists which could lead to undesirable outcomes that in turn could lead to backsourcing (Denning, 2013) and (Wei & Peach, 2006). Some of the risks which need to be minimized to limit backsourcing include full or total outsourcing (Nattem & Proveniers, 2012): "high outsourcing cost, poor service quality, loss of control, changes in management, or changes in company strategies" (Kotlarsky & Bognar, 2012).

Kotlarsky and Bognar's (2012) research on backsourcing in Europe provides detailed examples of outsourcing deals gone wrong due to inaccurately managing risk. Their work adds to the current body of knowledge as it was conducted in a different region and with a larger sample, while not contradicting other authors who also research risk management, such as Nattem and Proveniers (2012), who focused on risk of scope of services to define risk. Kotlarsky and Bognar (2012) also focused on problems leading to backsourcing. However, their risk findings were limited to research in only two companies and focused more on the process, rather than the reasons behind the decisions to backsource. Although Gorla and Lau (2010) published their research two years earlier and went beyond Nattem and Proveniers (2012) and Kotlarsky and Bognar's (2012) findings. Gorla and Lau (2010) attempted to forecast the decision factors when reviewing whether to backsource versus outsource and found firms highly value vendor competence and vendor coordination when deciding to backsource. Interestingly, Kotlarsky and Bognar's (2012) findings indicated that high unexpected costs did not weigh on the decision to backsource. This is one of the few contradictory research stances discovered while completing this literature investigation.

Aman et al. (2012) found through their research that although cost may not be the driving factor behind deciding whether or not to outsource, we cannot ignore transactional cost theory, as it is imperative firms select cost structures to allow them to minimize transaction cost (Aman et al., 2012). Hence, Aman et al. (2012) has taken the stance between managing risk factors around cost being a key decision driver to backsource. Alternatively, Gholami (2012) felt strongly regarding the importance of managing the risk of client/vendor relations, budget and the rising costs of under delivering. Their work took the opposite stance from Kotlarsky and Bognar (2012) whose research indicated that a hidden cost or rising costs significantly weigh upon whether to backsource or not. Gholami's (2012) research takes a different approach when reviewing risk management and does not focus on cost management but prefers to investigate the pre-analysis risk management assessments companies fail to do prior to engaging in an outsourcing relationship. Gholami (2012) highlights the lack of risk firms are aware of when deciding whether to begin an outsourcing engagement.

Throughout my research on risk management outsourcing models, I am surprised to have not found an overwhelming amount of risk avoidance or risk management models for management applicability. For example, Juntunen et al. (2010) took the approach of comparing short-run versus long-run outsourcing gains, taking into consideration the impact of switching providers. Although their research is focused on shipping, the outsourcing findings should be easily applied across industries. Unfortunately, their model focused too much on the cost aspects of outsourcing and the risks of switching providers. On the other hand, Kremic et al. (2006) do provide an easily applicable decision flow approach that examines risk factors of making the decision of whether to outsource or not. They highlighted the importance of motivation, risks, cost benefits, and cost factors for outsourcing as applied to high-level decision flow criteria.

Although risk management within outsourcing is a relatively new concept (Shereazad et al., 2012), this chapter hopes to contribute and help build the backsourcing risk management body of knowledge. Shereazad et al. (2012) recorded ten major risk factors within outsourcing and their definitions. The ten types of risk factors included are schedule, technical, financial, vendor, culture, reputation, intellectual property, flexibility, compliance, and quality. If managed well the ten major risk factors should give the organization a competitive edge through outsourcing and also limits the need to backsource.

Shereazad et al. (2012) also provided a thorough overview of risks to manage, but it is difficult to deduce whether their rankings are from the perspective of the client or supplier. Suppliers want to also diminish similar risks but may have a different perspective. The study appears to specifically cater to the client's perspective. Regardless, it provides a wonderful basis scope to begin managing risks.

Aubert et al. (1996) introduced the four-tier IT outsourcing risk classification incorporating hidden cost, contract costs and lower quality of service as impacting on a firm's competitive advantage. They further point to cost variations and a lower quality of service provided as the major risk factors that potentially would lead to a diminished outsourcing relationship. As pioneers in outsourcing IT risk management, they went beyond that in 2004 by authoring *A transaction cost model of IT outsourcing*, where they were able to correlate unintended consequence risk factors and actual outcomes (Qin et al., 2012). Following the work of Aubert et al. (1996, 2004) one of the most complete studies on outsourcing risk management was created by Qin et al. (2012). Although their research focused on financial institution IT outsourcing in China, the model they created is applicable to any type of outsourcing across geographic locations. They created a relevant, yet simple flow showing that risk factors lead to risks, which then generate losses. Their model initially shares a process flow and clearly depicts the relationship between various risk factors.

2.2.4 *Backsourcing Metamorphosis: Outsourcing Strategy*

According to Chandler (1969) "Strategy can be defined as the determination of the basic long-term goals and objectives of an enterprise and the adoption of course of action and the allocation of resources necessary for carrying out those goals". Chandlers' definition is still quoted today by business strategy researchers such as Abdi and Awartani (2013) who studied balanced scorecards as a strategic management tool, and Ito et al. (2013), who researched inter-firm distance and its impact on corporate performance, resulting in a regression model that supports the conclusion that distance has an impact on sales. Although, the definition of strategy has basically remained the same, its applicability has significantly grown. Overall corporate strategy has rippled throughout company hierarchies and structures to now include corporate social responsibility strategy (Kilian & Hennigs, 2014), corporate law strategy (Bird & Orozco, 2014) and logistics strategy (Muhindo et al., 2014). Muhindo et al. (2014) provide a perspective ahead of their time through promoting part or full logistics processes, according to company need in order to remain competitive. Linder (2004) credits Nike's competitive outsourcing strategy, which allowed it to instead focus upon design and advertising, enabling the company to surpass Adidas in the footwear industry.

The industry is maturing and so are the outsourcing strategies. Recently trending is that organizations are moving away from deploying full outsourcing strategies that formerly included handing over their entire IT operations to large outsourcing providers and began implementing partial outsourcing models as described by Fedorenko (2014). His groundbreaking research has already proposed some alternatives to the backsourcing phenomena. His research studied logistics and what works best for customs trade, giving us the opportunity to expand their methodology into other fields and begin further researching partial outsourcing strategies. Additionally, we have Murphy et al. (2012) who was able to differentiate a firm's strategic position and describes when to select full or partial outsourcing model. Their study is significant because it considers various modes of outsourcing that include combining providers.

The importance of aligning corporate to outsourcing strategy has been thoroughly studied and supports the decision to align and incorporate the strategies (Fjermestad & Saitta 2005). Fjermestad and Saitta's (2005) research defines the importance of involving stakeholders as part of the decision to outsource and with ongoing outsourcing initiatives. They further proposed implementing a project board, involving suppliers and corporate management to align the outsourcing initiative to the business strategy. Fjermestad and Saitta (2005) research further helped the alignment of the implementation of information technology within outsourcing as a key transformation success factor. However, the importance of stakeholder alignment has now shifted from a strategic initiative to a critical success factor of a strategic outsourcing implementation (Hodosi & Rusu, 2013; Qi & Chau, 2013; Duhamel et al., 2014).

Solli-Sæther and Gottschalk's (2015) stages of growth research links maturity level and sourcing decisions by providing a progressive view of the outsourcing industry. Their research is brilliant in assessing the evolution of outsourcing, linking it to a company's sourcing strategy. They were able to define as IT demands shift, so will the sourcing needs. Their hypothesis resulted in that the level of maturity changes as companies gain experience in outsourcing and grows large enough to eventually backsource. They further described the evolution of outsourcing in the 1980s from an in-house staff function to now including backsourcing. However, it would be great to see their initial research expanded to cover partial outsourcing models that incorporate various aspects of the industry, such as mixing sourcing strategies to include partial outsourcing and partial backsourcing.

2.3 Conclusion

This chapter began with a quick overview of the benefits associated with outsourcing from both the client and the service provider perspectives. Outsourcing is a strategic partnership between both organizations and the strategic element that transformed subcontracting to become outsourcing. The term outsourcing is further reviewed to highlight the ongoing discussion within the industry that lacks full alignment on the outsourcing definition. The disconnect the term outsourcing has had rippled to the term backsourcing, as some authors misuse the term insourcing to describe backsourcing. As we are on the path to building a backsourcing body of knowledge we move on to the major costs that must be controlled to diminish the need for backsourcing. We review major cost-related success factors that may not be obvious to researchers working outside of the industry.

The cost control section takes a practitioner's perspective and helps the reader gain relevant knowledge usually attained after many years of industry experience. This consolidated industry perspective provides an overview of cost country paradigm, response time, warranty, price, provider financial stability as well as switching costs. We then look past the outsourcing veil to review the balance between service level agreements, commitment guarantees and expected quality. After reviewing the expected quality, we move to the liability of foreignness and caution on supplier selection. The selection process is vital to the success of an outsourcing relationship, as the supplier may have access to key internal processes and capabilities.

There is a risk the supplier may take what they have learned from the partnership and combine it to increase their own competitive market advantage to become a feared competitor. The areas covered so far provide an overview of advantages and controlling factors that must be managed to limit the need for backsourcing. However, backsourcing is thriving and the body of knowledge is currently forming. Hence, we move to the second part of the chapter to discuss the body of knowledge we are building.

The second part of the chapter began with an overview of the limited available body of knowledge within backsourcing and the justification for borrowing from outsourcing. We then begin reviewing the three most impactful outsourcing transferable academic communities that can lead to backsourcing if not performed well. These three areas are Critical Success Factors, Risk Management and Outsourcing Strategy. Each of the three areas is defined and list major authors in each field who have significantly contributed knowledge in support of a building new backsourcing body of knowledge.

Bibliography

Abdi, M. R., & Awartani, A. (2013). Business strategy and corporate identity using balanced scorecards. *Journal of Current Issues in Finance, Business and Economics, 6*(2), 213–235. Retrieved from http://search.proquest.com/docview/1626693094?accountid=42864.

Agrawal, P., & Haleem, A. (2011). Risk effect of it outsourcing on firm performance and value. *International Journal of Management and Information Systems (IJMIS), 16*(1), 55–68.

Ali, M., Al-Salti, Z., & Hackney, R. (2011). Factors impacting knowledge transfer success in information systems outsourcing. *Journal of Enterprise Information Management*.

Aman, A., Hamzah, N., Amiruddin, R., & Maelah, R. (2012). Transaction costs in finance and accounting offshore outsourcing: A case of Malaysia. *Strategic Outsourcing: An International Journal, 5*(1), 72–88.

Applegate, L. M., & Montealegre, R. (1991). *Eastman Kodak: Managing information systems through strategic alliances*. Boston, MA: Harvard Business School.

Aubert, B., Rivard, S., & Patry, M. (1996). A transaction cost approach to outsourcing behavior: Some empirical evidence. *Information and Management, 30,* 51–64.

Aubert, B., Rivard, S., & Patry, M. (2004). A transaction cost model of IT outsourcing. *Information and Management, 41,* 921–932.

Banerjee, A., & Williams, S. A. (2009). International service outsourcing: Using offshore analytics to identify determinants of value-added outsourcing. *Strategic Outsourcing: An International Journal, 2*(1), 68–79.

Bird, R. C., & Orozco, D. (2014). Finding the right corporate legal strategy. *MIT Sloan Management Review, 56*(1), 81–89. Retrieved from http://search.proquest.com/docview/1627695379?accountid=42864.

Chandler, A. D. (1969). *Strategy and structure: Chapters in the history of the industrial enterprise*. Cambridge: The MIT Press.

Cleary, S., & McLarney, C. (2019). Organizational benefits of an effective vendor management strategy. *IUP Journal of Supply Chain Management, 16*(4), 50–67.

Denning, S. (2012). Why Apple and GE are bringing back Manufacturing. *Forbes.com*. Retrieved June 16, 2014, from http://www.forbes.com/sites/stevedenning/2012/12/07/why-apple-and-ge-are-bringing-manufacturing-back/.

Denning, S. (2013). What went wrong at Boeing. *Strategy and Leadership, 41*(3), 36–41.

Duhamel, F., Gutierrez-Martinez, I., Picazo-Vela, S., & Luis, F. L. (2014). IT outsourcing in the public sector: A conceptual model. *Transforming Government: People, Process and Policy, 8*(1), 8–27.

Erber, G., & Sayed-Ahmed, A. (2005). Offshore outsourcing: A global shift in the present IT industry. *Intereconomics, 40*(2), 100–112.

Fedorenko, R. (2014). Development of outsourcing in the customs sphere. *Asian Social Science, 10*(20).

Fjermestad, J., & Saitta, J. A. (2005). A strategic management framework for IT outsourcing: A review of the literature and the development of a success factors model. *Journal of Information Technology Case and Application Research, 7*(3), 42–60.

Garg, N., & Jain, M. (2019). Outsourcing project management services: Making it work for IT or digitally outsourced projects. *IUP Journal of Business Strategy, 16*(4), 23–46.

Gholami, S. (2012). Critical risk factors in outsourced support projects of IT. *Journal of Management Research, 4*(1), 1–13.

Gottschalk, P., & Solli-Sæther, H. (2005). Critical success factors from IT outsourcing theories: An empirical study. *Industrial Management & Data Systems, 105*(5), 685–702. Retrieved from http://search.proquest.com/docview/234907751?accountid=42864.

Gorla, N., & Lau, M. B. (2010). Will negative experiences impact future it outsourcing? *The Journal of Computer Information Systems, 50*(3), 91–101. Retrieved from http://search.proquest.com/docview/287966343?accountid=42864.

Gulla, U., & Gupta, M. P. (2012). Deciding the level of information systems outsourcing. *Journal of Enterprise Information Management.*

Hodosi, G., & Rusu, L. (2013). How do critical success factors contribute to a successful IT outsourcing: A study of large multinational companies. *JITTA: Journal of Information Technology Theory and Application, 14*(1), 17–42.

Ito, T. A. K. A. O., Matsuno, S. E. I. G. O., Mehta, R. A. J. I. V., Sakamoto, M. A. K. O. T. O., & Ikeda, S. A. T. O. S. H. I. (2013, April). An analysis of inter-firms distances and corporate performance using DEC spatial model. In *Recent Advances in Energy & Environment Integrated Systems. Proceedings of the 2nd International Conference on Integrated Systems and Management for Energy, Development, Environment and Health (ISMAEDEH '13)* (pp. 80–85).

Iqbal, Z., & Aasim, M. D. (2013). Outsourcing: A review of trends, winners and losers and future directions. *International Journal of Business and Social Science, 4*(8).

Jensen, P. D. Ø., & Pedersen, T. (2012). Offshoring and international competitiveness: Antecedents of offshoring advanced tasks. *Journal of the Academy of Marketing Science, 40*(2), 313–328.

Juntunen, J., Grant, D. B., & Juga, J. (2010). Short-run vs long-run trade-offs in outsourcing relationships. *Strategic Outsourcing: An International Journal, 3*(3), 211–225.

Kilian, T., & Hennigs, N. (2014). Corporate social responsibility and environmental reporting in controversial industries. *European Business Review, 26*(1), 79–101.

Kotlarsky, J., & Bognar, L. (2012). Understanding the process of backsourcing: Two cases of process and product backsourcing in Europe. *Journal of Information Technology Teaching Cases, 2*(2), 79–86.

Kremic, T., Tukel, O. C., & Rom, W. O. (2006). Outsourcing decision support: A survey of benefits, risks, and decision factors. *Supply Chain Management: An International Journal, 11*(6), 467–482.

Larsen, M. M., Manning, S., & Pedersen, T. (2013). Uncovering the hidden costs of offshoring: The interplay of complexity, organizational design, and experience. *Strategic Management Journal, 34*(5), 533–552.

Letica, M. (2016). The effect of outsourcing activities selection on the benefits of outsourcing/UTJECAJ IZBORA AKTIVNOSTI NA KORISTI OUTSOURCINGA ZA PODUZECE. *Management: Journal of Contemporary Management Issues, 21*(2), 77–97.

Linder, J. C. (2004). Outsourcing as a strategy for driving transformation. *Strategy and Leadership, 32*(6), 26–31. Retrieved from http://search.proquest.com/docview/194373978?accountid=42864.

Malhotra, S. (2014). Impact of outsourcing on the organizations opting for it. *International Journal of Marketing and Technology, 4*(3), 115–122. Retrieved from http://search.proquest.com/docview/1520928652?accountid=42864.

Muhindo, A., Zhou, J., & Mzuza, M. K. (2014). Impact of logistics outsourcing strategy in oil and gas industry in Uganda. *International Journal of Business and Management, 9*(6), 187–198.

Murphy, P. J., Wu, Z., Welsch, H., Heiser, D. R., Young, S. T., & Jiang, B. (2012). Small firm entrepreneurial outsourcing: Traditional problems, nontraditional solutions. *Strategic Outsourcing: An International Journal, 5*(3), 248–275.

Murray, J. Y., Kotabe, M., & Westjohn, S. A. (2009). Global sourcing strategy and performance of knowledge-intensive business services: A two-stage strategic fit model. *Journal of International Marketing, 17*(4), 90–105.

Nattem, R. v., & Proveniers, A. (2012). Entrepreneurial cooperation. *Journal of Corporate Real Estate, 14*(2), 121–133.

Parahald, C., & Hamel, G. (1990). The core competence of the corporation. *Harvard Business Review, 68*(3), 79–91.

Peslak, A. R. (2012). Outsourcing and offshore outsourcing of information technology in major corporations. *Management Research Review, 35*(1), 14–31.

Qi, C., & Chau, P. Y. K. (2013). Investigating the roles of interpersonal and interorganizational trust in IT outsourcing success. *Information Technology and People, 26*(2), 120–145.

Qin, L., Wu, H., Zhang, N., & Li, X. (2012). Risk identification and conduction model for financial institution IT outsourcing in China. *Information Technology and Management, 13*(4), 429–443.

Saraeenia, E., & Monfared, J. H. (2015). Codification of strategy of customer relationship management system with CRM SCORE CARD case study of engineering, design and auto-part supply company for Iran Khodro Co. (Sapco).

Savitz, E. (2012). Outsourcing reversed: GM hiring back 3,000 people from HP. *Forbes.Com*, 37.

Shane, D. (2018). How China gets what it wants from American companies. CNN Business. Retrieved from https://money.cnn.com/2018/04/05/news/economy/china-foreign-companies-restrictions/index.html.

Shereazad, J. G., Gorod, A., & Sauser, B. (2012). Prioritization of outsourcing risks from a systemic perspective. *Strategic Outsourcing: An International Journal, 5*(1), 39–71.

Soils, A., Leavell, H., & Maniam, B. (2013). Outsourcing: Friend or foe to U.S. MNCs? *Journal of American Academy of Business, Cambridge, 19*(1), 337–342.

Solli-Sæther, H., & Gottschalk, P. (2015). Stages-of-growth in outsourcing, offshoring and backsourcing: Back to the future? *The Journal of Computer Information Systems, 55*(2), 88–94.

Steinle, C., & Schiele, H. (2008). Limits to global sourcing? Strategic consequences of dependency on international suppliers: Cluster theory, resource-based view and case studies. *Journal of Purchasing and Supply Management, 14*(1), 3–14.

Tajdini, S., & Nazari, M. (2012). IS outsourcing decision: A quantitative approach. *International Journal of Business and Management, 7*(2), 113.

Tan, K. M. (2018). Outsourcing and price competition: An empirical analysis of the partnerships between legacy carriers and regional airlines. *Review of Industrial Organization, 53*(2), 275–294.

Thakur-Wernz, P. (2019). A typology of backsourcing: Short-run total costs and internal capabilities for re-internalization. *Journal of Global Operations and Strategic Sourcing, 12*(1), 42–61.

Veltri, N. F., Saunders, C. S., & Kavan, C. B. (2008). Information systems backsourcing: Correcting problems and responding to opportunities. *California Management Review, 51*(1), 50–76.

Walterbusch, M., Martens, B., & Teuteberg, F. (2013). Evaluating cloud computing services from a total cost of ownership perspective. *Management Research Review, 36*(6), 613–638.

Wei, J., & Peach, B. (2006). Development of a risk assessment model for global information technology outsourcing. *Journal of International Technology and Information Management, 15*(4), 35-III.

CHAPTER 3

The Birth of an Industry from Backsourcing Pioneers

This chapter will take us on a journey together with industry leaders who have been around since the inception of outsourcing. Together we will uncover if backsourcing is a phenomenon or an industry evolution beginning to shape the future of outsourcing. As a part of this journey, we will uncover the tangible reasons why practitioners are beginning to backsource. We will be hearing from service providers as well as clients to capture both sides of the backsourcing origin story. The anonymous participants represent top companies from the pharmaceutical, retail, insurance, and aerospace industries. As an outcome of the conversations, this chapter captures the evolutionary transformation of outsourcing by examining three major areas. The three major areas that this chapter will cover in depth, which ultimately leads to backsourcing are: **Outsourcing Satisfaction Transforming Engagements, Location Strategy Defining the Future of Outsourcing**, and **Outsourcing Maturity Changing the Business Landscape** (Fig. 3.1).

L. A. Mederos, *The Future of Outsourcing*,
Palgrave Studies in Accounting and Finance Practice,
https://doi.org/10.1007/978-3-030-71407-9_3

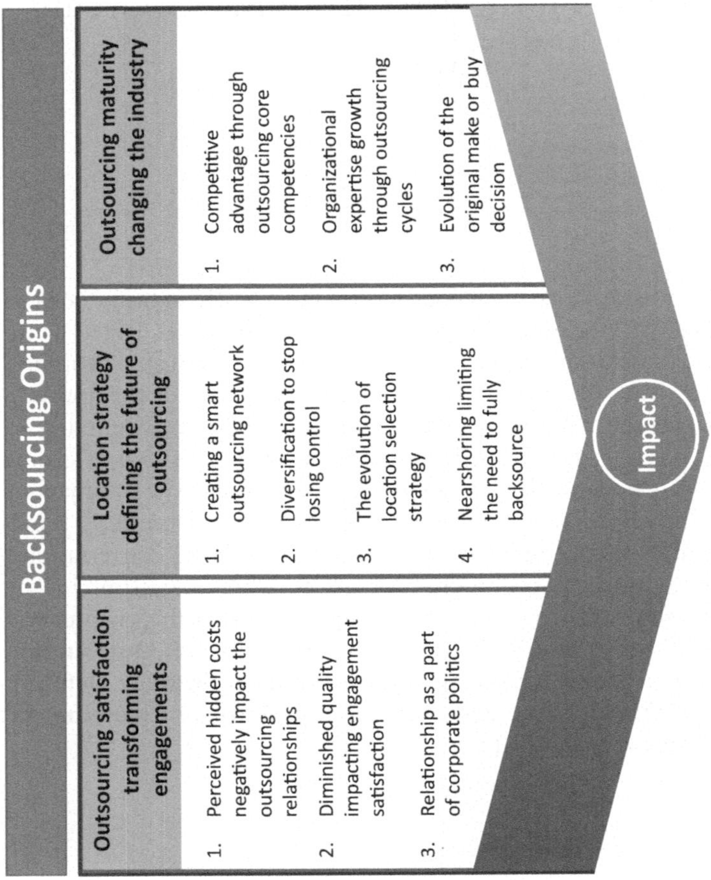

Fig. 3.1 Uncovering the backsourcing origins

3.1 Outsourcing Satisfaction Transforming Engagements

We begin the journey of understanding the background origins and what led to backsourcing becoming a growing business practice by assessing the relationship between engagement satisfaction and its impact on the outsourcing evolution. Outsourcing customer satisfaction management and improved services support organizations to improve their overall competitive position (Yoon & Kun, 2005). As we investigate creating an outsourcing strategy as a competitive advantage that reduces the need to backsource, we begin by taking a deeper look into outsourcing satisfaction as a practice to help us understand how it's application is shaping the future of the industry. After interviewing key outsourcing industry leaders, we begin to understand there are deeper complexities around engagements than only straightforward transactional behaviors. We have uncovered three major areas that can lead to backsourcing. These three major emerging areas that impact the satisfaction of an outsourcing engagement are: **perceived hidden costs negatively impacting the outsourcing relationship, diminished quality negatively impacting the engagement satisfaction** and **relationship as a part of corporate politics**. We will now cover three areas including direct quotes from practitioners as well as their impact on the industry.

3.1.1 Perceived Hidden Cost Negatively Impacts the Outsourcing Relationships

Increased costs within outsourcing can lead to decreased engagement satisfaction (Agrawal & Haleem, 2011). Outsourcing clients often find themselves dissatisfied with engagements due to their inability to budget for all possible associated costs (Agrawal & Haleem, 2011). Aligning on agreements and mutual expectations fosters longer term outsourcing relationships (Chen, Tu, & Lin, 2002). In addition, this investigation found that overall outsourcing satisfaction was negatively impacted due to misaligned expectations between service provider and clients due to hidden costs. The perception of hidden costs was found to be a significant reason that relationships were halted, and outsourcing clients began including backsourcing as part of their outsourcing strategies.

Perceived hidden costs can significantly impact outsourcing relationships as shown below through the interview of Participant 2 (P2). P2's interview associates the additional cost of outsourcing business as a hidden cost due to not originally budgeting for it. He was clearly not satisfied with his supplier due to their misalignment of his expectations. He describes below how he had to add expensive resources to the project in order to implement the solution which he was thought were included as part of the contract.

> **P2**: ...but sometimes [these hidden additional costs] I mean, I give you a case. For example, in the ERP that we're installing, there is a new POS solution, Point of Sale solution, okay? That is very, very new, okay? That even if you want to hire somebody out on the market that has expertise on that, you will not find it. Or if you find it, the costs are huge.
> [He was under the impression that the complete service was under contract. He does not appreciate having unpredictable hidden costs such as extended resolution lead times while cost is accruing hourly]

P2 perceives the additional variable costs as "hidden" because his organization had not budgeted for them as part of the overall solution cost. Conversely from the supplier's perspective, it could be that such costs are not hidden but variable and can be perceived as being upsell opportunities complementary to the contracted solution. Intrigued by the openness shared by P2, I asked him about any major cost deviations he had experienced. He responded with the following:

> **P2**: ...I would say that 20–25% deviations, either in terms of cost or time. This has happened!
> [20–25% cost and quality deviations can explain his frustration and dissatisfaction with the outsourcing engagement]

The 20–25% cost deviation experienced by P2 is definitely much higher than the documented industry average of 33% cost saving with only about a 6% deviation (Lee et al., 2012). P2 further explained his savings potential decreased due to the unforeseen costs. Another point made by P2 which caught my attention was that the organization he represented was quite elastic on costs. He was comfortable paying a premium for specialized services that were hard to find.

However, he clearly differentiated between operating costs and perceived additional costs which seemed to him, to be "hidden." As such, he differentiated two types of outsourcing. The first type was highly specialized niche skills which he was comfortable paying a premium and the second was to outsource low-level task-oriented services to focus on cost reduction. We will cover the first in greater detail later in this chapter. However, P2 revealed a growing dissatisfaction with spending his own time uptraining and developing the lower cost resources or as he refers to it, "getting them up to speed." He was also dissatisfied with the lead time for services to be rendered and their initial quality. In addition, he is not able to accurately assign a cost for the additional time he spends on rework due to quality corrections. Ultimately, his overall cost deviation increased by up to 25% from the original agreement. His perspective is important as it comes from the client's side and the part of the industry that fuels outsourcing demand.

Next, we learn about the other side of the story, the supply side of the industry. The comments below shared by Participant 17 (P17), an outsourcing executive with over 40 years of experience within outsourcing and currently working at one of the top five global service providers. Unfortunately, P17 is not the direct service provider for P2, but this perspective is important as it shows the supplier mindset when dealing with costs impacting overall satisfaction.

P17: ...the biggest cost normally is [ad hoc] labor, and that means that you have to find alternatives for those people.
[He is tasked with lowering client costs and has an increasing concern with low cost countries' increasing their costs which would ultimately impact the client's ad hoc services, not included in the contract]

Ad hoc services have a higher cost variability leading to lower satisfaction levels (Smogavec & Peljhan, 2017). P17 was tasked to provide additional services to the client from a country that was experiencing higher than budgeted costs due to their own outsourcing maturity and evolution. These rising costs would be transferred to the end client who was sourcing the ad hoc services. P17's comments below also indicate that misaligned cost expectations are a key risk of a successful long-term outsourcing relationship (Juras, 2007).

P17: Take [company name omitted] now some of our outsourcing customers now utilize cognitive data, utilize [well known product name omitted for anonymity] technology. They don't have that technology themselves. They believe that if they come to the company who has that technology, then they can actually get even better things through their outsourcing company.
[He is frustrated that clients expect services they are not paying for and will have access to because his company has a well-known line of business that provides that new technology. His cost of providing the service would severely increase if he met his client's "new" and unbudgeted technology expectations. He feels as if the client is expecting more than they contracted for and he can be provided within the original budget]

P17 was not satisfied with the overall client expectations or the status of their current relationship. Additionally, he is dealing with a counterpart on the client side who is also unsatisfied with the overall relationship. The counterpart expects to access services not contracted for nor included in the scope of the original agreement. The client views this misalignment as a hidden cost, and the supplier views it as out of scope but also understands it as the potential to cross-sell additional services. Either way, it still leads to outsourcing dissatisfaction due to costs not originally budgeted. Ultimately, this disconnect highlights that increased costs whether real or perceived can negatively impact the outsourcing relationship for both the supplier and client, which may lead to backsourcing.

3.1.2 Diminished Quality Impacting Engagement Satisfaction

Quality is a significant contributor to a successful outsourcing relationship (Soils, Leavell, & Maniam, 2013). This section relates how the perceived quality of outsourced services impacts the overall outsourcing satisfaction. This section also explores the transformation of outsourcing engagements by reporting on the experiences of practitioners. The premise through this section is overall outsourcing engagement satisfaction will be negatively impacted if the agreed-upon outcomes measures of quality are not met. The below examples attempt to dig deeper into the experiences of tenured outsourcing industry professionals to provide a complete picture of the relationship between quality and engagement satisfaction.

I was fortunate to have access to the Chief Information Officer (CIO) of a large global retail company to contribute to this research. We will refer to him as Participant 1 (P1). Although he is a global CIO, his P# classification here bears no relation to his importance as a research subject. The P# classification was used to allow participants' anonymity when I was worked with their data contributions. At the time of the interview, he had 19 years of experience within outsourcing in both the pharmaceutical and retail industries. He also worked throughout Europe and the US on key executive roles on both the supplier and client side of the outsourcing equation before becoming a client-side CIO. Below we review his response when I asked whether he had ever utilized backsourcing.

P1: Well the absolute answer is yes! And the word is called quality! So in the majority of the locations there is of course a reason why you backsource a process or activity or a workload or a production or so on and so forth, but I've got to say that sometimes, or lately the most common trend I see those in certain, it's just right before, quality! Quality is missing! Quality in overall terminology of the word quality! So, a good quality of finance is when you calculate location product or across manufacturing calculation of an item and it can be quite wrong.
[Values high quality and has been let down by outsourcing providers. He is dissatisfied with his providers due to quality failures in most of their outsourced services and believes that outsource providers do not value quality. It is the main reason his company is backsourcing]

Companies consider quality as a key feature in their value proposition (Lacity, Rottman, & Khan, 2010). Quality expectations must be met regardless of the location from which the outsourced products or services are being supplied. Similarly, P1 shared his view that quality was the main driver for him to backsource. The comments below highlight when the provider noticed a lesser quality in their overall processes ultimately leading to diminished outsourcing satisfaction.

P1: ...many companies are backsourcing and its because in order to be efficient in that business, you need to have very good process

outputs and the outputs of the processes which are executed over the last five to ten years I can say, it has been in a continuous decrease in quality.
[His sentiment toward outsourcers is they are lessening the quality year over year. He is disappointed with the providers due to lack of process focus and maintaining the quality measures agreed to in the contract]

It appears there had been an industry-wide acceptance of lower quality standards. In response to this phenomenon, organizations are beginning to refocus on quality within their outsourcing engagements. The below response is in support of outsourcing as long as the satisfactory quality meets the expected price point.

P1: ...only if the process is robust enough, mature enough, documented enough... then it will be...quality compliant to outsource...
[He does believe that if done correctly, outsourcing adds value. He is not against outsourcing; he is just against low quality outsourcing not meeting the original expectation aligned with price]

P1: ...the company spent three times more money trying to make those [outsourced] processes run. But clearly, they could have let those processes be housed and backsourced them... It's quite a very good example of a very, very big failure in outsourcing processes of the late 90's and it was from Switzerland to India.
[His past experience with low quality outsourcing negatively impacting the overall outsourcing satisfaction led to an outsourcing failure]

I observed that the more senior professional participants were more open with their answers and freely shared both successes and failures from which they learned. P1 was quite open by sharing his negative experiences around outsourcing quality that led to his support for backsourcing. Although, mutual expectations of both parties must be aligned when outsourcing (Chen et al., 2002), there was an unacceptable gap in P1's expectation of quality from his suppliers. There was a clear gap in service expectations between P1 and what the service provider was offering. This gap in service expectation was the main driver that led to the deterioration of the satisfaction in the relationship. Most significantly, P1 appeared to have lost faith in quality outsourcing and listed it as the main reason to backsource. His sentiments toward attaining the expected quality output levels were strong and were not based on one project but after a long history working with India where he experienced rework and quality failures while pursuing a cost advantage. Differing quality expectations proved to be a significant factor driving the backsource decision. Most participants ranked quality as one of, if not the main driver for backsourcing. Furthermore, most participants concurred that outsourcing satisfaction could not be attained unless quality expectations were also met.

3.1.3 Relationship as a Part of Corporate Politics

According to Misra (2004) corporate politics can take precedence over doing the right thing. This section investigates how an organization's internal staff maneuvering may negatively affect relationships on which the corporation's outsourcing decisions rely. We will review direct quotes from participants to show us how organizations deal with relationships and corporate politics as they play out during outsourcing engagements.

Participant 21 (P21) below, was an executive based out of Germany who had experienced a situation where the technical aspects of the engagement were satisfactory, but unfortunately, the relationship between the provider and client suffered. Although the services provided were being performed as agreed, the success of the overall project was in jeopardy due to the politics around managing their relationship.

P21: The relationship part by the way, is one of the most important for successful outsourcing [criteria]. I have seen where trouble started with relationship and with governance and not mainly on the technical side.

[He has seen contract problems due to lack of relationship management impacting the political landscape]

The interpersonal relationships formed and nurtured during outsourcing are integral to the success of engagements (Ulbrich, 2009). Hence, relationship maintenance is a key success factor and can lead to overall dissatisfaction of an outsourcing engagement and directly leads to backsourcing. The response below is from Participant 19 (P19), an executive with over 25 years of outsourcing experience and formerly had global responsibilities including as Chief Technology Officer (CTO) for a global health insurance company. At the time of the interview, he had an executive role at a top global outsourcing provider. His response sheds light on the importance of relationship management when dealing with corporate politics.

P19: Absolutely [corporate politics in outsourcing]. There's a lot of politics…because decision to outsource is made at the…top level and there is always politics. I think also decisions for outsourcing in some cases are made because they wanted to have kind of a change and were not able to execute…
[Acknowledges corporate politics but also sees how outsourcing can help execute key projects]

P19 shared an interesting perspective on how utilizing service providers can help an organization shape their future by implementing changes programs which they otherwise could not politically take on. This is an interesting perspective as there are two sides to the corporate politics game played within outsourcing. The first is that an engagement's quantifiable success may have no merit due to political adversaries gauging or even commenting on the project's success. However, conversely, as P19 mentioned above, politics can help organizations seeking to cut through their internal politics and deliver on projects that the company itself may not have been able to achieve internally. Similar to P19, with over 30 years of experience, Participant 16 (P16) has significant global experience in outsourcing and held various senior leadership roles. Below is his response in regard to experiencing corporate politics and their effect on outsourcing satisfaction.

P16: …from a corporate point of view, this strengthens some departments, I would bring it back to the leader. How did the leader get strength and influence when something gets outsourced?

> So that point of view, there might be for sure politics around for the [daily senior decisions] of outsourcing.
> [He clarifies, daily, relationships and corporate politics must be addressed as an ongoing part of outsourcing. It looks as if the higher people ascend on the corporate ladder, the greater the relationship factor and politics play a role in their ongoing success]

P16 also shared how corporate politics also play a part in the deal and are important to the relationship's success factors that drive outsourcing satisfaction. Relationship building allowed him to attain stakeholder buy-in and support for outsourcing success (Bennett, Verwey, & van der Merwe, 2016). Below we share an interesting perspective from Participant 7 (P7). He had a junior executive role on a $500 Million USD plus, global outsourcing deal and over eight years of experience on the supply side of outsourcing. I found it fascinating how she mentioned seeing leaders use corporate politics as a shield from making key decisions. Her words describe the situation below.

P7: ...because the decision makers were so high up in the organization that the...practical problems were not very effectively addressed...had operational execution issues. Because basically the highest management levels that actually had the decision-making power...were speaking through one of the strategy consulting houses.
[Senior management created a political layer between them and the operational resources through a consulting company]

Some leaders shield themselves from making decision as a strategy to avoid providing the wrong direction (Ulbrich, 2009). What I personally found outrageous was those leaders viewed indecision better than making a bad decision. Hindsight is 2020 but I can just imagine the type of political environment in which they were working, one where they prefer to slow down and bypass opportunities than face the repercussions for not choosing the best alternative. Unfortunately, the political layers negatively impact outsourcing engagements and do not end here. In another example shared, the IT department had no power to decline requests leading to an overwhelming cost increase. The company decided to bring in an outsourcing provider to deal with their internal struggle. One could say they essentially outsourced their internal corporate politics. Participant 15 (P15) was one of the executive resources the service provider brought into address the corporate politics of the deal given he had close to 20 years of experience in outsourcing within the pharmaceutical and airline services industry.

P15: ...The company cannot fix it themselves because they don't have power over the business and outsourcing is a very elegant way to make this somebody else's problem. Politically, that is very important...you should not underestimate internal politics!
[Using a provider to cut through the senior management internal politics]

P15's experience confirms the higher one climbs in the corporate hierarchy, the more corporate politics come into play (Bennett, Verwey, & van der Merwe, 2016). In this situation, P15 witnessed how an organization navigated the corporate political landscape by essentially outsourcing the problem. Ultimately, the way that political relationships are managed can mean the difference between positive or negative outsourcing satisfaction which can lead to backsourcing.

3.1.4 Impact of Outsourcing Satisfaction on Backsourcing

The outsourcing relationship satisfaction is a key contributor to the overall success of the engagement and advantage being sought (Yoon & Kun, 2005). This section provides insight about the significant impact outsourcing satisfaction has over the decision to backsource based on interviews with outsourcing industry professionals. We were able to see that backsourcing is now a tangible option for organizations that are experiencing lower than expected outsourcing relationship satisfaction levels. Three areas emerged which have the most significant impact on achieving overall outsourcing satisfaction and could lead to backsourcing are: **perceived hidden cost negatively impacting the outsourcing relationship, diminished quality negatively impacting the engagement satisfaction** and **relationship as a part of corporate politics.**

Perceived hidden cost was shown to negatively impact the overall client satisfaction when clients experienced an unplanned cost increase. We were able to explore both sides of the story as well as the "perception" by interviewing both clients' and service providers' in this research. For example, clients experienced a decrease in outsourcing satisfaction due to unexpected and unbudgeted cost increases impacting their overall expenses. This cost misalignment put outsourcing clients in an unfavorable situation so they had a larger demand for services than the budget planned to cover them. On the supplier side of the story, there are two major aspects impacting upon overall client satisfaction. The first is that ad hoc charges are not included in the contract and can have a significant financial impact on the engagement if such services are needed. Additionally, seeking highly specialized services can add to the originally budgeted expense if not included in the original contract. Additionally, outsourcing service providers shared situations where they witnessed unrealistic client expectations in regard to receiving services or products which were never part of the original agreement.

The interviews revealed the perceived **quality of service provided** by outsourcing providers had a significant impact on the overall relationship. Some participants shared their perspective on expecting various levels of quality and indicated that such decreases in quality were the main reason for backsourcing. They further added that decreased quality of outsourced processes was increasingly becoming the norm.

The third major area that emerged driving the overall outsourcing satisfaction was **relationship as a part of corporate politics**. We saw decisions to outsource being made at a senior level and unfortunately, sometimes the tangible success criteria of an engagement were disconnected from the project impact it provided, due to the political environment surrounding the initiative. This was interesting as it shows how relationship management can have a detrimental effect on a deal even when services are meeting expectations. Furthermore, we learned how organizations may use outsourcing to bypass internal corporate politics or use it to add additional layers between senior management and front-line resources to hedge against the potential for making the wrong operational decisions. We were able to share how political relationships have an impact on the overall success of the outsourcing engagement which may ultimately lead to backsourcing when not managed appropriately. Outsourcing satisfaction must be managed in order to achieve successful engagement and diminish the need for backsourcing. As an ultimate outcome of the interviews we can conclude the **potential to backsource is increased when outsourcing satisfaction is decreased** (Fig. 3.2).

3.2 Location Strategy Defining the Future of Outsourcing

According to Sao and Gupta (2013), the locations from where outsourcing services are provided have been heavily criticized since the nineties as being a major factor for sub-par outsourcing capabilities. We will explore location strategy as part of this section and its evolution as it impacts backsourcing. Outsourcing can be performed in a local, near shore or offshore environment. Local outsourcing may be geographically located within the same country or the same city. Nearshore is basically how it sounds considering that the shore of a country could be water or its physical borders. Offshore is geographically located further away from its regional neighbors and possibly in a different time zone. This section provides commentary from industry leaders sharing with us the evolution of location strategy and how companies are now leveraging near and offshore locations as part of their backsourcing strategies. We will review four major areas that lead to backsourcing when considering location strategy. The four emerging areas are creating a **smart outsourcing network, diversification as a means to stop losing control, location selection increasing backsourcing risk**, and **near-shoring limiting the need to fully backsource**.

3.2.1 Creating a Smart Outsourcing Network

Supplier diversification is the practice of using multiple outsourcing providers for the same or multiple processes. Essentially it results in the client diversifying their vendor portfolio to not rely on one or a few specific suppliers. The practice of engaging with multiple suppliers can also allow organizations to attain better pricing, hedge against any unreliable supplier and ultimately improve profit (Feng & Shi, 2012).

Outsourcing dissatisfaction appears to have been the melting pot for innovation within the pharmaceutical industry. I had a conversation with Participant P26 (26), an outsourcing executive with over eight years of experience in the pharmaceutical industry including working on both sides of the outsourcing relationship. He was currently working on the

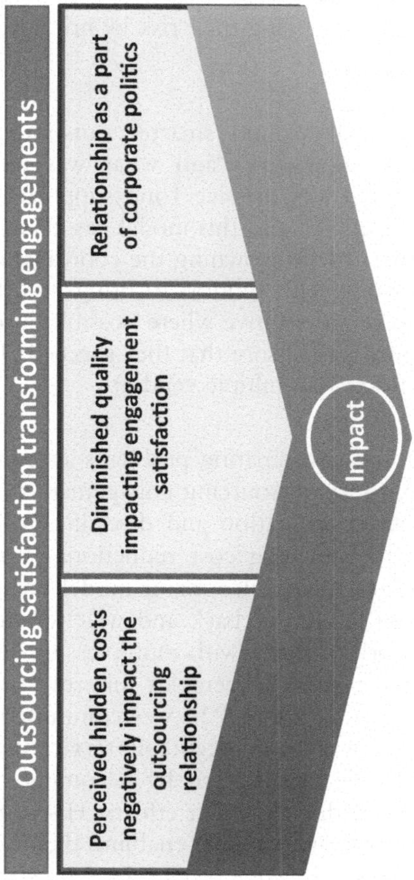

Fig. 3.2 Outsourcing satisfaction transforming engagement

client side for one of the top three pharmaceutical companies worldwide. The below shows how he has handled the risks of having one major supplier, as legacy outsourcing supports having one main outsourcing provider own most of the processes to achieve economies of scale. However, the economies of scale also bring complete dependency on the supplier's promise of delivery. Below we read how P26 explains the way his organization dealt with diversifying their risk by not having one main supplier.

P26: I would say it's all around smarter outsourcing... and if I compare back eight years ago what was pursued as an outsourcing service was massive [one supplier deals]. I just cared about the delivery and this model has changed to a joint model where the...client is owning the coordination.
[His company works with vendors to bring back their services but also to help vendors thrive where possible, also supporting them with resources to ensure that they succeed. They are now coordinating efforts via multiple vendors]

Vendor incompetence and coordinating problems account for significant cost impact and risk to an outsourcing engagement (Gorla & Lau, 2010). Therefore, supplier coordination and diversification in a multi-location network is key to achieving cost reductions (Konno, 2017). Participant 26 acknowledges their outsourcing model has evolved to a partnership where they no longer sit back and wait for deliverables as they once did but now work together with multiple suppliers in various strategic locations to ensure their deliverables fully meet the expected outcomes and lead times. In addition, P26 was committed to stepping in at any time if there ever was an unacceptable service deviation. This client-side support could only be achieved by becoming embedded in the supplier network and coordinating their efforts. His company implemented a multi-vendor coordination model enabling them to not rely on a single vendor. They also developed a vendor support structure where they are ready to step in and "bail out" any struggling vendor.

P26: ...if you see that the vendor struggles in the implementation phase because they need some more relays in the transition then you can bring back some transition ownership tasks, back to

> the company, to the client. So, you aim the vendor to be more efficient in the deployment, so it goes in our interest.
> [His company developed a model where they step in and support under-performing vendors]

The approach described by P26 above is a **smart outsourcing network** where the client steps in and supports underperforming suppliers to decrease the discrepancy between expectation and overall delivery of service. However, P26 had to implement solid service level agreements (SLAs) in order to hedge against their suppliers deviating from their commitments (Malhotra, 2014) and (Soils et al., 2013). P26's organization went beyond the set expectations and teamed up with the supplier to assure the SLAs were followed and supported them in their efforts. Coordinating the various vendors empowers them to have their fingers on the outsourcing pulse. This allowed them to develop an interesting vendor management model that fosters coordination while stepping into take back services that need the client's support. Initially, this could be interpreted as backsourcing, but it was only used for a limited time and with the focus on business continuity supporting the suppliers through a challenging time.

3.2.2 Diversification to Stop Losing Control

Losing control as used in this section, refers to when a client who is sourcing services or products and lost control of either their influence, decision power or even the overall processes necessary to providing a service or goods to their own customers. The evidence below shines a light on the impact that such loss of control is having on engagements and how organizations are using cost as a means to justify backsourcing control. This section covers how **organizations are diluting their historical one supplier outsourcing engagement to now diversifying and using multi-vendor / multi location strategies to regain control**. The evidence shows how executives and professionals are reacting to the loss of control facing outsourcing customers today and their response. The reporting below attempts to reveal shifts in control between client and supplier.

Participant 9 (P9) shown below also has both client and provider knowledge with over 10 years of professional outsourcing experience. P9 felt strongly that backsourcing was the road to regain control of confidentiality, loss of process and decision control within the pharmaceutical industry. **Loss of control is a key reason for companies to change their outsourcing strategy** (Kotlarsky & Bognar, 2012). Below is the response by P9 when I asked him if he was bringing back services in-house or just changing suppliers.

P9: …When they do backsourcing, they want to keep the control…So basically, they use internal resources for backsourcing. Also, you need to engage external capabilities to have the strategy to backsource, you know, in place to take the control and then you can continue. The company can continue internally…. Another one would be the loss of control…Because I mean as I mentioned before, pharma is really, you know, confidentiality. That's the business.
[Contractors are bringing services back, not fully in-house]

P9 reports witnessing outsourcing clients using contractors to help bring services back from suppliers. They broke out of the one supplier model and engaged with multiple vendors. The backsourcing efforts were not focused on bringing the overall processes from the various suppliers back in-house but instead at diluting the supplier control by bringing back management and coordination activities. He shared dissatisfaction with his current outsourcing engagement and stressed that control was a major reason for his client to backsource. He was also concerned that key decisions were being made by the service provider at locations where the client no longer has a strong presence. Making these decisions by the supplier could lead to the client losing confidentiality through further losing organizational control over decision-making. This was highlighted by having resources shift from the client to the service provider. It is common that resources shift employers from client to supplier as part of an outsourcing contract. However, these resources took their institutional knowledge and their ownership responsibility. Sometimes the same staff continued to work on their previous responsibilities which were now out of scope, from a supplier perspective. We dig deeper into decision control with the help of Participant 19 (P19) who was an outsourcing services provider executive and describes this scope shift below.

P19: One is to see the blurring of the companies I mean towards their customers so the ecosystem [control] is changing. I think this has an impact because if you don't know exactly where your responsibility ends then its better.
[Decision control lines are becoming fluid between supplier and client. Responsibilities are becoming blurred]

P19 views this scenario positively given his organization can take control of blurred responsibilities in order to make an impact and have the client rely more on his services. Alternatively, professionals representing the client perspective mentioned that having one main supplier limited their decision-making ability since the supplier makes most decisions for the outsourced services. Ultimately, this **loss of control resulted in outsourcing clients diversifying through going away from one main supplier and using multiple suppliers within multiple locations** while using cost as justification.

P19: Then maybe also it could be that through the unbundling of services they consider that they have a chance to be [more independent], achieve even more cost savings because I mean the bundling of services as a full service provider offered you to basically... you have the chance to absorb some or the subsidized part of your services...the demand or requirement to get control back.... and procurement gets more and more strong.
[He has seen clients unbundle their services to 'unbundle' the control and use cost to do it. They now want to have in-house cost control measures in place. He is seeing procurement departments get stronger and stronger through implementing this strategy]

Suppliers have been diversifying their provider locations to attain cost advantages by taking advantage of low-cost countries in offshore locations. However, it appears that clients are now also taking the diversification strategy to impact their own operating costs. Professionals interviewed confirmed this approach by admitting that they were also using cost as a means to diversify their supplier base in order to limit control. More so, they were **using supplier diversification to also bring**

services back by employing contractors and not necessarily bringing services back in-house, as shown below.

> **P19**: It's astonishing to see them in companies which are traditionally in the outsourcing area that kind of slice and dice some stuff, but the coordination is being done by subcontractors... I mean I have noticed this in the various industries and large companies that I have come across which range from a more or lesser, you know, range through this sourcing model and they basically took it back [control]. But then if you look, if you really check who was working, you know, with your peers that you're working with it's not necessarily an internal resource and many optic cases it's basically a contractor.
> [Backsourcing was not done through the company directly, but through a contractor. The **company retained decision control but did not fully backsource the services**. They took control back by breaking away from one major supplier to using multiple]

P19 witnessed something different than most participants had seen. He had access to more privileged information due to his wide network of contacts and senior level. He saw an organization backsource services that were spread across the globe to regain control. We can see how **companies are separating outsourcing services from one or a few key suppliers to multiple suppliers**.

This section covered how organizations are breaking up the control of one or few suppliers by diversifying their portfolio to **dilute the main supplier's control**. We heard from practitioners how they are losing key decision-making capabilities and how their sourcing strategies are evolving to reduce the supplier side control. This outsourcing evolution includes outsourcing clients backsourcing the control and coordination capabilities but not fully backsourcing the complete processes. The aim of this advanced sourcing strategy is to dilute the power from one major supplier and spread it across multiple providers while separating the control and coordination from all of them.

3.2.3 *The Evolution of Location Selection Strategy*

Organizations have the option to implement a location strategy to take advantage of emerging economies and an expanded talent pool with lower wage costs (Mrsik & Kostovski, 2017). Location strategy is defined as a strategy that targets the most optimal locations for contracting outsourcing services. The multiple layers of location strategy are particularly interesting from the vantage point of **three separate streams of thought** that emerged from my conversations with industry leaders. The **first group** supported outsourcing regardless of location. The **second group** were hesitant to outsource anything further than to a nearshore location. With the **third group's attitudes** being somewhat of a hybrid, they were comfortable with outsourcing certain processes regardless of location. However, they were hesitant when it came to higher level expertise. This last group found a balance to continue outsourcing higher level services but in a nearshore environment.

The first example shown below highlights the **positive sentiment independent of distance to home country**. Participant 9 (P9) with over ten years of experience in the pharmaceutical industry, in both outsourcing and backsourcing is an industry expert (client) and consultant (outsourcing provider).

P9: I don't think [location makes a difference] to be honest. I don't think that because you deliver it from China or from India will provide an un-satisfaction of these services. What I think is your organization and the capabilities and the skills you will use that can provide a different outcome, not the location. I'm not agreeing with the location. I'm agreeing that the location will have a, the resources or the... priority is just to have all the tools in place and to have a deployment of, and training of your capabilities in the outsourcing countries.

[He feels that location is not relevant to outsourcing as long as the outsourcing company has set up the infrastructure to do so]

The recent growth in technology has allowed outsourcing locations not to play as significant of a role in location strategy as they previously did (Sao & Gupta, 2013). P9 shared the legacy globalization perspective where offshore outsourcing location selection does not necessarily sway the decision to backsource. However, the opposite perspective was shared below by P19 who discussed why it was **not possible to outsource certain services to offshore locations**. He suggested companies should caution against offshore outsourcing in certain sectors due to strict domestic regulations.

> **P19**: [locations play a role] Yes absolutely…the decision is driven by the regulators. I mean if you are in the regulated market being in the insurance. Insurance, for example in Germany where they have the certain codes or the paragraph 2 or 3 which is actually asking the company or our clients to be fully aware of everybody that has access to their data and specific data.
> [Domestic regulations limiting location strategy]

P19's location limitation experience is an outcome of regulations, such as Germany's EU data legislation which has been domestically interpreted much more strongly than the EU dictates (Sao & Gupta, 2013). Given P19's expertise, he guided his clients through domestic outsourcing and how to avoid breaking regulations. His hesitation to offshore outsource even in a nearshore environment is justified due to governmental regulations limiting locations where the data is accessed. However, there is a third stream of thought around location strategy that is not completely against outsourcing in an offshore location covered below.

Participant 5 (P5) with over 10 years of experience in outsourcing was the country Information Technology Leader (ITL) for a large global insurance provider. His views clearly represent **the partial support and deterrence to outsourcing that some participants highlighted depending on service criticality**.

> **P5**: …it depends on the service you are providing! Okay, if you're a simple help desk service I don't believe the location matters. It's a help desk, pure simple help desk. But if it is regarding service, regarding core applications and so on, location matters.
> [No business-critical outsourcing]

Outsourcing clients have used this approach in the past and often use locations through placing selective outsourcing bids for specific services to minimize project risk (Herzfeldt, Wolferstetter, Böhm, & Krcmar, 2017). P5 supports outsourcing for low-level repetitive tasks but not for business-critical processes as a risk mitigation mechanism. The impact of service as viewed from a location strategy is threefold. The first group have a legacy perspective and fully support offshoring regardless of locations. The second group does not believe in offshoring and may or may not have fallen into this group due to government regulations limiting offshoring behavior. While the third group is innovative as they employ a hybrid strategy of selective partial offshoring depending on the business criticality and level of risk associated with offshoring.

Organizations engage in offshoring to attain a specific competitive advantage they otherwise would not have domestically attained. However, response time is critical as it makes the difference between the company seeking that advantage or a competitor beating them by a small margin. We will now embark on a journey of learning from the mistakes made by seasoned industry leaders who have experienced lead times delays to such an extent, it has fully shaped their perspective and opinions on using a future location strategy.

Participant 22 (P22) is an executive with only seven years of outsourcing experience. However, he had become a subject matter expert on contract creation due to his specialized pharmaceutical outsourcing experience. He had become the wizard of contract management due to constantly being able to work among some of the most brilliant minds who shaped the industry we know today. Originally, I met P22 when we were both service suppliers, he had been recruited by the client at the time of this interview. He officially had left the dark side. Or at least that was our fun icebreaker. I asked him various questions from my interview guide and specifically about his personal experience in time zone management as shared below.

P22: I think time plays a bigger role but that normally coincides with location. So people want to have the feeling that whatever they've outsourced is still close to them but they get the benefit of outsourcing…India [delays] where you're on a different time zone, different continent, I think we are seeing a lot of outsourcing to low cost countries. But within Europe where that is not so much an issue… you don't have the distance…and the time differences that outsourcing can bring.

[He has experienced lead time delays impacting service and is using nearshoring within Europe to avoid the time zone delays. He is not particularly worried about offshore outsourcing, but is concerned with time zone differences]

P22 found a way to continue outsourcing **but hedged against the time zone limitation by implementing nearshore outsourcing**. Nearshoring practices are often adopted when turnaround times can affect the success of deliverables (Slepniov, Brazinskas, & Brian, 2013). At the time P22 understood the major risk his organization was facing was related to their supply chain lead time. In response, he designed a contract to reduce the risk associated with offshoring by limiting the variable lead time through engaging with a neighboring country's lower cost service providers. This is significant because their former offshore service provider may have thought P22 was backsourcing, but instead, he was restructuring his supply chain to take advantage of their regional opportunities.

3.2.4 Impact of Location on Services Leading to Backsourcing

There is a significant impact on outsourcing decision-making when it comes to considering location strategy that can lead to backsourcing. This section allows us to see the outsourcing industry evolving from the legacy single supplier model, often seen in large IT outsourcing engagements, to the diversification approach we are discovering. We can now see the outsourcing evolution coming into age through the creation of a **smart outsourcing network, diversification** as a means to stop losing control, **location selection** increasing backsourcing risk, and **nearshoring limiting the need to fully backsource**.

The **first major evolutionary factors** leading to how location strategy defines the future of outsourcing focuses on the creation of a **smart outsourcing** supplier network. The evolution of the maturing of smart outsourcing has completely reconfigured our view of outsourcing. We learned in this model that an organization steps away from the legacy or sole supplier model to expand its supplier relationships. The organization would have to expand its supplier network by breaking out a process area that previously would have gone to one main major supplier and now distributed the services throughout multiple service providers. There are two major reasons attributed to making this change in outsourcing strategy. The first is the perception that the company backsourcing services, but in reality, they are only backsourcing aspects of the previously outsourced processes. We learned that in this specific model the outsourcing client was bringing services back in-house, while simultaneously using a third party to manage the multiple suppliers to whom they have dispersed the remaining services. This proves that backsourcing itself is a diverse topic as the smart outsourcing model aims to backsource control, but not the actual process areas. The second point of discussion around smart outsourcing is an evolutionary industry leap to organizations **developing sourcing models where they partner with their diverse supplier network and loan resources or jump in when there is a substantial risk of not meeting key deliverables**. This demonstrates that the outsourcing industry has greatly departed from its origins and is now much more than a strategic relationship between a major sole provider and client.

We continue to dig deeper into how organizations are diversifying their outsourcing strategies to stop losing control as it often emerged from the conversations with a key contributor to backsourcing. Naturally the **second major evolutionary factor** in regardsto how location strategy was defining the future of outsourcing is **loss of control**. Organizations changed their overall sourcing strategy due to losing control over influence, decision-making power, and/or processes leading to a change in location and/or supplier.

We learned there was a control shift from client to supplier due to the blurring lines of responsibility after employees transitioned from working for the client to service provider, taking their skills and capabilities with them. Overwhelmingly the outsourcing clients said they were concerned with losing control over what made them successful if they continued to outsource larger portions of their business. Through these conversations, we discovered some organizations are now **backsourcing in order to retain control** or bringing control back to the client's side of the equation. Companies are now changing their location strategy by implementing outsourcing engagements with smaller scopes that allow them to retain their control over influence, decisions, and processes.

The **third major** evolutionary factor regarding how location strategy is defining the future of outsourcing is around **location selection**. We shared the three streams of thought around the location strategy from the participant interviews. The first is the legacy perspective of fully supporting offshore outsourcing regardless of location by using structured and documented processes and SLAs. The second is the opposite where organizations choose not to engage in an offshore strategy due to some countries placing restrictions on data access and key essentials. The third stream captured my curiosity the most, as it takes advantage of capabilities from the previous two location strategies. The third stream of thought in practice, is what we refer to as the **hybrid location strategy**. The hybrid location strategy supports offshoring lower skilled repetitive work throughout the world similar to the first stream of thought but promotes backsourcing or nearshoring for business-critical processes.

The **fourth major** evolutionary factor regarding how location strategy is defining the future of outsourcing was focused on **nearshoring limiting the need to backsource**. Participants interviewed on this topic were straightforward and unfortunately not as innovative as the previous evolutionary factors but still remain significant. In general, all participants shared the belief that outsourcing provides a competitive advantage. However, this advantage is diminished when they experience time zone delays due to proximity issues. These delays have driven organizations to pull out of offshore locations to search for regional partners that can provide similar cost structures without the risk of delays. This was significant as we learned some organizations may appear to be backsourcing, but actually, are changing their locations strategy to include nearshoring.

3.3 Outsourcing Maturity Changing the Industry

This section shares the evolution of the outsourcing industry and how maturing organizations are dealing with this new landscape. We will begin the section by going over how a minority of organizations are going against the norm and beginning to outsource their previously untouchable core competencies. We will continue this organizational outsourcing maturity by going over how organizations are learning from multiple outsourcing cycles. Then we will review how organizations are starting to revisit the make or buy decision from a different perspective. There is more of an interrelated mix in the overall make or buy decision which is different from the legacy cost-focused perspective focused around fully making or buying the entire service area. Organizations are rebalancing their sourcing models and bringing services back in order to remain competitive regardless of cost.

3.3.1 Competitive Advantage Through Outsourcing Core Competencies

A **core competency** is defined as a company's unique contribution to the market difficult for a competitor to imitate, including diverse capabilities that allow for strategic advantage (Ljungquist, 2007). Core competency theory within outsourcing is focused on outsourcing all areas other than what is core to the business (Perera, Ahamed, Rameezdeen, Chileshe, & Hosseini, 2016). Most of the research around core competencies is focused on maintaining the integrity of core competencies as a justified business need (Modarress, Ansari, & Thies, 2016). Core competencies are widely regarded as what truly make an organization unique and allow it to thrive in a sea of competitors. However, candid conversations with industry leaders revealed there are some companies going against the tide and beginning to outsource their core competencies. As this is a dissenting position, let's begin with the commonly accepted perspective, or dare I say, the classic core competency strategy. We begin with Participant 22 (P22) below who supports the long-standing sentiment expressed by most research participants when asked if he had seen or had experience with an organization that outsourced some of their core competencies.

P22: I haven't seen no! I mean the typical things that I've seen they outsourced sort of supporting services.
[He has not seen companies outsource their core competencies]

In support of P22's viewpoint, most participants responded to that question with surprise and asked why I would even consider asking questions around outsourcing core competencies. They did not specifically address why I would ask that question but their tone and sometimes pause before they responded with a confident, "no" as they answered. I remember one participant even took a deep breath to compose himself in disbelief that I would even dare ask such a question. I must admit even I began to doubt the relevance of this question after the tenth "no" answer from a disappointed participant, possibly wondering if I had ever worked a day in the industry. Luckily, I have been told I can be quite stubborn so continued to search for the points of transformation within the outsourcing industry. Although I continued asking if the participants had been involved in outsourcing core competencies, I had given up on the significance of this question. However, I had an interesting conversation with Participant 15 (P15), an executive in the aerospace industry and he had a different perspective on core competencies as shared below.

P15: ...core comp is very subjective... and shrinking... But what I am trying to tell you is that 80% of the [core] tasks which are required to be developed [in-house], they have been outsourced and they just keep the 20% which is the competitive advantage.
[Core competencies shrinking. Companies are beginning to strategically outsource portions of their core competencies as long as they retain the perceived portion to allow them to remain competitive]

His perspective shows how his company is now managing core competencies differently than most organizations. In order for organizations to stay competitive they must review and update their core competencies, not solely identify them (Ljungquist, 2007). P15's organization is evolving by reassessing their core competencies but and going as far as re-scoping them. He felt confident in their reassessment and provided a specific example below.

P15: I am currently in the aviation business and I could say that ticketing and many of the core functions of aviation are today outsourced... but it is being done by another company for everyone. So, it is no longer a competitive advantage to do it yourself.
[He has been a part of outsourcing core competencies. A shared core competency is no longer a competency if another business can provide it at a lower price point with better quality]

We now have two perspectives where most participants sided with P22 and only one additional participant shared the same viewpoint as P15. Only P26 had the same dissenting viewpoint on how outsourcing core competencies were evolving. This supports that although most organizations are following the same path in not outsourcing their core competencies, two different respondents shared their innovation in dealing with core competencies. Essentially, outsourcing is a means to achieve a competitive advantage. It makes sense as organizations continue to assess their competitive landscape, understanding that what made them **competitive yesterday may slow them down tomorrow**.

3.3.2 Organizational Expertise Growth Through Outsourcing Cycles

Processes are interrelated actions, activities, or functions carried out by a group (Costello & Molloy, 2009). Structured processes include the documentation and uniformity of such practices. A well-documented outcome of outsourcing is organizations with a well-structured and documented environment to hand over the services to the service provider. Organizations learn from the previous cycles to become wiser and reap benefits from the overall learning during the rounds of outsourcing (Solli-Sæther & Gottschalk, 2015). P15 witnessed has seen this outsourcing phase evolution and shared some insightful thoughts below. He recalls the initial phase of **outsourcing is usually the hardest for organizations due to the change management issues required to restructure labor** and **process implementation** since organizations may not have developed structured processes before outsourcing. We previously reviewed the control aspect of supplier diversification, but this section reviews how organizations understood they had lost control over their processes. The response below captures the shift in organizational maturity and lessons learned as a result of having standard processes in place after the first round of outsourcing.

P15: The first gen you always have to fight with not having the right standards in place ...after the first generation of outsourcing [the client] usually ends up in a highly standardized environment.

[The first cycle of outsourcing is the hardest. After they understand how to do it, they are better off structurally and have also gained outsourcing experience]

P15's statement means although the organization may experience pain during the initial transition stage, ultimately it should be in a better position by having structured processes in place as part of outsourcing. Many organizations take advantage of this opportunity and structure their processes and capabilities as part of the engagement. Ideally, the outsourcing client owns their process documentation and is ready to either backsource the specific process areas such as application development or server capacity requests or hand them over to an alternative supplier. This clarifies the first step in backsourcing is outsourcing itself. The response below from P15 captures the learning evolution after multiple growth cycles, breaking out the supplier scope and handing over different sections of their processes to various providers.

P15: Next generation of outsourcing will run different… the more experience the more is the possibility of backsourcing. Next gen will do it different and in smaller portions.
[He believes companies are becoming smarter and will outsource portions of their business but not an entire process area]

P15's response above captures the legacy one supplier model discontent but specifically how being involved in multiple outsourcing cycles gave them the unique advantage. Now they have well-structured processes and in-house senior professionals with significant outsourcing experience ready to challenge the status quo. P15 further described how having a well-documented environment gave them more clarity as to what works well and which areas they no longer impacted. Ultimately outsourcing facilitates backsourcing in that organizations can end up with a more structured and visible environment. Furthermore, having structured processes allows organizations to consider alternative suppliers by having a documented "ready" to go transfer environment. Now we can see that the **outsourcing evolutionary journey is not only traveled by service suppliers, but a highway also accompanied by clients**.

3.3.3 Impact of Outsourcing Maturity Level Ultimately Leading to Backsourcing

This evolution and maturing of outsourcing is a key contributor to organizations beginning to change their sourcing models to now include backsourcing as a part of their evolution. The **three outsourcing maturity factors** changing the industry are through organizations **outsourcing core competencies**, learning through **outsourcing cycles** and the evolution of the original **make or buy decision**.

The first evolutionary factor is that organizations are maturing and transforming what they consider core to their business as a competitive advantage. The legacy core competency management strategy is based on the untouchability of core competencies when it comes to outsourcing. However, we were able to speak to two brave souls who dared to go against the business norm and are **restructuring core capabilities to those that will make them more competitive tomorrow**. Companies are beginning to carve out their core competencies by redefining what truly makes them fundamental to their business in response to organizational evolution. This is significant to outsourcing because organizations are becoming more cautious about how they manage and label core business processes. In addition, some outsourcing companies have begun to focus on shared core services as in the airline industry example. Companies would be at a disadvantage if they kept performing a core competency in-house when most of the industry is getting the advantage of lower prices and higher quality processes from suppliers. It also shares another angle of where the industry is shifting to by expanding the overall outsourcing services and providing alternative possibilities to outsource.

The **second major factor** helping to transform the outsourcing industry is how **organizations are becoming smarter through learning from multiple outsourcing cycles**. The first round of outsourcing takes the most effort by both the supplier and the client. This is where the processes are structured, and the environment is constructed so it can be outsourced. And it also leads to the client gaining a well-structured environment that can either be backsourced or served on a platter to the competition. Additionally, clients would have restructured their organization to deal with the skills shift to the outsourcing company as well as learned how to manage them. This environment also sets organizations to be in a better position in the future to work with multiple providers by preparing the groundwork for what could later turn into backsourcing.

The **second major factor** helping to transform the outsourcing industry is a progression of the first cycle of outsourcing in that companies are **now becoming smarter in what they chose to outsource** and how they manage those processes. Organizations are **no longer outsourcing everything that is possible**, but rather learning from past mistakes and beginning to limit their outsourcing practices solely to portions of their business.

The **third major factor** transforming the outsourcing industry is the evolution of the make or buy decision in outsourcing. The cost seeking advantage provided by outsourcing is no longer as strong as it once was. Some organizations are seeking a balance of services between their procurement and their internal production to remain competitive and control their success. Organizations still seek outsourcing through this approach but reassess what they produce inside vs. what they outsource. Implementing balanced outsourcing would typically lead to organizations **letting go of cost focused decisions and moving closer toward value driven capabilities**.

3.4 Conclusion

Outsourcing has been continuously evolving ever since the first IBM and Kodak strategic outsourcing deal that gave birth to the industry. Solli-Sæther and Gottschalk (2015) further highlighted that the outsourcing maturity would essentially evolve into backsourcing. We have discovered that the industry is evolving but not into a separate stage that only covers backsourcing. We have discovered a more **complex reality where organizations are not only backsourcing but also changing their entire outsourcing models**.

The experiences and lessons learned shared by professionals serve as the foundation for this chapter and to discover the creation of three major pillars and their effect on outsourcing's evolution. We began this chapter by reporting on outsourcing satisfaction to understand the significance of placing more responsibility on both suppliers and clients. This significance is presented through having professionals from both the client and service provider sides. We were able to discover how the overall level of **outsourcing satisfaction** needs to be managed by both the service provider and the clients to increase engagement satisfaction and limit the potential to backsource.

We then learned and understood the outsourcing story to understand more about backsourcing and that it is not a phenomenon within the outsourcing industry itself, but part of its' evolution. This realization came to light through uncovering how **location strategy** was defining the future of outsourcing. Organizations are taking full advantage of multiple strategic locations by partnering with a diverse network of suppliers allowing them to step away from the legacy one supplier model. This diversification allows them to limit the control once exercised by service providers.

We finished the chapter by exposing how some organizations are developing strategic alternatives to their previous core competency models due to their own **outsourcing maturity**. Outsourcing as an industry is maturing and so is the experience attained by client organizations who have gone through various outsourcing cycles. Ultimately, the outsourcing industry is maturing and evolving into much more than it used to be and more complex than we once thought. The entire outsourcing industry is changing, and it is no longer geared toward transactional exchanges or functional partnerships focused on providing services at a lower cost than an organization could internally produce.

Bibliography

Agrawal, P., & Haleem, A. (2011). Risk effect of IT outsourcing on firm performance and value. *International Journal of Management & Information Systems (IJMIS), 16*(1), 55–68.

Bennett, K., Verwey, A., & van der Merwe, L. (2016). Exploring the notion of a 'capability for uncertainty' and the implications for leader development. *SA Journal of Industrial Psychology, 42*(1), 1–13.

Chen, Q., Tu, Q., & Lin, B. (2002). Global it/is outsourcing: Expectations, considerations and implications. *Advances in Competitiveness Research, 10*(1), 100–111.

Costello, C., & Molloy, O. (2009). A process model to support automated measurement and detection of out-of-bounds events in a hospital laboratory process. *Journal of Theoretical and Applied Electronic Commerce Research, 4*(2), 31–54.

Feng, Q., & Shi, R. (2012). Sourcing from multiple suppliers for price-dependent demands. *Production and Operations Management, 21*(3), 547–IX.

Gorla, N., & Lau, M. B. (2010). Will negative experiences impact future it outsourcing? *The Journal of Computer Information Systems, 50*(3), 91–101.

Herzfeldt, A., Wolferstetter, T., Böhm, M., & Krcmar, H. (2017). From products and service to IT solutions: Nine principles for managing IT solutions. *E—Service Journal, 10*(2), 1–22, 76–77.

Juras, P. (2007). A risk-based approach to identifying the total cost of outsourcing. *Management Accounting Quarterly, 9*(1), 43–50.

Konno, Y. (2017). Impact of "product scope" and "customer scope": Suppliers' diversification strategy and performance. *Annals of Business Administrative Science, 16*(1), 15–28.

Kotlarsky, J., & Bognar, L. (2012). Understanding the process of backsourcing: Two cases of process and product backsourcing in Europe. *Journal of Information Technology Teaching Cases, 2*(2), 79–86.

Lacity, M., Rottman, J., & Khan, S. (2010). Field of dreams: Building IT capabilities in rural America. *Strategic Outsourcing: An International Journal, 3*(3), 169–191.

Lee, C. K. M., Yeung, Y. C., & Hong, Z. (2012). An integrated framework for outsourcing risk management. *Industrial Management & Data Systems, 112*(4), 541–558.

Ljungquist, U. (2007). Core competency beyond identification: Presentation of a model. *Management Decision, 45*(3), 393.

Malhotra, S. (2014). Impact of outsourcing on the organizations opting for it. *International Journal of Marketing and Technology, 4*(3), 115–122.

Misra, R. B. (2004). Global IT outsourcing: Metrics for success of all parties. *Journal of Information Technology Cases and Applications, 6*(3), 21–34.

Modarress, B., Ansari, A., & Thies, E. (2016). Outsourcing in the Persian Gulf petroleum supply chain. *Strategic Outsourcing: An International Journal, 9*(1), 2–21.

Mrsik, J., & Kostovski, N. (2017). Offshoring accounting services: New opportunities for developing countries. *Accounting and Management Information Systems, 16*(1), 132–146.

Perera, B. A. K. S., Ahamed, M. H. S., Rameezdeen, R., Chileshe, N., & Hosseini, M. R. (2016). Provision of facilities management services in sri lankan commercial organizations. *Facilities, 34*(7), 394–412.

Sao, D., & Gupta, A. (2013). Threats to the international trade regime: Economic and legal challenges arising from anti-offshoring measures across the globe. *The International Lawyer, 47*(3), 407–439.

Slepniov, D., Brazinskas, S., & Brian, V. W. (2013). Nearshoring practices. *Baltic Journal of Management, 8*(1), 5–26. https://doi.org/10.1108/17465261311291632.

Smogavec, T., & Peljhan, D. (2017). Determinants of outsourcing satisfaction: The case of slovenian SMEs. *Economic and Business Review for Central and South—Eastern Europe, 19*(2), 203–245, 270.

Soils, A., Leavell, H., & Maniam, B. (2013). Outsourcing: Friend or foe to U.S. MNCs? *Journal of American Academy of Business, Cambridge, 19*(1), 337–342.

Solli-Sæther, H., & Gottschalk, P. (2015). Stages-of-growth in outsourcing, offshoring and backsourcing: Back to the future? *The Journal of Computer Information Systems, 55*(2), 88–94.

Ulbrich, F. (2009). How interpersonal conflicts influence IS-sourcing decisions. *Strategic Outsourcing: An International Journal, 2*(3), 208–222.

Yoon, Y., & Kun, S. I. (2005). An evaluation system for IT outsourcing customer satisfaction using the analytic hierarchy process. *Journal of Global Information Management, 13*(4), 55–78.

CHAPTER 4

The Future of Outsourcing: Strategic Outsourcing Controls and the Backsourcing Evolution

4.1 Case Studies: Discovering the Future of Outsourcing Through the Birth of Backsourcing

Outsourcing is a young industry and is in the process of maturing to its full potential. This chapter will review the progress of outsourcing's maturity from the perspective of four different industries and their transformations. We will explore how the future of outsourcing is currently being defined by presenting four individual case studies. We will dig deep to uncover the obstacles the companies overcame to correct previous outsourcing mistakes or errors. We will also review how their businesses recovered by using non-traditional outsourcing strategies. Each company is an industry leader representing great success. The company names will remain anonymous due to competition. I was especially careful to not provide any specific company's highlights since they are industry giants in their respective fields and could easily be identified. This anonymity allowed me to gather honest data that will help to shape the future of the outsourcing industry. The future of outsourcing is currently being defined by key industries adopting distinct outsourcing strategies to achieve their respective goals. The different outsourcing applications range from the classical one supplier full outsourcing model, to a hybrid backsourcing strategy which could easily be viewed as the smart

L. A. Mederos, *The Future of Outsourcing*,
Palgrave Studies in Accounting and Finance Practice,
https://doi.org/10.1007/978-3-030-71407-9_4

outsourcing that represents the next phase in the outsourcing evolution. The four industries we will study are the **Pharmaceutical**, **Insurance**, **Cookware**, **and Aviation**. The industries are as diverse to provide an unbiased view of what is taking place across the world of outsourcing.

Sometimes my friends ask, "how did you fall in love with the world of outsourcing." It is definitely not the business practice I planned to pursue instead it is an industry I found that life steered to by studying international business. During my studies, I developed a hunger to understand how some economies thrived while others did not. My interest provided me with a way to fall in love with the world of international business. I also realized outsourcing often creates international opportunities that exert a positive financial impact to benefit many economies throughout the world. Shortly after finishing my MBA I was fortunate to join IBM which back in the 1980s invented outsourcing with Kodak. This opportunity allowed me to work with industry pioneers and key outsourcing decision-makers from leading global organizations. Together we have created four case studies to give us a clear perspective on outsourcing today and how it is evolving into something much more than we could have imagined.

All the companies participating in the case studies are Fortune 500 except for the company from the cookware industry. However, they are a prominent well-known large global company based in France. The case study company selection process had a minimum criterion of accepting only multinational organizations who were renowned global leaders within their respective field and had engaged in global outsourcing. Currently, the pharmaceutical company is globally ranked in the top five according to Forbes 2020 (Hansen, 2020). The Aviation case also includes one of the most respected airlines in the world. The companies who agreed to participate in this study are representative of their industry and have been in business longer than their industry's average and leading in sales and market size. Table 4.1 provides an overview of the industry and company code for reference and confidentiality.

The cases begin with a quick overview of the company to share the impact of their significance within their industry. Then we will review their previous outsourcing environment and the obstacles they overcame including direct quotes from the professionals and continue with the innovative actions taken that were against classical full outsourcing standards. The reason we should care about these case studies is because they prove outsourcing is currently morphing into a greater strategic advantage

Table 4.1 Case study industry tracker

Industry	*Company code*	*Case study number*
Pharma	Pharma Co.	1
Insurance	Insurance Co.	2
Cookware	Cookware Co.	3
Aviation	Aviation Co. & Aviation Supplier Co.	4

than could have been imagined at the industry's beginnings. We will read how backsourcing is not just a phenomenon occurring due to a specific business problem or industrywide event but is embedded in outsourcing. This integration has presented the foundation from which one can prove that backsourcing is the next phase in outsourcing's evolution. We will see how all companies representing their respective industries are engaging in some form of backsourcing. **Backsourcing is defined** by repatriating the processes that were once outsourced. Although, we may sometimes associate backsourcing with bringing back resources, it actually is the act of bringing back the actual process. Ultimately, this chapter conveys the evolution of outsourcing from the perspective of four different companies who represent their industries. However, the Pharmaceutical industry case study provides a complete snapshot of how outsourcing and backsourcing have morphed into a new Hybrid Backsourcing Strategy that defines the next phase in the evolution of outsourcing. The below graph represents an overview of each industry we will cover in this chapter. The chapter will also end with the below graph, but it will then include the main reasons why each industry represents a specific evolution (Fig. 4.1).

4.1.1 Pharmaceutical Industry Case Study

According to sales and market cap Pharma Co. is one of the largest multinational pharmaceutical companies in the world. Originally it gained significant experience in outsourcing with the goal to lower its overall operating costs while focusing on their core competencies. With their headquarters located in a small Western European country from its inception, their geographic location meant it had to rely on outsourcing both domestically and internationally to thrive. Pharma Co. also had experienced outsourcing professional leading key departments and currently has two outsourcing strategies in place. The first is a Hybrid Backsourcing

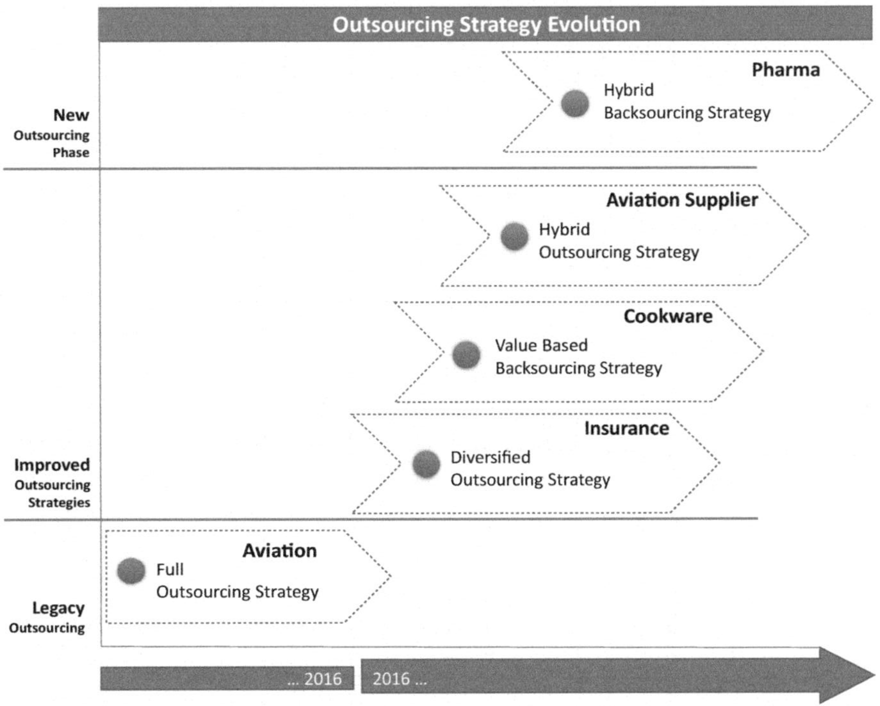

Fig. 4.1 Outsourcing strategy evolution

Strategy applied to their information technology organization and the second is the typical, yet exceptionally mature classical outsourcing strategy being implemented by their clinical trials division. A **Hybrid Backsourcing Strategy (HBS)** is an outsourcing strategy that includes backsourcing as part of the overall diversified strategic sourcing relationship.

The company's IT department had gone through multiple outsourcing cycles that resulted in thinning of their internal environment and lacked control of key processes and the power to make key decisions. An **Outsourcing Cycle** is the completion of the entire full outsourcing contract from beginning to end. In addition, their retained staff did not have industry and institutional process know-how to succeed in the new environment. They handed over the keys to the castle by outsourcing key roles and the key talent who knew how to make successfully deliver. However, Pharma Co. did have experience in outsourcing and could rely on their institutional knowledge of what failed and was beneficial to the company after the completion of each outsourcing cycle. Their niche expertise allowed them to develop an innovative outsourcing model that balanced supplier risk, internal expertise, cost control and decision control.

Retaining the Best Resource Balance Formula for Resources

Initially Pharma Co. decided to enter into a full IT outsourcing relationship focusing on output-driven cost reduction activities to allow the company to work on their core competencies. It had recently completed a multiyear outsourcing relationship with one of the world's largest outsourcing providers notable as one of the first global companies to provide outsourcing services. Both companies were large reputable global organizations. However, being engaged in a full outsourcing relationship meant that Pharma Co. no longer needed to keep senior specialized information technology staff on their payroll. As with most large outsourcing engagements, the outsourcer would directly hire or through a third-party retain key resources who had specific customer technical knowledge. The **outsourcer** is the service provider contractually responsible for providing the outsourced services while the **outsourcee** is the client purchasing the outsourced product or service. The client / outsourcee would no longer have to provide the services in-house or retain resources and instead pays the outsourcing provider/outsourcer for such services. The joint client and provider effort of transferring resources is usually part of the first phase of an outsourcing engagement called the transition and transformation stage.

The effort of assessing the required skills could sometimes lead to the outsourcer not having enough resources with the best client-specific know-how to provide the expected quality services. Conversely, the opposite could occur if the most skilled resources with deep client expertise are transferred over to the service provider. The latter is a service provider's dream but may place the client at risk of losing operational control and specifically, their decision-making capabilities. For the service provider this is the best result as it ensures the client(s) needs them. However, there is a fine line between having the right talent, headcount or not having enough resources who possess the client-specific knowledge. The best time for a client to negotiate this labor balance is during contract negotiation when the service provider would prefer to get the signature to begin the engagement but does not want to retain too many existing employees.

Hiring-on too many client resources limit profit maximization, specifically in situations where the service provider may be under contract to keep such resources for a specific amount of time. Depending on the country, the required amount of time could be many years even if the resource does not have to work. The **retained organization** includes the staff the client agrees to retain on their payroll after the outsourcing engagement begins. The retained staff must manage the outsourced service levels and also serves as the liaison between various departments throughout the company. As such, the retained staff serves as the bridge between various departments within the pharmaceutical company and the company providing the outsourcing services.

Prior to the handover of outsourced services, the skills needed by an organization are much different than those it requires post the transition and transformation phase. While staff of the pre-outsourced IT department may possess deep technical capabilities, the post outsourcing environment requires the management of services to be provided along with the transition from the actual technical work to driving and coordinating results.

Although Pharma Co. spent significant time designing their post outsourcing environment, they quickly realized made a mistake. Pharma Co. had retained some of their top-performing resources but unfortunately found out they were not skilled to thrive in the new environment. In addition, to not retaining the right skillset, Pharma Co. also failed to retain the right scope for the outsourced roles. The **outsourced role**

scope is less forgiving as it describes the work performed by the organization broken down by tasks and overall responsibilities owned by those roles. Pharma Co. was in the difficult situation where they retained an extremely technical talented organization who lacked the soft skills needed to manage the required deliverables.

Additionally, the retained organization roles and responsibility scope impeded them from taking a contractual hard stance due to most of the documented and agreed power resting on the service provider side. The role responsibility design shielded them from any blame if deliverables were not met, but also limited them from making any significant impact. Furthermore, the retained organization could not support internal stakeholders during urgent situations or make any tangible changes without the approval of the service provider. Pharma Co. had essentially outsourced their own decision support, decision control, and approval process.

Having lost capabilities to impact decisions internally also politically hindered the retained staff. Politically the retained staff did not have power to drive projects and increasingly received less support and internal buy-in of their recommendations. The other side of the coin resulted in the service provider commenting that they would often be liable for deliverables they did not fully own. Ultimately, Pharma Co. was in a challenging situation due to outsourcing control of its information technology decision-making power and expertise.

Designing the Future, from Failure to Success

Pharma Co. a global pharmaceutical company with many large departments that have adopted two disparate outsourcing approaches. Unlike the information technology department, the clinical trials organization had taken full advantage of augmenting their capabilities and globally sourced hard-to-find skills to move faster through the stages of their clinical trials. The organization responsible for clinical trials had to use outsourcing as a key advantage to meet deadlines or at least find the skills needed to perform the highly specialized project-based activities. It would be both extremely difficult and expensive for Pharma Co. to recruit and hire the highly skilled resources needed to fulfill project-based deliverables it would probably not retain after the project completion.

Outsourcing clinical trials may appear to be a competitive strategy but that advantage was lost after industry competitors also outsourced trials whenever possible. However, Pharma Co. understood this niche and how difficult it was to attain resources with highly sought-after skills for short-term work. Pharma Co. had to constantly create long-lasting relationships with niche outsourcing providers able to continually provide resources with skills exactly when needed. Hence, outsourcing of this nature could be considered survival niche outsourcing. The survival aspect literally applies as Pharma Co. develops lifesaving drugs in addition to the need to attract the best resources to survive and thrive in a highly competitive industry.

Pharma Co. had two major outsourcing strategies in place when it completely overhauled its outsourcing strategy. The clinical trials organization had a **progressive outsourcing strategy** which occurs as organizations outsource all parts of their business that make sense with no regard to backsourcing. This strategy was also applied to recruiting the best talent regardless of price point.

The below quote is from the interview transcript with a clinical trials medical director with close to 30 years of experience in outsourcing including global responsibilities. He highlights the need for outsourcing regardless of price to hire specific core skills to fulfill specific departmental objectives.

> People think that outsourcing is cheaper than managing resources in house, but that's not how it really is. For some things, companies are willing to pay more, even though it's expensive to outsource! But then there are certain expectations that we want from that project, which are then better obtained from external parties compared too internal….sometimes the company thinks that, okay well, it's like 15 people, but it's to bring something to the market for the patients, then it's all [worth] doing it. (Anonymous, Personal Communication, August 3, 2016)

He feels so strong about his mission to help patients that cost is secondary as long as results are achieved. His search for world-renowned capabilities drives his progressive outsourcing strategy so far as to pay someone 15 times the market rate if it means bringing a drug to market. Honestly, I was surprised when he mentioned paying someone the equivalent of 15 people and immediately realized I had selected the wrong profession! I can also imagine that pharmaceutical companies are currently investing significant amounts in the race for the global COVID-19 vaccine.

While the clinical trials organization dove deeper into their progressive outsourcing strategy, the information technology department desperately needed a change. Pharma Co's IT department lost its control and believed it had potentially over outsourced. However, it had a secret weapon no one expected! Pharma Co. had full ownership of its processes, process descriptions, and all documentation around all outsourced areas. Owning the process allowed it to have full visibility into which areas it made sense to own, to hedge ongoing risk. Although the decision to own the processes documentation was at a multi-million USD cost to Pharma Co., it allowed them to eventually backsource.

Understandably Pharma Co. was not satisfied with their outsourcing environment and sought change initially by replacing their Chief Information Officer (CIO). The below quote is from a key leader of the retained IT organization. The pharma IT leader refers to the CIOs backsourcing strategy. In the quote below he highlights how backsourcing or as he calls it, "internalizing" the knowledge will be the differentiation for future success. Backsourcing became a key strategic initiative for the new CIO whose focus rested on strengthening the internal organization once again. This driver was supported by key stakeholders who wanted him to quickly strengthen their position.

> The new CIO outlined in the recent town hall that he envisions increasing the amount of "internalizing" the resources that are currently outsourced in specific areas due to the fact that he feels the need of internalizing this know-how that currently is in the hands of the external providers and making it a know-how that remains internal to the company for various reasons...this is a new direction changing in the past couple of months from what was led primarily by the previous CIO. But now with the new CIO things seem to be changing in another direction. Specifically within IT that [backsourcing] seems to be the case because yes as I said, a lot of this know-how has been externalized in the past years, and there seems to be now a feeling that, that did not necessarily meet certain requirements the company has, reasons for which the new direction seems to be pointing more into internalizing. (Anonymous, Personal Communication, August 4, 2016)

The IT leader provides additional support to the popular backsourcing strategy with the quote below. He feels strongly that **outsourcing brings an initial reduction in labor and operating costs but eventually a**

second wave will arrive of non-budgeted costs that reduce the long-lasting benefit. Additionally, long-term outsourcing costs not budgeted may include server maintenance and added services such as capacity monitoring applications which have not been contracted. Additionally, a service provider may define an outsourced offshore ratio when negotiating the contract to meet a profitable price point. This **offshoring resource ratio** is the numerical relation of high-cost country resources as compared to the lower-cost country. Basically, based on the number of a lower-cost country's resources the service provider uses, your labor cost will be lower. Unlike the clinical trials organization where they experienced a high-level of offshored outsourced services, the information technology department has experienced a significant reduction in quality.

> Now this seems to be done mainly based on let's say high-level strategic decisions, not necessarily having brought into consideration the cost for the whole outsourcing in the long-term. So, in the short-term, you had a strong reduction in price, and costs in operations. But with time it seems to be more and more clear that the cost increases around quality in countries in which resources are cheaper. You do feel an impact in the quality that is delivered by these outsourced components within the organization. I've seen it on my projects for example or in the services that I've had to interact with once they've moved on to other countries. So, I think the cost reductions are just short-term cost reduction improvement. If you add up the amount of cost and quality lacking for the long-term, it just does not make sense. (Anonymous, Personal Communication, August 4, 2016)

He has also experienced differences in quality and work culture between offshore outsourced personnel in Eastern Europe and South East Asia, as quoted below. He shared frustration with the Asian resources serving as order takers, but they would not provide added consultative value or openly oppose recommendations, even if they knew it would not make sense to implement.

> There's a lot more micromanagement needed for our outsourced services in Southeast Asia due to the way in which they interact on a day-to-day basis, whereas our counterparts in Eastern Europe may be, you know, you can expect from them more from a consultancy component. They come up with ideas and suggestions on how to do things, which obviously helps the project whereas Southeast Asian, they just follow orders. (Anonymous, Personal Communication, August 4, 2016)

Ultimately, Pharma Co. created an internal study to assess vendor risk and understand how to hedge against it. The study pointed to key vendors that would severely impact the pharmaceutical operations if they did not meet the agreed deadlines. As an output of this study, they decided to create a program to remain in continuous communication with their suppliers and when necessary would jump into assist with meeting their deadlines. This was an emergency only temporary **supplier risk avoidance support** where Pharma Co. would take over, lend resources, and even provide funding in order to limit unacceptable risks. Pharma Co. was the only organization included in this chapter that implemented such an umbrella risk mitigation program. Interestingly, the vendors believed they were part of a greater team and gladly handed over control of their operations and processes because they knew it was temporary and due to a critical situation. The quote below is quite important as the newly retained staff leader refers to the company's decision to pursue a mixed approach highlighting their new strategy to seek an innovative solution that maximizes the best of both outsourcing and backsourcing.

> The company brought back some services and resources, but it does not constitute a full backsourcing model. But I would say more often what is needed is for the vendor to provide some outsourcing services. (Anonymous, Personal Communication, September 14, 2016)

Formulating the Future of Outsourcing: Hybrid Backsourcing Strategy

Pharma Co. information technology department realized regardless of reaching original cost targets, they had serious problems in regard to supplier risk, internal expertise, cost control, and decision control. They clearly understood they needed to make a seismic change to thrive. This seismic change arrived with a complete change of outsourcing strategy that would not only change their entire environment moving forward but would simultaneously birth the next phase in the outsourcing evolution. The strategy they developed and implemented is the **Hybrid Backsourcing Strategy** which focuses on the following four areas (Fig. 4.2):

1. **Restructure for Talent**: Assess which areas of the business lacked the skills to manage the outsourcing relationship and drive results. This would entail building up some of the capabilities they had transferred back over or lost due to the outsourcing agreement and

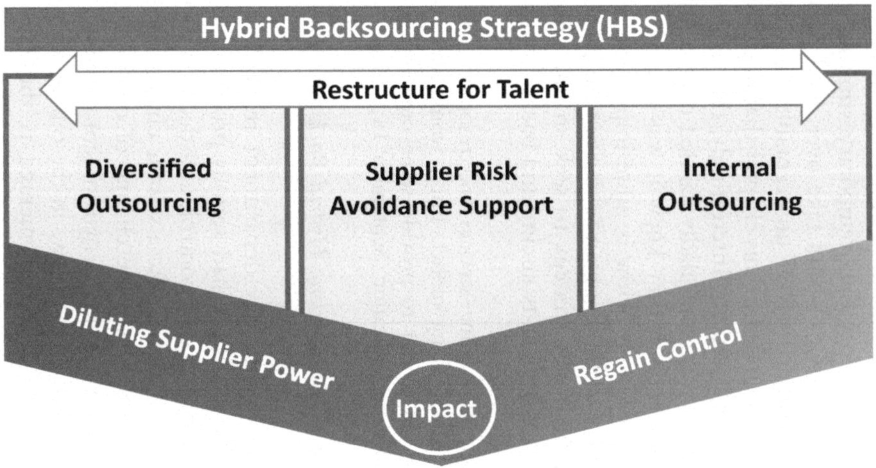

Fig. 4.2 Hybrid backsourcing strategy (HBS)

rebalancing of scope activity ownership transferring between client and service provider.

2. **Diversified Outsourcing**: Spread the outsourcing services from one main supplier to multiple. It was originally preferred to engage with one major supplier to take advantage of economies of scale. However, transferring most service to one supplier may also transfer the control and decision-making capabilities.
3. **Supplier Risk Avoidance Support**: The temporary management of supplier processes in order to limit unacceptable risks. This can also include providing funding and labor in order to assure that deliverables are met.
4. **Internal Outsourcing**: Utilize its multinational strength by employing its own resources throughout the word to provide IT services internally at lower market-based costs. Pharma Co. is large enough with locations throughout the world to take advantage of low-cost country resources already embedded in the corporate culture with strong loyalties to the company.

Pharma Co. realized that it had to find a way to bring back control and realized that the best opportunity to take charge of their future was when the 5-year outsourcing agreement was coming to an end. They took this opportunity to meet with various potential suppliers and although most were skeptical at first to make such a unique change, they were ultimately pleasantly surprised.

Pharma Co. **diluted the supplier responsibility by contracting with multiple vendors to provide various services previously provided by sole outsourcer**. Ultimately, Pharma Co. realized that it had to bring back control and having multiple stakeholders instead of just one allowed them to dilute their previously supplier gained power. This allowed Pharma Co. to have multiple outsourcers provide competing services formerly provided by one service provider. However, the key to this strategy was not to create chaos. They had to assure the control and decision-making transferred smoothly to Pharma Co. Arguably, the most important part of their innovative strategy was **they maintained the management of the various vendors in-house**. This meant they back-sourced the key control mechanism while creating an environment of competition across the various outsourcers.

Pharma Co. attained diversity of outsourcers by their initial decision to retire from the main service provider itself and hire staff from the open market with some of the key skills they had lost. At first by making a skills assessment Pharma Co. grew stronger and then built the capabilities in-house by hiring key talent. Building this key core strength was essential to implementing the Hybrid Backsourcing Strategy and to lead from within. Their innovative strategy was largely possible because they previously paid to have their key processes returned to successfully run their operations. The ownership of process documentation provided clarity about the processes occurring on the supplier side. The documentation offered more clarity into their decision-making and identified roles it needed to own so they could backsource the capability.

The third strategy change helping to define the future of outsourcing was able to be implemented due to their global reach and multiyear outsourcing institutional knowledge. Pharma Co. already had production sites and operations throughout the world in many of the same cities where initially the main supplier had been providing outsourced services. Additionally, some of the retained staff already had experience leading offshore resources from the same lower-cost countries where the outsourcer conducted business.

Conclusion of a Completely New Way to Do Business Globally

Pharma Co. implemented a unique Hybrid Backsourcing Strategy that not only allowed them to regain control of their operations but also expanded its reach to their suppliers, and completely changed the power dynamic. Pharma Co. initially was able to dilute their supplier control by implementing a Diversified Outsourcing Strategy where they diluted the decision control owned by one major supplier and engaged with various outsourcers through multiple smaller contracts. Then they used their newly created backsourced management and strategic coordination capabilities to control their own service providers. This control shift was especially successful due to the implementation of the Supplier Risk Avoidance Support program. This program allowed Pharma Co. to take control of a supplier's process with the intention of providing temporary support on mission-critical deliverables. Service providers welcomed the coordination and participation in the program as a business requirement and the added benefits of full alignment with their client. This unique strategy has also diversified their outsourcer network while increasing their own control and knowledge.

The second strategy Pharma Co. implemented is within the clinical trials organization. The strategy used by clinical trials is less innovative but still unique and uses a niche outsourcing approach where cost is not a determining factor to recruit talent. The main purpose of the second strategy was to temporarily find the specific skills and talent it needed around the world without the risk of fully employing resources it would only temporarily need to augment their existing staff. However, in the pharmaceutical industry this is not considered a strategic advantage as most organizations now use this strategy. Unlike the IT organization, location was not a deterrent as long as the talent with the skillset could be recruited.

Unlike most organizations, Pharma Co. is in a fortunate situation to apply multiple outsourcing strategies to solve problems within the company. It is large enough it does not have to maintain one global outsourcing strategy and has empowered the different divisions of the company with the ability to define their own future. This freedom to define and design has fostered the creativity through budget autonomy and departmental mission allowing it to take on their division's fate by using department-specific decision-making on a global scale.

The application of this Hybrid Backsourcing Strategy (HBS) potentially could be the most innovative outsourcing strategy in the world as it merges backsourcing, outsourcing, internal offshoring, external offshoring, process ownership, stakeholder management, and hiring the right skills to return and control the success of the company. The Hybrid Backsourcing Strategy has achieved so much success at Pharma Co. currently they are assessing the potential impacts to implementing it in other areas of the business (Table 4.2).

4.1.2 Insurance Industry Case Study

Insurance Co. is one of the top five largest global insurance companies. They had internally provided global Information Technology support throughout the organization for quite some time. They struggled with uniformly consolidating their IT environment across global regions with users frequently ignoring their suggestions and change management's recommendations to adopt new tools. Basically, the IT department was facing global resistance on every step after trying to implement something new as directed by global headquarters. Insurance Co. was not sure if they should continue facing significant internal resistance after pushing for change or simply work with an outside service provider to handle the

Table 4.2 Pharma: Why should we care?

Overview of strategy	*What was implemented*	*Industry significance*	*What was backsourced?*
1. Pharma Co. set the new outsourcing benchmark by departing from legacy outsourcing through the creation of a comprehensive outsourcing strategy that has its **foundation** on **backsourcing** 2. The **Hybrid Backsourcing Strategy (HBS)** combines aspects of supplier diversification, backsourcing and internal outsourcing to provide a completely new way to outsource	1. They implemented **backsourcing of key areas** and began **internal outsourcing** 2. Implemented **supplier diversification** to **dilute** the one supplier **power** 3. Implemented **a risk avoidance strategy** that would temporarily take over a supplier's processes when needed 4. Backsourced **management** and **strategic coordination** of various outsourcers	1. Innovative strategy **brought control** and **decision power back** to the company. HBS **sets the new standard** of how to outsource for success 2. The HBS **can be applied to any global company seeking to diversify their sourcing strategy** while creating an in-house talent force to be feared	1. Control and coordination of their own processes 2. Control of processes provided by supplier 3. Key capabilities and skills

headaches that come with such a large global IT consolidation of services and processes within a political and divided corporation.

This case is structured to help us understand how the lack of will to make decisions impacts and deteriorates a fragmented relationship between global and regional leadership and impeded global change. Furthermore, the direct words from key company leaders provide us with a view into the evolution of outsourcing at one of the largest insurance companies in the world. This will help us understand how the company began implementing a global legacy one supplier outsourcing strategy but shifted to modern diversified outsourcing.

Ensuring the Worst Political Landscape
Insurance Co. began using a classic make or buy model from the manufacturing industry and adopted it for their insurance services environment. While working with the model they decided it would be best to engage with an outsourcing strategy firm to assist in making the decision of whether to outsource. Similar to the old saying that went something like "*nobody ever got fired for hiring IBM.*" I'm not suggesting they used IBM, but the leadership was well aware of the company's highly political environment and decided to use an outside firm to guide them in their decision and to take responsibility. The outsourcing strategy firm was tasked with assisting them in their decision whether to "**make or buy**" global IT outsourcing services. If they chose to "**make**" it would entail continuing to provide the services in house, while choosing "**buy**" would result in engaging with an outsourcer to provide services externally.

The outsourcing strategy firm performed a complete study going beyond what was originally proposed by Insurance Co. and came back with the recommendation to "buy" global IT services. As can be expected after such a decision, Insurance Co. had to internally gain buy-in from IT department leaders and other key stakeholders had to agree or disagree with the findings. There was an ultimate agreement with the recommendation, and they decided to go through with seeking an outsourcing company that was large enough to handle outsourcing at a global scale.

After the usual bid and proposal process conducted by large organizations of this size, they decided to go with one of the largest and oldest outsourcing providers in the world. The typical multi-million-dollar deal for a full global information technology outsourcing engagement can range from forty to one hundred million USD. This deal was no different as it included one of the largest global insurance companies requesting the help of one of the largest information technology companies to solve their global outsourcing and internal politics demands.

The **initial driver to outsource was the failure to internally consolidate its worldwide information technology organization and the decision to transfer the responsibility to an outside company**. However, the contract's goals were not only to cut through the political layers but also to **deliver services at a lower cost than internally producing them, while implementing new technologies**. Internal politics may be one of the most sensitive and underrated problems associated with accomplishing a successful outsourcing engagement. Internal politics play an exceptionally large role when trying to attain buy-in from influential local key players. Local players sometimes will have more decision-making power than other company staff may realize and could delay implementation through passive resistance. **Passive resistance** occurs when an employee or group of employees delay a project or milestone by being unresponsive or not supportive of the desired approach or outcome.

There are some organizations that rest significant control at the local leader level, as in this case. Insurance Co. required the signoff of local leadership to mark regional phases completed as part of the service transition from the client to the service provider. This required the outsourcer to jointly work with the local country leadership, operations, and project staff to meet the various project requirements. The global outsourcer was also tasked to work with not only the information technology organization but also with the legal and human resources teams. This was to assure both contract requirements were being met to avoid any potential service level agreement penalties when following local country regulations during the transfer of labor from the client to the service provider. This labor transfer is normally expected with projects of this size when the resources transfer their employment from Insurance Co. to the global outsourcer.

Not surprising given the corporate political environment, various local leaders resisted the transition in defense of local law and requested an exception from joining the new globally consolidated organization managed by the outsourcing company. The impact of their actions was taken quite seriously by both the service provider and Insurance Co's. retained staff, given that local country buy-in and support was essential to their success. Arguably, the most astute resources to deal with internal company politics are those who work inside the company and understand the politics. However, another alternative the Insurance Co. relied upon was that the resources arriving from outside would come into the organization and cut right through the internal politics to get the job done.

Too Insured to Make a Difference

Insurance Co.'s significant issues with their internal politics served to impede the entire organization from achieving large-scale success. It was believed an outsourcing company would be in a better position to positively impact the disruption and then regional leadership could accept an environment designed and pushed by the global headquarters. Insurance Co. attempted to outsource their regional and country-specific problems but made one destructive choice. The senior leaders at Insurance Co. attempted to ensure themselves personally from failure by employing an additional consulting company to serve as the barrier between the global outsourcing company and the headquarters. Hiring the outside company meant local management had inserted two outside layers between them and their internal headquarters as a buffer before having to take a stance, provide support for a potential decision or even provide guidance. The political environment was so broken that the global outsourcing company had to meet with the intermediary company to obtain approval of key agreements between them and the local country management. The intermediary consulting company would then take those agreements for approval to management at the global headquarters. The quote below was taken from an interview with one of the global headquarter-based leaders on the global outsourcing supplier side.

> You were talking with a whole chain of people that had no decision-making power that were externals themselves. And those layers then filtered the information till it actually reached somebody on the client side who was able to take a decision, but who was, at least from my perception, too high up in the organization to effectively and timely do so. (Anonymous, Personal Communication, September 12, 2016)

The supplier side leader openly discussed their discontent due to the lack of trust and the deteriorating relationships they were trying to build with regional leaders to make the change they were contracted for. The costly added layers created frustration up and down the entire communication chain while increasing the lead time to make any significant decision. It seemed as if there were competing justifications for entering into an outsourcing relationship. As a result, the global supplier questioned whether they would be able to take advantage of their economies of scale by using their offshore centers to meet the agreed low-cost price points. However, due to the relationship and communications breakdown it was challenging for the outsourcer to maintain their targeted timeline due to the communication toll gates created by the Insurance Co.

The communication problems continued throughout the engagement and ensued in increased costs. The quote below was taken directly from a case study participant working at the global outsourcing supplier. He had seen the labor cost increase due to having to staff a higher number of resources at headquarters in lieu of lower-cost local region technical capabilities due to the communication barriers.

> Usually in the contract, for price reasons, the intention was to offshore much more than was afterwards offshored in the operational realities of the contract itself, and that was due to operational issues arising. Allot of the operational issues are, well, communication issues in nature, from what I've seen. Not technical issues or skill level issues. A lot of what I've seen are communication issues and, you know, understanding, being close enough to the client to really understand what the needs are and what the priorities are. (Anonymous, Personal Communication, September 12, 2016)

The initial contract price points an outsourcer identifies as profitable needs to be achieved in order for the outsourcer to remain profitable. The reason the contracted global outsourcing company took the contract and could forecast a profit was due to using their global offshore capabilities. This competitive capability allows it to service Insurance Co. at a lower price per head than if it provided same services internally. This ratio imbalance started to eat at the outsourcer's profits and served to spread the negative relationship sentiment.

The quote below was taken from a senior leader at Insurance Co. During the conversation, he acknowledged the company made some past mistakes and it was continuously learning from them. He also mentioned the overall outsourcing contract had been updated to handle some of the local political restraints. He mentioned the company needed to change their outsourcing strategy and although they were not seeking back-sourcing services so soon after beginning such a large-scale project. They were in turn implementing a supplier diversification strategy and beginning to understand their true in-house capabilities.

> The strategic goals of the sourcing project are being redistributed in order to have a work balance between what an outsource supplier or what an incumbent supplier or what's done in-house, have been adjusted from where the project started at the beginning to try and focus the delivery on those areas where either the new supplier or the incumbent suppliers, or in-house are strongest and most able to deliver. So, the project started off with Plan A and what's been implemented is Plan C. And I guess its kudos to all of the organizations that they recognized that I am willing

> to be flexible in terms of adjusting the objectives. (Anonymous, Personal Communication, August 4, 2016)

Flexibility is imperative for large organizations to thrive and especially when dealing with multiple countries and stakeholders. As shown by the quote, even though it was not the original intention to make multiple changes to the plan, it is imperative for an organization to learn from their mistakes. And be flexible enough to work together with multiple vendors to create a joint strategy beneficial to all companies involved in the outsourcing engagement. The iterations are important, and he is grateful the global outsourcing company was willing to reduce scope so other suppliers could jump in and help.

When a full outsourcing engagement is implemented it means the outsourcee, itself will no longer need specific resources. Such resources may be laid off, transferred to the outsourcer, or their responsibilities may change from owning the actual process to more of a relationship management role. For example, it is not uncommon for a local country CIO working for Insurance Co. with multiple subordinates in his reporting line to end up either becoming a relationship manager or transferred to the outsourcer, and reclassified as a service manager supporting their previous employer. However, the outsourcer may be under contract to retain their employees for a specific amount of time depending on country or contract terms. The responsibility is placed on that resource as to whether they can secure their position with the global outsourcing after the contract ends. As one can imagine, this shift creates employment uncertainty and deviates a previous executive career path to more of a specialized information technology subject matter expert. This career uncertainty and deviation from one's career objectives served to enhance the discontent toward global outsourcing within the Insurance Co. The quote below provides insight into the fear some employees begin to experience as they begin an outsourcing engagement. When their anxiety increases about the uncertainty of their career a lot of the hesitation may arise about whether to fully support to an outsourcer arriving to take over their responsibilities.

> People who are working internally within an organization will feel abandoned when they are outsourced! If they really want a career in technology, then it might be enhanced by going to the vendor. Will that be seen as a positive? To a degree that becomes vendor specific. So, for example, if the vendor is well recognized, well known within the industry and has a

> reputation of building good technical skills, of building people's careers, as the greats of Google or Apple get into the outsourcing business, I think people would welcome it. And where it comes to some of the lower-end suppliers in the business, then it's certainly not perceived as being particularly career-enhancing for the people who are impacted by it. (Anonymous, Personal Communication, August 24, 2016)

The above quote provides genuine insight into the mind of an employee whose career may drastically change when as a thriving regional executive they are unwillingly transferred to another company. Some of these regional executives thrive in the new organization and they become leaders within the global outsourcing provider. However, more often what I have seen is local Chief Operating Officers or Chief Information Officers are not able to find their footing as a service provider and leave soon after their contract allows.

No More Decision Stagnation

Soon after the outsourcing engagement started, Insurance Co. realized it had relied heavily on the global outsourcer who also faced substantial pushbacks from multiple key local country managers. This pushback led to both the outsourcer and Insurance Co. failing to deliver on key milestones that if missed included associated financial penalties. As costs were increasing on both sides and milestones missed, both the outsourcer and Insurance Co. realized their current communications chain and overall communication structure needed to change.

They worked together to rectify the communication breakdowns of their relationship and internally the Insurance Co. realized they had to quickly act. At this time, they both began reviewing the current state of the engagement and overall relationship. By understanding the agreement's problems, they realized a full and complete information technology outsourcing deal may have been too ambitious an undertaking for any one company to fulfill. Through the outsourcing improvement assessment, they jointly concluded that the original contract covered too large of a scope and needed to be further broken down incorporating multiple local suppliers to fully provide specific services at the required quality level.

Normally, one can assume an outsourcer prefers to provide full outsourcing services to a client. A full outsourcing relationship looks great on a balance sheet for the outsourcer with an additional multi-million

USD revenue added to their books. The global outsourcer welcomed the reduced scope as it allowed the focus to be on data center and server hosting services instead of low value, time-consuming maintenance work with much lower return on their investment.

Insurance Co. also took ownership responsibility for their political situation and improved its outsourcing model. During this initiative they discovered a major breakdown in communication and barriers created leading to hesitation by staff to accept the organizational changes. With the creation of multiple obstacles to decision-making a culture of **decision stagnation** emerged encouraging all to not make any. Decision and especially joint decisions between the outsourcer and outsourcee are imperative to mutually keeping the relationship fruitful. This is especially amplified when local country influencers are involved.

Local country influencers often have power to push back and reject adopting new corporate decisions or recommendations. Adoption was futile without the joint support of local key stakeholders. The major communication breakdown emanated from its senior staff who were using multiple outside consulting companies to internally communicate decisions to their own staff and other vendors. Using so many layers to communicate created confusion and implementation delays.

Conclusion that Leaves Flexibility to Succeed

Insurance Co. faced decision stagnation due to their attempt at outsourcing internal political issues. They engaged with a global outsourcing provider to provide a solution to both global IT consolidation and to eliminate the internal political disconnect. Their senior leadership exacerbated their problem with internal politics by contracting an external consulting company as their communications solution provider to ease tensions between them and the entire organization, including with the contracted global outsourcer. This additional layer was detrimental to the IT global technology consolidation as the global firm was unable to receive the senior leaders' confirmation or approval of timely decisions necessary to making an impact. Insurance Co. understood that it needed to improve it operations and went through multiple outsourcing iterations until it found the right model that best fit them.

This global strategic improvement was possible in part due to having internal leaders restless in driving needed change as well as having a global outsourcing provider who was flexible enough to work with them in redefining what was originally contracted. The outsourcer's contract flexibility was significant to the outsourcing strategy because they ultimately agreed to reduce scope mid-contract. The reduction of scope meant that Insurance Co. would adopt a supplier diversification strategy directly impacting the global supplier. Insurance Co. distributed various processes to local suppliers, but most global spanning responsibilities remained with the initial large global outsourcer.

Insurance Co. changed its full outsourcing model from the legacy one supplier model to utilizing multiple vendors to provide niche services around the world. Having multiple suppliers allowed the main outsourcer to focus on key scope areas while no longer having to worry about what they considered low-value work. They welcomed the new defined scope as it allowed them to deliver much-needed quick wins to local country leadership. Insurance Co. will continue to outsource and has further found that the more it outsources the better and more skilled its leaders have become at managing the outsourcing relationships. They will also be much more selective of the processes chosen to hand over after mistakes led to paying millions USD.

Insurance Co. significantly increased their outsourcing management skills and is taking advantage of it by managing to new diversified supplier landscape. They have reduced their risk exposure by implementing a supplier diversification strategy while maintaining control and coordination of the various supplier. However, are not implementing a macro backsource strategy. This also proves the typical full outsourcing projects of the past may no longer be relevant in today's global business environment (Table 4.3).

4.1.3 Cookware Industry Case Study

Cookware Co. is a top-tier global cookware manufacturer and retailer. The company has a presence in over 50 countries and around 2,000 employees with global headquarters in Western Europe. This case study was created together with multiple layers of the organization in order to attain a complete and holistic view of the current backsourcing strategy. The interviews were with key participants including the Chief Information Officer (CIO), IT leadership, and IT management with day-to-day operational responsibilities. The purpose here was to capture both the strategic view as well as the operational impact.

Table 4.3 Insurance: Why should we care?

Overview of Strategy	*What was implemented*	*Industry significance*	*What was backsourced?*
1. Insurance Co. applied a **Supplier diversification strategy (diversified outsourcing)** to **regain decision capabilities** and **reduce risk** of a sole supplier not meeting specific deliverables	1. Global contract **was broken out to include multiple local suppliers**. Global supplier agreed to reduce scope to areas they could succeed 2. Will no longer outsource at will and became selective on what processes to outsource 3. Local suppliers provided local retained staff with the political significance to signoff on a globally led strategy	1. It provides a record of both the supplier and the client **diverting** from the legacy one supplier **outsourcing benchmark** 2. Global outsourcer supported reducing scope and giving work away to local suppliers 3. Insurance companies looking to diversify no longer need to follow the aged one supplier model and **can define an outsourcing balance that works best for them**	Control and coordination of various suppliers

The company built a solid reputation by manufacturing in-house high-quality durable top-selling products. In addition to their high-quality manufacturing standards, Cookware Co. offers a lifetime warranty on its core products. This resulted in a strong brand and product differentiation as their high-quality manufacturing standards were part of their DNA. The company was founded 100 years ago and throughout the organization's corporate culture focused on high-quality production and attentive customer care.

The case begins with a review of their current over outsourced environment due to a never satisfying hunger for outsourcing. We will then hear the words spoken from participants that were living this environment to further help us understand what change took place. We will also see how the company sought guidance from an experienced CIO to help them implement a new outsourcing strategy. No one inside the company would have predicted this CIO would not only solve their problems but go on to define a new method to backsource.

Getting Burned by Over Outsourcing

As Cookware Co. pursued corporate-wide cost reductions it continually began outsourcing more and more of its information technology infrastructure and respective services. The company took advantage of outsourcing and offshore outsourcing, especially in recent years to work with centers based in China, Thailand, and Portugal resulting in quickly reducing costs. As Cookware Co. started to have cost reductions associated with outsourcing, it continued to seek additional processes to outsource. Cookware Co. wanted to take advantage of its global reach and send their manufacturing processes to lower-cost countries by offshore outsourcing. Cookware Co. began to realize outsourcing's positive impact to their bottom line soon after their first outsourcing cycle. This quick cost reduction fueled their hunger to continue outsourcing wherever possible.

Cookware Co. also began defragmenting its IT infrastructure operations and outsourcing most of it to third-party vendors focusing on significant cost reduction. Cookware Co. saw the financial impact of outsourcing and continued to progressively outsource each process until their ever-changing savings targets were achieved. Ultimately, this strategy resulted in a fully outsourced environment with no attention to their core capabilities or long-term strategic direction. They found their environment had been fully outsourced including IT infrastructure and hosting services to less than capable vendors.

Soon after the handover of services to the main IT outsourcing provider the IT-retained organization and the finance department started having an increased number of ticket counts. **IT Ticket Counts** are the records of work orders to be completed by the IT department. Each IT ticket meant both internal and external resources needed to work on IT-related problem reported by a staff member. The issues ranged from resetting sign on credentials to restoring servers hosting key financial systems. All these tickets generated two common factors that were not good news to the company. The first common factor was that they all had a financial burden associated with fixing them. The labor cost to fix tickets was exponentially increasing as the ticket number grew from week to week. The second and most alarming common factor was the tickets resulted from having an outsourcing vendor whose selection was heavily based on cost reductions. Unfortunately, this limited financial focus resulted in the selection of an outsourcer whose quality did not match Cookware Co. long history of high-quality products.

Cookware Co. quickly found their operating cost significantly increasing as costs to fix issues landed on their scope due to the way their outsourcing contract was drafted. They were also forced to continue providing services internally running a dual IT environment for longer than they had budgeted for, to assure that their systems did not fail. The unplanned cost diminished the original cost savings which were decreasing by the day to the continuous vendor-related missed deliverables and server failures. They needed a significant strategic change in order to stop the financial bleeding and hired a new CIO to help them navigate the environment they were in and cast them to safety.

The new CIO that Cookware Co. recruited brought the coveted combination of expertise around strategic outsourcing from both the client and service provider side. He understood the company's financial situation due to outsourcing mistakes and immediately conducted a global assessment. The results revealed the company had over outsourced its IT processes and had no set control structure to guide specific outcome from their service providers. His unique previous client and service provider perspective allowed him to focus his efforts on a value-based backsourcing strategy. Although the CEO believed in the new value-based IT strategy, the other board of directors did not agree with his revolutionary approach to backsourcing. It was then recommended that he attain a second opinion through an external third-party management consulting firm.

The reputable strategy firm hired by Cookware Co. showed that they had systematically begun a trend of outsourcing as much as possible regardless of fundamental need or profound long-term benefit to the organization. The consulting firm supported the CIO's initial hypothesis which helped him attain the support he needed to implement a companywide outsourcing strategy change. Interestingly enough, gaining buy-in from the rest of the organization was much easier to attain at the lower levels because they were eager for change and drastically wanted some type of improvement. Sadly, at that point they figured that it could not get any worse. They went full steam on their client-driven value backsourcing strategy and decided to bring back 100% of IT-related activities that had some type of direct client value. The umbrella reason for the decision was that they had lost control of being able to provide their clients with timely quality products.

Trouble in the Kitchen

Of course, Cookware Co. did not attain the forecasted cost reductions since their original outsourcing strategy failed to implement controls and structure. The company lost their focus on the long-term and on quality. And the expected labor cost reductions were not achieved due to the SLAs not including specific contract controls. The problems that Cookware Co. faced were compounded by their initial attempt to implement a diversified outsourcing strategy by using multiple service providers. However, later it was found across all regions only a few of those processes had clear uniform instructions. Essentially, **there was no set benchmark on how to accomplish a goal, what the goal looked like, or even if achieving the goal was worth the effort**.

Immediately, the company began a process documentation project to set uniform global metrics across regions. After the company began to document and maintain standards the process influenced and increased workers' moral and became a key success factor for all regions as everyone rallied toward the same goals. Their backsourcing strategy did permit for outsourcing of projects and non-client value work but not their business as usual resources that had a downstream impact on the clients. **Business as usual (BAU)** are the key resources needed to run the day-to-day operations. The exception for project-based outsourcing was due to having access to key skills that were needed for only a limited time but most important, because they believe that they will have greater control over quality. Considering outsourcing projects after their negative experience shows the long-term of corporate maturity at Cookware Co. However, such outsourcing initiatives were limited, with defined scope and well-documented measurable processes. Below we can see how the group new CIO shows his cautious support for outsourcing.

> Outsourcing is required because there is certain repetitive tasks that they do which does not add value to the core business and only if, and I will repeat myself, only if the process is robust enough, mature enough, documented enough and has backing of a professional quality outsource company. Then it will be successful and financially feasible and quality compliant to outsource. (Anonymous, Personal Communication, July 26, 2016)

Cookware Co. recognized their **IT core capabilities** as technology-related abilities that are fundamental to running their organization but also separate them from their competitors. Their motto became "*the more vital the BAU is, the more reason to have it performed in-house*". Somewhat of a long modo, but at least we can say that they were backsourcing IT and not marketing! Cookware Co. found itself chasing that initial outsourcing cost savings taste through what some leaders compared to indiscriminatory outsourcing. **Indiscriminatory outsourcing** is the continuous outsourcing of processes with little effort on due diligence. **Core competencies** could be processes or skill areas where key resources are needed to support a special product or service that sets the organization apart from others. The core competencies aim to provide a competitive advantage central to a product or service provided.

Cookware Co. implemented a distinctive backsourcing strategy in that they did not backsource its IT operations to the home country where they housed their headquarters. The company decided to backsource its IT operations to Barcelona, Spain, to create a global command center closer to home, while maintaining the lower-cost operations and increased control. In Barcelona they recruited highly technical skilled resources and also supported a limited regional IT operation for hubs so they could serve different cultures and time zones. The backsourcing strategy proved so successful they were able to reduce their development team from 30 outsourced resources in India to only ten based in Spain. This was the result of increased quality-related rework, miscommunication, and regional face-to-face interactions.

Surprisingly, the Group CIO was still open to outsourcing certain processes. However, he preferred outsourcing short-term projects with set end dates instead of long-term key BAU operations. The quote below reflects his frustration about the diminished quality of the processes he was bringing back.

> Quite regularly in my day to day job I see a lot of outsourced processes which are supposed to be running smoothly and working properly. They do not work. They do not function correctly! So obviously, that malfunction is directly affecting the output or quality of the outsourced process. If the output of a process is not at the right quality, then your entire supply chain suffers from beginning to end. (Anonymous, Personal Communication, July 26, 2016)

The group CIO had a magnitude of experience leading global initiatives for close to two decades. He was an outlier in that he was both an IT executive and a strategic business leader. With his strategic cross-boundary perspective, he united Cookware Co. by creating a communications plan focused on gaining continued support for the backsourcing movement and increasing their revenue. His perspective deviated from the typical IT role as only a supporting function. Typically, a **supporting business function within** an organization provides support to other core business functions. However, with his innovative perspective he managed to push Global IT out of the kitchen and onto the living room floor. By improving the ERP system, he was able to connect key areas which allowed sales and manufacturing to continuously communicate speak while maintaining their deep focus on client satisfaction. This unification of its businesses earned him a seat next to the CEO, not only as the technology SME but as a trusted business adviser.

While speaking with another IT leader he mentioned while some companies may attempt to use outsource staff to augment their management layer, Cookware Co.'s strategy to empower resources by hiring them. He described his support of that strategy by explaining how much easier it is to work with peers who possessed the needed core skills but also were aligned with the company mission. He mentioned this strategy reduced many of the competing personal agendas that added no value to clients. Through his quote below that offshored resources lack motivation, for example, he cited much longer response times compared to Spain-based backsourced resources. He also believed if the outsourced support was not geographically located nearby, the outsourcee faced greater hurdles.

> I would say a strategic, cultural point of view, that [Cookware Co]. always tries by default to, I would say the more managerial roles and tasks to be higher, then resources are to be hired in-house. Based on offshore sites, typically in IT, typically India; I would say that the quality and the time response that we are facing is not the one that we would have expected....Something that you maybe can fix in two days with an on-shore or near-shore center maybe can take you five, six days in an off-shore center. (Anonymous, Personal Communication, July 11, 2016)

Global outsourcing entails working with diverse cultures and understanding of verbal and non-verbal communication styles are equally diverse. Understanding these subtle and sometimes not so subtle differences can make or break relationships. Culturally, verbal, and non-verbal communication presents a challenge when trying to discern meaning and what exactly is being implied. One person may not fully understand the desired expectation of the communication and the other person may not understand what is being accepted in an agreement. Misunderstandings based on communication create significant frustration and additional delays.

Finally Cooking with Gas: New Value-Driven Backsourcing Model
Cookware Co. encountered difficulty when depending on their providers to maintain consistent service and quality standards. The company experienced a significant increase in backlog orders when their enterprise resource planning system failed which generated tension among globally dispersed order fulfillment regions. The **Enterprise Resource Planning (ERP)** system sourced by Cookware Co. was meant to unify inventory, planning, purchasing, and sales. Unfortunately, they had lost their capability to fulfill orders on time resulting in dissatisfied customers throughout the world.

We may find it hard to believe that the reason grandma failed to receive that beautiful cooking pan in time for her birther was because of an IT issue. Unfortunately, it was! It was also an IT issue that time you rushed out to the store hoping to buy your significant other the casserole dish they mentioned for months before their special birthday, and find out it was out of stock at the store had been for weeks. And I'll add quite candidly, as a shopper my customer satisfaction level plummeted after visiting three stores and none had the product I was looking for in stock.

Client satisfaction as a metric, provides the company a way to assess their clients' level of happiness following their brand interaction or purchase. Luckily, the company already had a customer service evaluation process in place to gauge client satisfaction and link sales to order fulfillment ratios. As this measure fell it proved to be vital for the company to realize they had a significant problem stocking enough inventory for potential sales. Their timely realization 1 forced changes by recognizing their progressive outsourcing strategy was not meeting their expectations or increasing sales as they had anticipated. With Cookware Co.'s 100-year business history they quickly realized they needed to act. Cookware Co. had its pulse in their industry and moved quickly to avoid permanently damaging their brand. Unlike many organizations that view IT as a supporting organization, Cookware Co.'s IT department was considered an internal core function.

Cookware Co.'s new CIO quickly realized the IT department needed to create a more seamless delivery process between their clients and throughout their supply chain to assure the company was manufacturing the amount of product precisely forecast by sales. Cookware Co. faced more cultural and communication issues after outsourcing to India. The IT leadership also discovered corporate communications were not easily understood or translated by its low-cost country service provider representatives. This miscommunication led to a large amount of rework and internal frustration which resulted in extending project timelines and of course, increased labor cost.

Cookware Co's. challenges with transcultural communication negatively impacted their operations and resolution lead times. **Resolution lead times** are vital to a company's success as they measure the time it takes to apply a solution. We can assume the longer it takes to fix a problem, the lower the satisfaction score will be lower. Cookware Co. had an informal satisfaction score, and it was especially useful in capturing the resolution lead times were taking much longer than expected. The resolution lead times were linked to labor costs. The company's assessment captured the total time spent working on a problem using offshore outsourced resources and found total time spent resulted in much longer than domestic or nearshore outsourced resources.

This labor cost finding was shocking as the lower cost country resources were one-third the cost of the home shore resources. The labor cost of most key major projects was more expensive than working with resources in the high-cost country location. The outcome of their international labor cost exercise caused the company to realize it would cost less to hire high-quality skilled resources in-house, and by backsourcing regionally rather than continuing to offshore.

The new CIO understood the current obstacles facing the company and also how the company's core mission was based on client value. In response, he applied an innovative **Client Value-Driven Backsourcing Strategy** focused on bringing back only processes that added direct client value and only those processes. This strategy combined three areas with a client-driven focus which led to increased quality and long-term cost management (Fig. 4.3).

1. **Fully Documented Processes & Structure**: The creation and documentation of processes is a key aspect of this strategy as it sets the foundation of what the processes that help the organizations

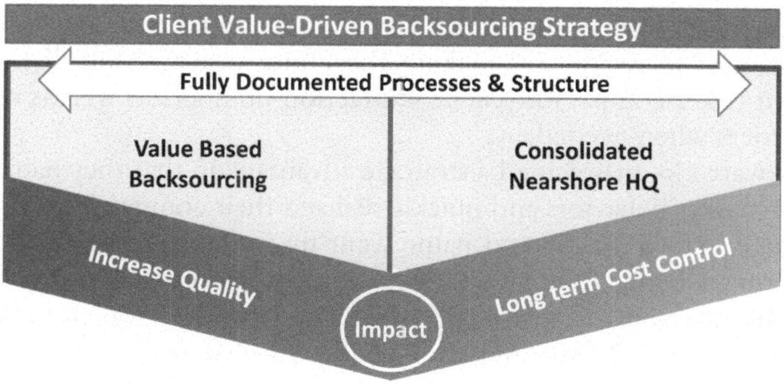

Fig. 4.3 Client value-driven backsourcing strategy

thrive should be. Process scope is a critical success factor as it is vital for an organization to understand what processes should be owned internally, owned externally, and what does a perfect scenario looks like.

2. **Value-Based Backsourcing:** The assessment of what value means to the business their clients. This strategy focuses on reviewing the client priorities and assuring and the company owns all value chain processes that directly impacts the end client's decision to purchase.
3. **Consolidated Nearshore HQ**: It may not always be feasible to directly backsource to the high-cost home country. However, creating a nearshore location that mirrors the home country's culture and environment takes advantage of highly skilled resources at a fraction of the cost.

The client value-driven backsourcing strategy applied at Cookware Co. increased the quality of all client value added processes. This focus should further ripple throughout the organization and maintain labor cost at bay. Cost management was also an output of the strategy as it created a strong environment where cost was tightly managed.

Conclusion of a "Well-Done" Backsourcing Strategy

Cookware Co., a leading global cookware company that initially benefitted significantly from outsourcing and subsequently required more and more outsourcing of their core processes to achieve their ever-changing cost reduction targets. They quickly started seeing that the new progressive outsourcing recipe was making the entire organization ill through increased ticket counts, low client satisfaction numbers as well as missing fulfill orders when needed.

Cookware Co. maintained a strategic advantage in that they had a keen sense of market behaviors and quickly realized their company was burning for change before their brand name went up in flames. The CEO had a reputation of being fully aware of his kitchen's potential and took the unpopular decision to replace the CIO. The new CIO was not afraid to go against the norm, and frankly I would say that he preferred a good discussion with substantially based opposition than the typical "yes sir" response. He quickly took charge and understood the complete environment through running a study that resulted in him having laser focus on backsourcing all processes that had direct client value.

The analysis revealed the original cost reduction targets were not met due to miscommunication resulting in significant rework. This problem drove up labor costs so much that the benefits of using offshore teams considerably diminished. Along with the cross border and cultural miscommunication issues which lead to extended timelines and damaged fulfilling customer orders. The cross-border miscommunication was hedge not by backsourcing to the home country but the neighboring country of Spain which had an ample amount of highly skilled resources hungry for work. As a result, Cookware Co. dramatically began backsourcing 100% of their IT core processes that had a direct client impact including hiring resources. They will continue to outsource project-based work but only with an end date.

In conclusion, Cookware Co's top leaders agreed their brand was at risk due to their lack of direction to continuously reduce costs. They understood change was inevitable if they wanted to remain competitive. This change came with a complete change in their outsourcing strategy to bring back control of their IT operations by backsourcing all processes that added to client value. Implementing such a strategy took significant buy-in from senior stakeholders supported by a detailed analysis proving that backsourcing would bring back the control over their quality, resolutions lead times and labor cost management. Although initially the strategy was unpopular it was overwhelmingly successful. The company no longer had a global order fulfillment issue, ticket numbers fell to an all-time low and client satisfaction rose higher than it was when they deployed their initial progressive outsourcing strategy. Their labor costs

Table 4.4 Cookware: Why should we care?

Overview of strategy	*What was implemented*	*Industry significance*	*What was backsourced?*
1. Client Driven Value Backsourcing focuses on bringing back processes that add direct client value and focused on only bringing back those specific processes	1. Company stopped a discriminatory outsourcing strategy and began focusing on client value 2. Backsourced IT operations to nearshore location 3. Keeping control and representing HQ at lower labor costs 4. Implemented process controls and structure	1. This **strategy combines** both **value creation** with **backsourcing** 2. It already shows a growth from a standard backsourcing strategy to one that focuses on client value	All processes that added value to the client

are not as low as when they outsourced the global IT organization but are lower than before starting outsourcing and surprisingly lower than when backsourcing began. The organization has a new perspective toward backsourcing and is beginning to backsource their manufacturing capabilities (Table 4.4).

4.1.4 Aviation Industry Case Study

A good friend once told me that "*if you find a good story, chase it till the end of the landing path*" He also happened to be a pilot, so the metaphor seemed appropriate. The case study we will cover next will share an industry's evolution from the one supplier outsourcing best practice to the new and evolved diversified outsourcing strategy concentrating control and coordination in-house. This case will begin with studying the airline industry by going deep inside the outsourcing strategy of one of the largest airline companies in the world, hearing the words directly from senior decision makers to then following that chain of services to uncover how the airline supplier is transforming to remain competitive.

The case study is about one of the top five European-based airline companies and in 2019 was cited as one of the largest global airline companies based on the number of passengers and crew. The case study reflects a different outsourcing strategy than used by other industries. The large airline company, which we anonymously refer to as Aviation Co. was taking advantage of its global reach by utilizing low-cost hubs to maintain its airplanes in addition to simultaneously having access to top skilled resources. As a leader in the aviation industry their outsourcing model representative of a large legacy airline company. They were executing a mature outsourcing strategy not focused on back-sourcing. We follow their service supply chain to review one of the largest Aviation Suppliers worldwide. Aviation Supplier Co. is one of the world's top technical providers for the aviation industry, employing over 3,000 global resources who service aircrafts, engines, and do line maintenance. Aviation Supplier Co. supports over one thousand aircraft with an extensive global network of logistic centers in London, Zurich, Abu Dhabi, Singapore, and Melbourne and more. Aviation Supplier Co.'s outsourcing model is currently evolving from an outsourcing relationship with one large information technology infrastructure provider to smaller transactions with multiple technology suppliers. Aviation Supplier Co. **owns the integration and coordination** between their data centers and various information technology server management providers such as the network and applications including SAP.

The case is structured so initially we will hear directly from executives representing both the aviation company and the aviation supplier. By navigating this process, we will review and understand why the aviation company continues to use a traditional one supplier strategy. We will then transition to the supplier side and in more detail review their transition to a more complex diversified outsourcing strategy. We will dig deep to understand how they are taking their aged full outsourcing strategy and transforming it into a strategic advantage. The participants whom I interviewed for this case study each have over 30 years of outsourcing experience including a former Chief Technology Officer and Chief Architect for top Fortune companies. Due to the level of expertise, they have contributed significantly to the findings of this case study as well as further helped to show how outsourcing as an industry is evolving.

Do We Take off Outsourcing or Is There Trouble on the Landing Path
Aviation Co. was fully supportive of outsourcing and continuously sought to uncover additional areas to outsource including their core competencies. The case study findings show they were not focused only on reducing costs but sought strategic partnerships to provide them with a strategic advantage over their competition. The company seeks to further outsource areas such as the booking systems which was once a core business capability. This previously thought of core competency lost its edge once it was serviced faster and cheaper by an outside vendor. Additionally, it stops becoming a competitive advantage once most airline companies in the industry outsource the capability. At this point booking stopped being a core capability and transitioned to one that airlines were able to reduce cost while having access to better systems provided by external vendors.

Aviation Co. sought outsourcing partnerships that provided them with a competitive advantage, but the cost reduction had to remain. This is noteworthy to point out because their main objective was not solely to reduce cost, however, it was expected as part of overall improvements to service. Essentially, the cost savings was an unspoken accepted understanding that any outsourcing competitive strategy should be attached to a cost reduction as well. This strategic outsourcing pursuit lead them to outsourcing their complete information technology infrastructure.

Outsourcing as a profession is maturing and Aviation Co. is fully growing the capabilities in-house to manage their outsourcing providers. Doubling down on outsourcing has permitted them to develop **advanced outsourcing management capabilities in-house which led to higher and tougher demands from their providers than other companies which did not build such capabilities**. They have also fine-tuned their outsourcing selection processes which filtered out vendors that would not fully commit or provide specific capabilities they sought. This was a lesson learned from previous outsourcing engagements which resulted in failure due to not having the specific requirements of what success would look like from the beginning. This selection process even includes an area for additional priced competitive advantage benefits that the potential supplier can offer. For example, when they were entering an outsourcing relationship with an outsourcer who was well known for their information technology advancements, they quickly demanded cloud mobility expertise and help with improving their overall environment. I had a conversation with an executive with over 30 years in the outsourcing industry from the supplier side who mentioned the below.

> The client wants to reduce their costs. This is mostly their main objective. This allows them to spend more elsewhere within their own company. Secondly, we bring experience in technology to the table and with that comes innovation into play. We help them stay competitive in the market through providing them cloud mobility capabilities that they don't have. (Anonymous, Personal Communication, August 19, 2016)

The above example supports the decision Aviation Co. made to continue supporting a progressive outsourcing strategy. This continue to outsource where possible strategy allows the airline company to divert capital where it is needed the most while partnering with key companies that provide them with "something special." Long-lasting organizations combine their internal capabilities with industry strengths and strategic partnerships.

The quote below is from an airline outsourcing executive who fully supports offshore outsourcing with the caveat the outsourcing engagement has to be fully documented and standardized. And he clarifies his position on standardization as one of the most important aspects of a successful outsourcing engagement since if the work is, more could be replicated and improved.

> Location does not make any difference. When you need to shift from one location to the other. You always have, at the beginning, I would say, yes, a challenging time because you need to [shift the] workload....if you do it right, and if you really stick to the standardization, what is necessary...I do not see that big difference. (Anonymous, Personal communication, August 4, 2016)

The aviation industry's specific strength other industries may not possess is the ability to easily move their major product from country to country. Their supply chain model allows them to move their planes requiring maintenance to the least expensive location, as part of busines as usual. For example, a plane traveling from Germany to the Philippines can be serviced in the Philippines. The work will still be done with all the rigorous safety requirements and takes advantage of the Philippines' lower-cost labor. The company that performs those rigorous safety checks was the aviation supplier who provides services to airlines such as Aviation Supplier Co. Although **Aviation Co**. had a full outsourcing strategy that was working well, their **Aviation Supplier Co**. was facing obstacles it needed to overcome.

Aviation Supplier Co. had to re-think their outsourcing model due to major obstacles that arose out of their full outsourcing relationship. **Aviation Supplier Co. was involved in a full IT infrastructure outsourcing engagement that resulted in the cost of doing business significantly rising and simultaneously lost control of their internal decision control**. Ultimately this led to the retained staff losing influence over key projects and the prioritization of deliverables within their own outsourcing environment. Initially, they gained the usual first-class labor cost reduction benefits from the full IT outsourcing engagement, but unfortunately, the low-cost journey did not last long. In addition to dwindling cost benefits of outsourcing, Aviation Supplier Co. realized they also lost their decision control power.

Aviation Supplier Co's initial obstacle was that it had failed to fully assess which areas truly needed to be outsourced and took flight on a full IT infrastructure outsourcing journey. Although historically sound, the one supplier service provider model was too rigid for Aviation Supplier Co. The company's senior IT leadership team struggled with their new ability to adjust to timely business issues by utilizing their service provider. The quote below describes how the company was restricted from receiving key needed services to run their operations due to contractual limitation.

> They came back because they were not satisfied with the single provider approach. You're limited to delivering the processes and standards which were made up in the contract, in the outsourcing contract, maybe three years before. They lose flexibility. They lose speed and today, sometimes not capable, due to standards, contractual standards, to manage special non-standard requests. (Anonymous, Personal Communication, September 5, 2016)

One would imagine that a key benefit of outsourcing would be the flexibility to pivot resources. However, this flexibility was limited due to the outsourcer being limited to providing only the services that had been agreed to three years earlier. The strong legal walls that the original terms of the agreement left both the IT provider and client in a situation bound only to support what was previously agreed to. The outsourcing contractual environment was so restrictive and slow that it did not foster the creation of many additional service requests. It further generated a loss of faith and control in request management as well as the ability to make quick decisions that impacted business results. The quote below reflects on location selection as not solely a detriment on its own however it may no longer be financially feasible to provide the specific requested outsourced service from the home country. However, the art in this offshoring advantage is the flexibility to quickly mobilize the workforce when needed.

> Outsourcing from Switzerland is not feasible from a cost perspective. It is far too expensive. You are going to a near shore country and what my experience is wherever you go it helps when you don't select too many different locations. Ideally you have the whole service from Poland and then you can manage and then these people where they can work together. Of course, you have local social media and possibilities to communicate nowadays. But still it helps if those that provide the service are in the same location. And where this location is, is makes no difference if they have the right skills. (Anonymous, Personal Communication, September 5, 2016)

The major mistakes Aviation Supplier Co. made before making changes to their outsourcing strategy was handing over its decision control to the outsourcer and then experienced rising operating costs. The short quote below from a seasoned professional who provides outsourcing services highlights how restrictive cost management had become. **The increased cost of outsourcing restricted the organization from being able to invest in other areas of the business.**

> I mean they are just; they have their rules that they need to follow but they go where it's cheapest. I mean that's what they do. (Anonymous, Personal Communication, August 4, 2016)

Natural Evolution into a New Outsourcing Strategy

Aviation Supplier Co's executive leadership desperately needed to take control of their future by replacing their Chief Information Officer (CIO). The new CIO's strengths did not include a deep technical background instead he had more skill in business and stakeholder management. This hiring strategy mirrored their needs to recruit a fast-acting technical leader that understood their business.

The quote below is from an outsourcing service provider with deep aviation outsourcing industry knowledge and expertise including decades of working with clients across multiple industries. His quote shines much light into the overall outsourcing strategy evolution that he was a part off firsthand. He openly discusses obstacles that Aviation Supplier Co. faced through losing their IT business knowledge by relying on the legacy outsourcer. The environment where control was handed over to the outsourcer was not hidden, but an actual strategy that we are now learning to have been a destructive one. He further highlights how Aviation Supplier Co. was bounded by their contracted process arrangements. In this case, the processes were contracted in a way that it hindered the company through not allowing Aviation Supplier Co. the flexibility to request additional services, when needed.

> They were looking for an all-in-one provider or a provider who could manage all of their IT globally. So, they thought they'd get rid of the IT problems, of course, because it got to complex. And by doing that, after a couple of years, when they were or became aware that a single-provider approach, they experienced that they lost dynamic, of course, in the change business. So, they couldn't follow the business changes so quickly on IT as they were expecting. So, you're not so flexible anymore. (Anonymous, Personal Communication, September 5, 2016)

He further mentioned how important the "interlink" between the various stakeholders was in the new organizational structure. The new organization structure also needed to have new capabilities starting with the new CIO as well as the rest of the retained organization who would now serve are the bridge between business requirements and how technology would help them achieve their goals. Furthermore, the new organization had to include technical and stakeholder management responsibilities.

> They also became aware after the years, that they lost all of their IT business knowledge. Which of course, got closer and closer to the real business or more connected and integrated, which was also not very good for them or they were bound into processes which made them do a lot of effort, losing time, et cetera or keeping standards, which were not fitting or matching the requirements they had after a while. So, they started to backsource, which means, they understood that it may be better if they used internal, so called, retained organization. Which is usually, you take the very best people, knowing your own business and also parts of IT, in the high-level perspective and to interlink and manage the providers to get the IT and the business requirements together. Because usually the IT provider knows the IT and the business knows the business. But the

> interlink of these both disciplines, this was usually the problem. So, they started to source in or backsource. (Anonymous, Personal Communication, September 5, 2016)

Aviation Supplier Co. completely changed their power position by pitting potential service providers against one another by creating bidding wars on price for potential contracts. Aviation Supplier Co.'s business is very price sensitive and cost is a key differentiator in vendor selection. Now Aviation Supplier Co. may use the market to their advantage by engaging in smaller deals with a variety of vendors competing for their business by included increased service at lower prices.

The following quote is significant as it shares how the supplier side is also evolving in response to the industry's new supplier diversification and backsourcing initiatives. The executive supplier side leader providing services to Aviation Supplier Co. highlights how the outsourcers themselves are moving away from providing full IT outsourcing solutions. He further provides a background on the overall outsourcing industry shift to pulling back on a full outsourcing model while focusing on more scalable and flexible options such as mobile cloud capabilities which would allow the service to be scalable with little effort. Interestingly, he also commented on how the industry is evolving naturally toward the new outsourcing scalable specialties as a response to client demand. The respondent also mentioned that there has not been a widely communicated strategy based on the new environment where organizations are backsourcing as part of business as usual but have gradually understood this to be the new reality. Essentially, there has not been an overly communicated announcement that the industry is evolving but more and more clients as changing the way they engage in outsourcing which is currently defining the future of the industry itself.

> I think it has been evolved kind of naturally. I need to be able to react quickly and I need to abandon from the idea to have IT outsourced to one company for a 5-10 years contract and stay there and so they probably and that's what I think it's also started to change in that respect it is the line. The strategy has evolved and has not been that clearly communicated to all the decision makers within our clients and it just kind of happened to happen. Unfortunately, for the supplier that means the transaction that were big and large at one time is now becoming more and more OTCs or over the counter. I also see, you know, that there is a lot of functionality which is now back to our client. It's the integration of the services the

> coordination of the different type of vendors and services. They also do at the moment I mean what I see is that they like to have – to be in the owner of their data centers and their assets being able to flexible, flexible, you know, switch the service mobile to send it to give it partially or in total to another supplier.(Anonymous, Personal Communication, August 24, 2016)

Taking Back Control of Your Flight Plan

One of the biggest drivers for a company to make a seismic change is a problem large enough that it makes the company focus on their core capabilities. Aviation Supplier Co. had to deal with making a change due to increased costs and their lack of flexibility. Aviation Supplier Co. had to be nimble enough to change service locations and set up support staff as fast as possible where needed in order to support aviation companies such as Aviation Co. who was benefiting from their outsourcing relationship. Aviation Supplier Co. was hoping to achieve this flexibility advantage at a low cost while having the technology infrastructure to do so quickly. Unfortunately, they had established a long-lasting one supplier relationship so cemented in bureaucracy and processes that there was no room for quick thinking and reaction. This overly processed and overly bureaucratic environment led to them completely rethinking their outsourcing environment.

Aviation Supplier Co. decided to end their relationship with their main supplier and backsourced their entire IT infrastructure capabilities including data center services. The idea behind this against the grain strategy was a desperate move to bring back control of their operations and attain the ability to move quickly when needed, without the complex request environment that had been created over the years.

Aviation Supplier Co. believed because they owned their data centers their staff could quickly take action quickly and not worry about aged IT infrastructure contract drafted to address last decade's problems. The backsourcing decision was initially received with some concerns by their senior leaders but quickly gained a bottom-up buy-in as more and more resources where hired-in and ready to immediately help multiple stakeholders without the previous lagging vendor request management processes. Aviation Supplier Co.'s motivation was not to drive innovation but instead to change their outsourcing model by focusing on cost and control. However, they do have an interesting backsourcing model. Aviation Supplier Co. is **bringing back control by diluting the services that**

were once provided by one supplier and outsourcing them to various outsourcing providers.

The outsourcing strategy change removed Aviation Supplier Co.'s dependence on a single infrastructure supplier who even had difficulty getting a new server up and running or onboarding key support staff. However, their strategy was not a simple backsourcing vs. outsourcing strategy. They implemented a hybrid approach which addressed all of their main concerns. They took back ownership of their data centers but have contractors manage the multiple vendors that provide various services within the data center, such as network, cloud computing, SAP, capacity management, and server maintenance. Hence, they are using a hybrid outsourcing model where Aviation Supplier Co. is using subcontractors to manage and coordinate the different services that were once provided by one supplier. The main difference is that those services are now broken out and contracted out to multiple service providers. The **Hybrid Outsourcing Strategy (HOS)** begins with a foundation of documented processes and structure that aligns diversified outsourcing, backsourcing key processes and outsourcing of vendor management as the three main contributing pillars described below. The output of this strategy is to increase internal flexibility while structuring a foundation of long-term cost control management.

1. **Fully Documented Processes & Structure**: The creation and documentation of processes is a key aspect of this strategy as it sets the foundation of what are the processes that help the organizations thrive, what processes should be owned internally, owned externally, and what does a perfect scenario.
2. **Diversified Outsourcing**: Spread the outsourcing services from one main supplier to multiple. It was originally preferred to engage with one major supplier to take advantage of economies of scale. However, transferring most services to only one supplier also may transfer the control and decision-making capabilities.
3. **Backsourcing Key Processes**: The company took back control of key IT infrastructure capabilities to ensure their IT readiness.
4. **Outsourcing Vendor Management**: The centralized project management and coordination of multiple outsourcing providers managed by another external subcontractor.

Aviation Supplier Co. implemented an interesting form of backsourcing as they outsourced their vendor project management. **Vendor project management** is the coordination and management of the work performed by multiple service providers in order to collectively meet the goals and deliverables of the client company. Companies who bring back their control after outsourcing typically employed in-house key resources to manage the formerly outsourced capabilities. Aviation Supplier Co. also outsourced the management and coordination of their vendors who had taken over the processes previously owned by the one legacy outsourcer. **Legacy outsourcer** is the long-standing outsourcing service provider. Their diversification strategy included outsourcing the vendor management. However, that subcontractor that was coordinating and managing the vendors was completely separate from any of the other companies that were providing services becoming a trusted representative of Aviation Supplier Co.

Conclusion to Flight and Backsource Safely

The aviation industry has a supply chain built with offshoring capability which is unlike other industries. This capability to transport their products, airplanes, to a maintenance hub located in lower-cost country to work on is unlike any other industry. The large airline company which participated in this study was not interested in backsourcing and instead outsourced their core capabilities where possible. Internally they built a wealth of knowledge about outsourcing management and have moved past engaging with vendors solely for cost advantages. Price reduction is basically a conversation starter as the potential vendor must bring more to the negotiation table than cost savings. Following this case study, we moved to the aviation supplier's environment to see how they could continue to feed that increasing demand for lower cost while requesting additional services.

Aviation Supplier Co. was involved in a multiyear full IT outsourcing engagement with a global supplier under a strict governance contract. The long-term contract limited their ability to add-on additional services or requirements emanating from current business problems. New requests on issues not contractually agreed on years before would take so long to be processed they would lose their urgency by the time they were approved. In addition, the company began to see rising costs in their outsourced environment due to their restrictive contract and its lack of flexibility. Ultimately, key business stakeholders had to fix their IT operations were forced to make changes beginning with their CIOs departure to changing an entire outsourcing strategy that included backsourcing their data center, key skills, and vendor management capabilities.

The company decided to completely shift away from their sole supplier strategy and implement a **diversified outsourcing strategy with backsourcing at its core**. This Hybrid Strategy allowed the breaking apart services provided by one service provider and sought new providers They opened their bidding processes and sought new providers offering flexible terms and additional services at lower price points to whom they would outsource their multiple smaller scope areas. However, their main concern was to regain control in case they had to make significant and timely changes to their operations. They addressed this concern by backsourcing the coordination and management of the various service providers. In addition to splitting the services to multiple suppliers, they also outsourced the management of the suppliers. The company they used to coordinate the various vendors was separate from all others in that they did not own any other responsibilities and was often perceived as an internal partner due to their strong relationship and loyalties. Unfortunately, it is too soon to gauge the long-lasting success of Aviation Supplier Co. evolved outsourcing strategy. However, at the time of this publishing, the stakeholder sentiment was positive toward the backsourcing focused strategy due to its cost reduction and bringing back flexibility and control over their success (Table 4.5).

4.2 Conclusion

The relatively young outsourcing industry has grown into a multibillion-dollar industry by 2020 and continues to evolve. This chapter conveyed the evolutionary story from the perspective of four different industries. The four industries studied were **Aviation**, **Insurance**, **Cookware**, and **Pharmaceutical**. These specific industries were selected because they are all independently capturing a section of that evolution ranging from the most advanced pharmaceutical industry to the aviation industry showing how the airline remains focused on legacy outsourcing.

Pharmaceutical industry: The chapter began with a Pharmaceutical industry case study that reviewed the most advanced outsourcing strategy being used today. Their strategy is so novel that it should be defined as a completely new phase within the evolution of outsourcing. The top five

Table 4.5 Aviation: Why should we care?

Overview of strategy	*What was implemented*	*Industry significance*	*What was backsourced*
1. Aviation Co. took advantage of a progressive outsourcing model focused on a mature full outsourcing strategy continuing outsourcing all areas where possible **2. Aviation Supplier Co.** took advantage of both a supplier network as well as internal capabilities through a **Hybrid Outsourcing Strategy** creating a balance of what they own and what they outsource	**1. Aviation Co.** Implemented a progressive outsourcing strategy increasingly demanding continuous improvements from their suppliers **2. Aviation Supplier Co.** Implemented a diversified outsourcing strategy while backsourcing certain key processes a. Using subcontractors to manage and coordinate the different service that were once provided by one main IT supplier b. Increased flexibility and cost management control	**1. Aviation Co.** Proves that outsourcing continues to provide ongoing benefits within the right environment **2. Aviation Supplier Co.** using subcontractors to manage and coordinate the different services that were once provided by one main IT supplier a. Provides a clear differentiation between how an Aviation company is maximizing suppliers and how the supplier **had to evolve** in order to remain competitive	1. Key processes 2. Control and coordination of various suppliers

pharmaceutical company that we studied is setting the new benchmark on how to outsource. They have implemented the Hybrid Backsourcing Strategy (HBS) that brought back key processes to the company as well as created an internal outsourcing organization to supply itself. It further created a risk avoidance strategy where they would temporarily take control of a supplier's process to assure there were no supply interruptions. The HBS can further be applied to any global company seeking to differentiate themselves while taking back control of their success.

Next, we covered the **Cookware industry** where we learned how a leading global company implemented a backsourcing strategy focused on value processes. This case study is also significant and shows that companies applying a "backsourcing" strategy are doing a lot more than simply the opposite of outsourcing. Their innovative Value-Based Backsourcing strategy set the benchmark on how to backsource with structured value.

Chasing the outsourcing evolution wave took us to the **Insurance industry** where we uncovered diversified outsourcing and how this was the first jump from the classical one supplier model that chased economies of scale. The Insurance Co. case study taught us that both the client and service providers is open to the outsourcing evolution and were willing to reduce scope to focus on what makes them successful. All case studies focus on the story of one company at a time, except the Aviation industry.

The chapter ends with the **Aviation industry** case study and follows the service chain of a top global airline and an airline service provider. The case conveyed how two companies within one industry are taking advantage of two different strategies. The Aviation Co., a top global airline company is applying a mature legacy outsourcing strategy with a progressive outsourcing. They are not focused on backsourcing and continue to improve their management of outsourcing relationships to attain greatest benefit of doing business with their suppliers. Conversely, we share a company providing services. With this company's story we learn how it had to evolve and restructure by applying Hybrid Outsourcing Strategy (HOS). HOS that takes advantage of both internal network and external suppliers to achieve the flexibility and long-term cost control. The image below captures the evolution of the outsourcing industry and how different each strategy is when compared to the original classic and now "legacy" outsourcing benchmarks.

The industries selected to be part of this research are significant because they all represent a stage within the outsourcing evolution. Each case study further provides an overview of how that industry compares to others (Fig. 4.4). Most of the changes represent slight advancements except the pharmaceutical industry who has reinvented outsourcing by the implementation of the HBS. The below graph visually represents this industry evolution and reasons (Fig. 4.5).

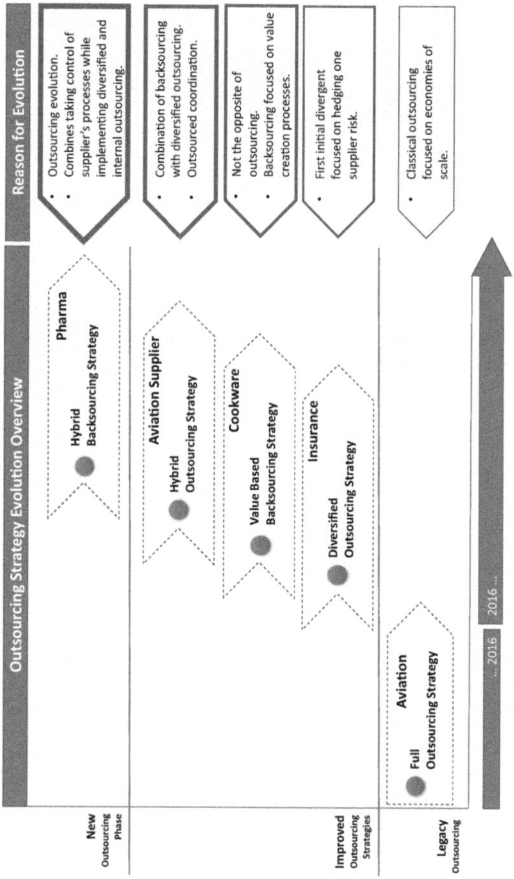

Fig. 4.4 Outsourcing strategy evolution overview

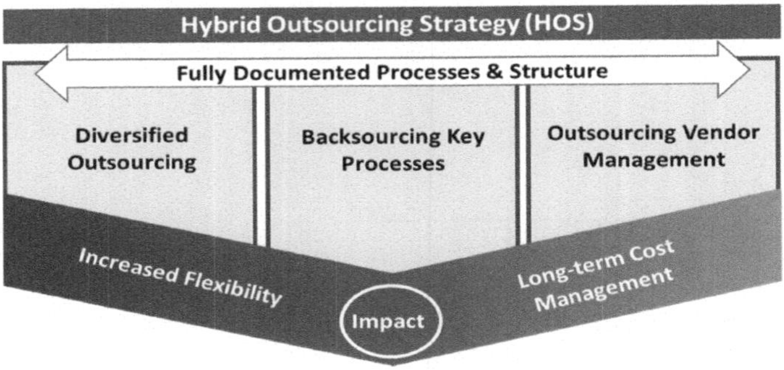

Fig. 4.5 Hybrid outsourcing strategy (HOS)

Bibliography

Hansen, S. (2020). *These are the world's largest drug and biotech companies*. https://www.forbes.com/sites/sarahhansen/2020/05/13/these-are-the-worlds-largest-drug-and-biotech-companies/#218842192d72.

CHAPTER 5

The Development of a New Outsourcing Theory Uncovered by Backsourcing

Outsourcing as an industry recently has made an evolutionary jump forward. Diverging from the past has clearly occurred in the Pharmaceutical and Aviation industries. Both industries have shown that they are simultaneously maximizing classical outsourcing as well as breaking off and developing their own evolution of outsourcing as a strategic powerhouse. This chapter will cover the historical significance of how both industries had an independent progressive supplier relationship that has led to their significant industry outsourcing perspective and innovation. We will especially see how their strategic sourcing innovations impacted the outsourcing evolution, as a whole.

The chapter opens with an overview of the pharmaceutical (pharma) industry's early years and examine companies like Merck who were able to take advantage of rudimentary outsourcing relationships to attain a strategic advantage that keeps them strong, a century later. We will review how outsourcing is evolving within the pharmaceutical and aviation industry into something greater than solely seeking a cost advantage.

The chapter continues to describe on their evolutionary path by reviewing the progression of outsourcing as an industry. Outsourcing as an industry is reviewed from two new perspectives. The first is **Outsourcing as a Key Element**, where we see the first major steps lead to the outsourcing evolution where the goal was to take "out"

L. A. Mederos, *The Future of Outsourcing*,
Palgrave Studies in Accounting and Finance Practice,
https://doi.org/10.1007/978-3-030-71407-9_5

of the company by outsourcing. The second and more mature process shared led to **Backsourcing as a Key Element** which covers key value driven processes that are brought "back" to the company. We will also review each area and reason for the evolutionary jump that led to the new outsourcing phase called **Hybrid Backsourcing**. The chapter will then conclude with another evolutionary view from the control's perspective. The industry is evolving and so are the controls that will help organizations reach success (Fig. 5.1).

5.1 The Significance of the Pharmaceutical Industry on the Future of Outsourcing

This section provides a historical journey up to the modern pharmaceutical industry from the industry's beginning with the sales of drug store remedies during the Victorian era to the global industry it has become. We will read how outsourcing has been part of the industry longer than we realize and how the pharma industry has become one of the most innovative industries defining the use of backsourcing strategies today. The section opens with a historical overview of the pharmaceutical industry and its financial significance. We will then review how the industry set the outsourcing benchmark to create a completely new stage of outsourcing.

5.1.1 From Leeches to Today's Pharma and Sourcing in Between

Today's pharmaceutical industry resulted from apothecaries moving away from distributing botanical-based remedies such as morphine, to manufacturing their own drugs in the middle of the nineteenth century. Imagine if you lived during the Victorian era when leeches were commonly used to alleviate various ailments. Now imagine its a few months later and you have a sore throat and return to the same pharmacist and he suggests you drink an opium-based syrup to alleviate your ailment. I can imagine that if we knew its side effects, we would have not chosen the bittersweet drug-based option. This move toward drug-based solutions was cemented by Friedrich Sertuerner.

Friedrich Sertuerner, a pharmacist apprentice discovered morphine in the early 1800s. He was not yet a full-fledged pharmacist when he made the discovery that helped to build the pharmaceutical industry. His discovery marks the origin of using natural products chemistry and

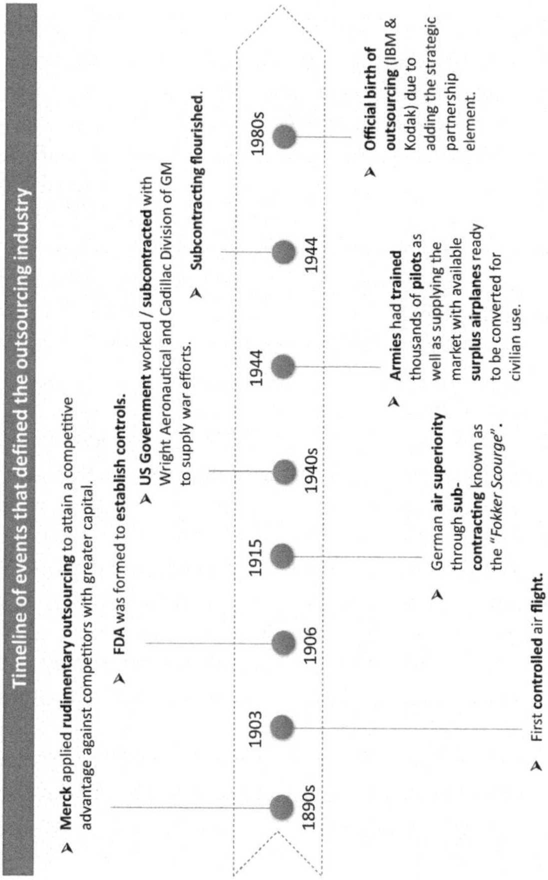

Fig. 5.1 Timeline of events that defined the outsourcing industry

pharmacology (Lever, 2007). Natural product chemistry is the study of chemicals created from living organisms while pharmacology is the science of drugs from creation to how they affect us. For example, Merck is one of those key pharmacies hose business was created during the Victorian era and transformed into what it is today.

Merck's roots can be traced back to 1668, and in 1827 Emanuel Merck led the change from a pharmacy business to a research-based industrial organization (Matos et al., 2020). This transformation created the modern pharmaceutical industry where pharmacies and distributors began to manufacture drugs. By the 1890s, Merck became a pharmaceutical powerhouse thought the use of a combination of external inventors and university partnerships to develop new products and focused its internal scientists on production efficiencies (Burhop, 2009). Merck had to innovate to compete and thrive against other companies with greater OR more capital (Burhop, 2009). **Merck arguably applied a rudimentary outsourcing model** where they could improve efficiencies internally while relying on strategic university partnerships for continuous innovation.

The **pharmaceutical industry's purpose** is tasked to discover, create, and manufacture medications, vaccines, and drugs to help cure, treat, and/or mitigate symptoms associated with ailments or diseases. There are various governing bodies throughout the world dedicated to assuring our safety by evaluating and supervising the industry's output. Some of the controlling agencies include the Pharmaceutical and Medical Devices Agency for Japan, as well as the European Medicines Agency in Amsterdam with a greater scope that includes the entire European Union. The US's also governing body is the Food and Drug Administration. The **Food and Drug Administration (FDA)** was formed by the Pure Food and Drug Act of 1906 which protected US citizens from ingesting adulterated and misbranded drugs (FDA.gov, 2018). The FDA evolved and includes consumer protection with the Federal Food, Drug, and Cosmetic (FFDC) Act of 1938 establishing quality standards for drug manufacturing. In 1962, the FFDC was amended to protect the public convey trust in the reliability of drugs. This meant pharmaceutical companies would have to prove their drugs were safe and effective. Although highly regulated, as of 2019 the industry grew to a substantial $1.3 trillion USD industry with favorable projections (EvaluatePharma, 2019).

The **worldwide pharmaceutical revenue** is divided between the US holding about 33% with Western Europe holding about 22%, while China has now broken into the top 3 with 10% (Statistica, 2020). Global sourcing played a large role in worldwide pharmaceutical sales growth. India provides the world with about 20% of generic drug manufacturing and between 2005 and 2016 the US realized a savings of over 2 trillion USD (Shetti & Khanna, 2019). The pharmaceutical industry has taken advantage of outsourcing capabilities by extending manufacturing to include contract research and information technology.

More than ever before pharmaceutical companies are engaging in contract research outsourcing as spending reached approximately $80 billion USD by 2017 (Getz, 2018). **Contract research outsourcing (CRO)** is defined as a service provider supplying contract-based work for clinical trials and clinical research in new product development. Outsourcing clinical trials and research provides pharmaceutical companies with access to key niche research capabilities they would otherwise have or need to retain beyond the specific trial. Pharmaceutical companies have been able to achieve greater efficiency in drug development timelines and assured validity of products by outsourcing parallel analytical trials (Haigney, 2019). Pharma has taken advantage of outsourcing within the CRO space to achieve a competitive advantage, but it does not stop there. Pharma also partners with some of the leading technology companies to gain an information technology advantage.

Within the pharmaceutical industry information technology outsourcing has helped innovate by allowing a focus to remain on its core capabilities and cost efficiencies. In 1997, Novartis Pharma signed what then seemed like a enormous $57 Million USD IT outsourcing deal with IBM, seeking cost savings through their strategic partnership (IBM, 1998). Novartis is not the only pharmaceutical company seeking a cost advantage through outsourcing. Roche established a shared service center in Poland to provide services previously supplied from higher cost countries including the USA and Switzerland, and AstraZeneca established centers in China, India, and Mexico (Fierce Biotech, 2016).

Through researching how outsourcing was evolving through various industries I noticed that the pharmaceutical industry was addressing outsourcing from a unique maturity perspective. I was fortunate enough to run an independent case study at one of the largest pharmaceutical companies in the world. The company has a long history of ranking within the top 5 in the world and one for setting industry best practices benchmarks. The next section goes into detail how the pharmaceutical industry is currently defining the future of outsourcing through a foundation based in backsourcing through the Hybrid Backsourcing Strategy.

5.1.2 Current Outsourcing Evolution Within the Pharmaceutical Industry

The pharmaceutical industry has developed an innovative outsourcing strategy that is applicable to any industry. The Hybrid Backsourcing Strategy (HBS) is redefining the outsourcing industry because it is not just a different way to apply outsourcing as a cost advantage or outsourcing for a specific objective. This revolutionary outsourcing strategy empowers large organizations to break free from reliance on large outsourcing suppliers. This reliance often means handing over control of global processes and power over controlling key business outcomes. The HBS is significant in that it is not just a way to outsource focused on a single objective. The HBS completely changes how an organization engages with suppliers as it focuses on three different pillars with a cross foundation on restructuring for the right new environment talent. The three pillars are diversified outsourcing, supplier risk avoidance support, and internal outsourcing.

Diversified outsourcing is the first pillar and significant on its own as it departs from classical outsourcing by going away from the legacy one supplier model and dividing the large contract into smaller more controlled sections. The second pillar is a completely new model on how to engage with suppliers. The **Supplier Risk Avoidance Support Model** encompasses a completely integrated supplier network where the company purchasing outsourced services monitors and coordinates the milestones of various outsourcing providers. The outsourcing client coordinates the various smaller suppliers who have the opportunity to service them. This opportunity became available by implementing the first stage which also diversified the risk of relying on one main large supplier and instead dilutes their risk by breaking down the contract into smaller manageable sections. The smaller sections are grouped together and coordinated to meet the objectives defined by the outsourcing client. This coordination provides two key benefits. The first benefit is it fully aligns the suppliers with the client and each other to provide the contracted services. While the second benefit takes back control of their success by coordinating the list of providers.

By owning the coordination of multiple smaller contract areas, the company backsourced their control formerly handed over to one main supplier. Owning the coordination puts them in a situation to control their future by **activating the supplier risk avoidance model** when a supplier cannot meet a specific deliverable or key deadline. The client would be embedded in the supplier's process by providing resources and funding, if needed, to ensure the pharmaceutical company does not miss key deadlines that could impact people's lives. The supplier momentarily gives up power of their processes or operations to accept the support needed to complete the contracted product or service. The chart below shows the relationship between the supplier and the outsourcing client before and after the activation of the Supplier Risk Avoidance Support Model (Fig. 5.2).

The third pillar includes the implementation of internal outsourcing. **Internal outsourcing** is when an organization supplies itself with services or products from another area of the same company that can attain lower labor and/or operating costs. This is more specific to large organizations that have an international labor force with internal resources. The organization would utilize their international internal strength and take advantage of lower cost country labor rates through their already set infrastructure. This is also applicable domestically if labor costs differ enough to make a financial difference. Also, the company does not have to have the capabilities internally at the time of initially implementing the strategy as they can hire for the desired skillset. The foundation for this strategy is established on either retaining or recruiting the appropriate resources to lead the new organizational structure that has a stronger ownership balance on both backsourced as well as outsourced processes.

5.2 How the Aviation Industry Is Helping Outsourcing Take Flight

This section takes us on a historical journey through the aviation industry and its symbiotic partnership with external suppliers. This relationship helped countries gain wartime air superiority as well as decreased travel lead times so global commerce could take off. This century-long supplier relationship has created outsourcing management expertise to design one of today's most innovative outsourcing strategies. We will close the section by reviewing how one of the world largest aviation suppliers redefined outsourcing and is setting the benchmark for the rest of the industry to follow.

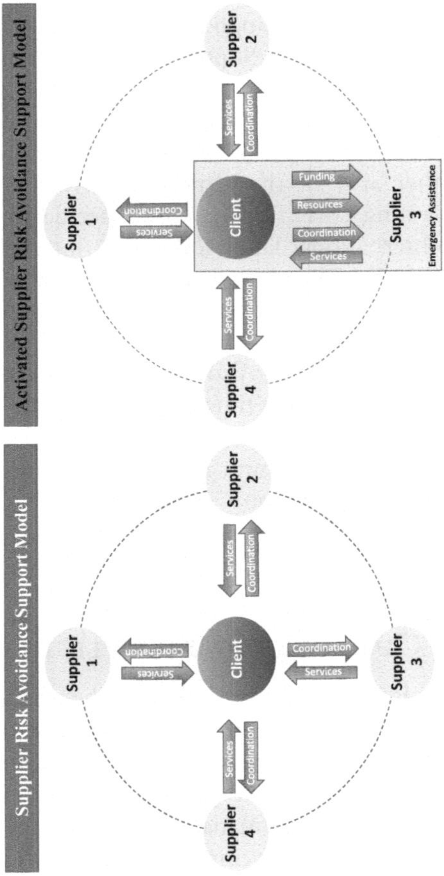

Fig. 5.2 Risk avoidance support model before and after activation

5.2.1 *Aviation Industry Market Maturity*

The aviation industry can trace back their history to many centuries ago when kites were flown. However, it took until the twentieth century for the commercial aviation industry to mature and unite the world by drastically reducing worldwide flight travel time. The commercial aviation industry sector is dedicated to flying passengers or cargo. Voyages that once took many weeks on a ship now take just hours to complete with air travel. Global proximity has stimulated companies to engage in international business much easier than ever before by reducing commuter travel time from one country to another, regardless of the oceans between continents. Although the idea of flight was conceived thousands of years ago, it is only recently humankind that was able to travel through the air. Wilbur and Orville Wright built and flew the first ever controlled flight (Frandsen, 2017). Controlling the plane's flight truly set them apart from all their competitors. The term heavier than air distinguished hot air balloon technology of the time from the heavier motor-powered fixed-wing aircraft being developed.

Ever since their first short flight in 1903, transportation changed forever thanks to aviation pioneers the Wright brothers. However, their astonishing achievement would not have been possible without George Cayley. Sir George Cayley is known as the "*father of aeronautics*" for inventing the basic principles necessary to manufacture a fixed-wing airplane (Pritchard, 1954; Ackroyd, 2011). During the last century aviation finally started to take off. However, it was not until the first world war the aviation industry boomed. The boom ushered in air combat as maneuverability and speed significantly improved by giving a competitive advantage to the side with the best technological advancement (bbc.com, 2014). Germany understood this war strategy but did not have the required in-country skillset to develop such technological advancements.

Germany engaged with the aircraft supplier company Fokker to help them gain a competitive edge against the French, British, and Americans who were also fighting to rule the skies. This subcontracting relationship was beneficial for the Germans as it led to their air superiority. Beginning in 1915, the "Fokker Scourge" translated as the "Fokker Scare" became feared after Germany fitted their first machine gun on an aircraft to shoot through the blades (Bechthold, 2017). The Fokker D.VII was such an advanced design it gave the Germans a deadly advantage over the Allies (Nijboer, 2016). This subcontracting relationship proved so beneficial that the Fokker D.VII was specifically listed on the cease fire Armistice Agreement of November 1918 which required handing over all Fokker D.VII planes to the allies (Tucker, 2014).

Throughout the first two decades of the nineteenth century flight technology significantly progressed from the first flight to controlling the skies over Europe. Just like businesses, governments seek competitive advantages or risk devastating results. However, the devastating results take on a different meaning during war time. The US government sought outside help by creating a plan for the Wright Aeronautical Co, and Cadillac Division of General Motors Corporation, to jointly manufacture with the Army Air Corps to focus on increased production and coordination (Haar, 1965). World War II efforts ultimately resulted in manufacturing more than 300,000 airplanes including 95,000 in 1944, catapulting the industry from 44th to number one in production value (Haar, 1965). According to the US Federal Aviation Administration, there were close to 300,000 pilots trained as a part of the War Training Service program alone (Kraus, n.d.) Ultimately, as a result of **World War II, armies trained thousands of pilots and supplies the market with available surplus airplanes ready to be converted for civilian use**. The airline industry blossomed and while global air transportation was considered luxurious, it was highly regulated. This strict regulation lasted for forty years through the Civil Aeronautics Act (CAA) of 1938.

The US aviation industry was highly regulated by the Civil Aeronautics Board (CAB) which controlled ticket prices, routes, trade practices, and which airlines entered the market (Siegmund, 1990). However, in 1978 President Jimmy Carter signed the Airline De regulation Act which opened up the airways to new market entrants, resulting in additional employment opportunities due to a greater number of routes (Thornicroft, 1989). The regulation resulted in reduced fares for passengers but unfortunately it reduced the airlines' ability to provide their high level of service (Brown, 2014).

By 2018, the global airline industry grew to $682 billion in revenue with a compound annual growth of 5.5% from 2014 to 2018 (MarketLine Industry Profile: Airlines in Global, 2019). By 2019, the global industry had grown to reflect an estimated $29 billion in net profit with North America making $16.9 billion, European carriers making around $6.2 billion and Asia-Pacific carriers landing in third place by earning a $4.9 billion net profit (Bonnassies, 2019). The aviation industry became significant to the world economy. However, it also has internal and external risks that can negatively impact its success. Some of the risks associated with the airline industry profitability include oil price volatility, as fuel prices can swiftly diminish a company's profit as well as passenger demand, ticket prices, and ancillary charges (Zarb, 2018).

Although these risks are significant to the success of an airline company, there has not been a greater threat to the entire industry as the novel Coronavirus. The International Air Transport Association (IATA) which supports global standards around safety and security has estimated the global airline industry will suffer a $113 billion loss due to the Coronavirus (Coronavirus hit for airlines could reach $113bn: IATA, 2020). The aviation industry has historically been a low margin one with companies seeking to lower costs where possible.

The aviation industry frequently seeks to lower costs by outsourcing key areas of their business ranging from airplane maintenance, to having a lower cost airline service an entire route where a low-cost competitor may be attempting to take over a market. Frequently, legacy airline companies respond to low-cost competition by engaging with a low-cost regional supplier to fly the lower cost routes (Tan, 2018). The low-cost regional outsourcing suppliers paint their planes to match the bigger and more known company and provide the resources to fly the planes and service the passengers. Additionally, the aviation industry trend is to outsource maintenance and technical services through mutually beneficial supplier and client partnerships (Holkeri, 2019).

5.2.2 *Current Outsourcing Evolution Within the Aviation Industry*

The commercial airline industry is comprised of both passenger and cargo transportation. The industry's growth is one of the significant drivers of the world economy. The industry's financial impact and a less discussed factor is its effect on spurring other industries to thrive. The civil aviation industry impacts other areas of the economy and is significant to the economic prosperity of a country (Arora & Mathur, 2020). For example, when I began consulting, I was on a Chicago-based team at IBM. A few of my colleagues lived in proximity to our downtown office, but many of them lived all over the US. The only requirement related to proximity was we needed to live close to a major airport. I was living in sunny Miami, Florida while my office was in the Windy City. This was especially funny because initially when I negotiated my contract freshly minted MBA, I was trying to land a challenging job to return Miami or somewhere on the East Coast. Nothing against San Francisco, which I love dearly, but my entire family was in Miami and I wanted to be in close proximity. Naively I forgot about salary negotiations and accepted the first salary offer when I heard I could work from anywhere, as long as it was close to an airport. As a young man with dreams of new experiences, you can imagine how excited I was to become a travel warrior.

The opportunity provided me a chance to work closely with various clients at their corporate offices while having the flexibility to travel home for the weekends. The airline industry provides consulting companies with the means to go after consulting opportunities with no regard to the distance from our corporate office. This opportunity allowed me to meet senior outsourcing executives within the aviation industry who agreed to let me conduct a case study at one of the top global companies large enough to accurately represent the industry. The novel Hybrid Outsourcing Strategy (HOS) is the compilation of over a century wide industry experience from that first flight to today's advanced outsourcing strategy.

The Hybrid Outsourcing Strategy coming out of the aviation industry is an evolutionary jump from legacy outsourcing focusing on three different pillars. The three evolutionary pillars are diversified outsourcing, backsourcing key processes, and outsourcing vendor management. The first pillar is diversified outsourcing mirroring the HBS in that both move away from legacy outsourcing by breaking large contracts into small manageable sections to be distributed throughout various outsourcing service providers. The second pillar is **backsourcing key processes**. The strategy does not focus on backsourcing all processes but is selective in that it focuses on certain processes that add specific value to the company. For example, the aviation industry is backsourcing key IT infrastructure areas that allows them to decrease the lead time to make changes that directly impacted their clients by not having to wait for a supplier approval on changes. This change returned the control they lost and flexibility they sought.

The aviation industry has built a wealth of knowledge managing vendors from its inception as it allowed them to gain a competitive advantage from the beginning. The industry supplier management expertise can be seen through the third pillar being **outsourcing vendor management (OVM)**. Implementing OVM resulted in outsourcing the management and coordination of the diversified outsourcing suppliers. They developed a network that allows them to keep control of the smaller contracts while using a separate subcontractor to manage the outsourcers as well as connecting them with the retained organization that represents both the newly backsourced processes as well as requests taking flight from internal business stakeholders. The three pillars have a strong foundation on process documentation and structure to understand what are the processes that add sustained value as well as what success should look like. Ultimately, the driving force behind the strategy development was to increase flexibility while assuring long-term cost control through having key backsourced ownership of certain processes while utilizing an advanced diversified outsourcing model that focused on sustained cost control with full control of variations through the creation of the outsourced vendor project management office.

5.3 Sourcing Evolution Setting the Foundation for Future Outsourcing Direction

Gottschalk and Solli-Sæther (2005) described the last three growth phases of outsourcing as outsourced, offshored, and ultimately backsourced as the most matured. Their research in outsourcing dwelled into a field not fully uncovered. Their innovative findings captured the maturity growth but showed no complete overlap in content between the stages. Recent years have proven that the outsourcing industry is going through an evolution where some organizations are applying a mixture of models breaking from history. The evolution of outsourcing can now be divided into two sections.

The first is where outsourcing is the key driving element while backsourcing is the driving force beneath the second section. The first part of the evolutionary growth that is driven by outsourcing can include **Subcontracting**, **Outsourcing**, and **Offshoring** as they are all handing over responsibilities to an outside company. The second section is driven by bringing a key element back to the company. The second covers **Diversified Outsourcing**, **Hybrid Outsourcing**, and **Hybrid Backsourcing**. Hybrid Backsourcing is where we can see the true evolution and clear-cut difference that will no longer be referring to history but making it (Fig. 5.3).

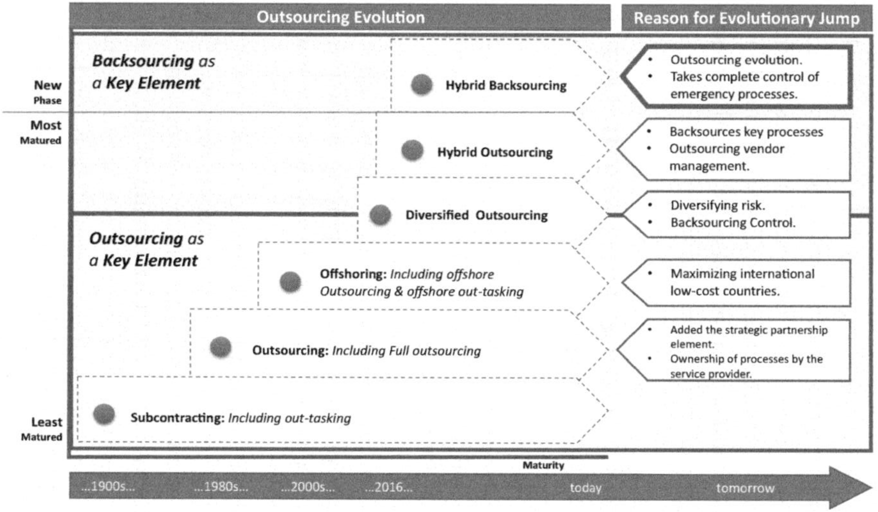

Fig. 5.3 Outsourcing evolution and growth

5.3.1 *The Past: Outsourcing as a Key Strategic Element*

The first part of the outsourcing evolution began with a foundation to take processes from the company and hand them over to an external supplier. We will refer to this as **outsourcing as a key element** since the focus is to take services out of the company. This section includes Subcontracting, Outsourcing, and Offshoring. By reviewing the pharmaceutical and aviation industries as examples, we can conclude the first evolutionary step after supplying services internally was to subcontract them.

Subcontracting is defined as engaging with a person or business outside of the company to execute a specific contracted work product. Subcontracting has been a competitive tool used by leading global organizations for longer than recognized. We have learned subcontracting has been around for over a hundred years. And probably began a century ago after Merck began to practice an outsourcing strategy by subcontracting with local universities to help create drugs. We also learned how subcontracting was used as a competitive secret during the second world war to gain superiority over other countries. **Subcontracting has a transactional focus** as it assures the agreed upon or contracted promise is accomplished. Subcontracting could mean the practice of adding staff during peak season or hiring a specific resource to manage a project for a limited time. Subcontracting relationships focus on providing access to resources for the short term and specific transactional tasks (Chaari & Leclere, 2012). What subcontracting agreements have in common is that clients own the process and the task or project focus defined by a limited objective.

The next level of industry maturity in subcontracting is out-tasking. **Out-tasking** is related to repetitive low value activities organizations would rather not have key resources spend time on completing. Out-tasking is holding an outside supplier responsible for a minor part of a specific process or task instead of the entire process area (Sanders, Locke, Moore, & Autry, 2007). Out-tasked activities can range from running a manual script, or racking servers on a data center instead of managing the entire data center. These activities may bring value to an organization and be part of their strategic road map, but alone are not strategic activities. For example, using low-cost vendors to perform tasks on a schedule may be part of an outsourcing strategy, however the task may not be essential to the corporate strategy.

Although subcontracting remains globally relevant. **Outsourcing evolved from subcontracting** when IBM agreed to the strategic partnership with Kodak and took over their processes and created the first official outsourcing relationship (Loh & Venkatraman, 1992). The business practice of subcontracting was replaced by a new practice, outsourcing, as a result of their revolutionary engagement (Applegate & Montealegre, 1991). **Outsourcing is defined** as a strategic relationship where an external organization brings value to another organization by contractually owning their internal processes for a specified time period. Outsourcing service providers seek economies of scale where they can provide multiple customers a specific service at a lower price point than if they internally generated those services.

Full outsourcing engagement occurs when a company hands over an entire process area to another company, for example the management of their information technology department. In practice, outsourcing is a strategic initiative pursued by both organizations. For example, I worked in a large global outsourcing engagement where the client sought our company's expertise to give them a strategic information technology advantage. They wanted us to own their entire infrastructure environment including the data centers and server farms. The company further wanted us to serve as their own internal IT leadership, even sitting on several stakeholder boards. We owned several vital client processes, and the relationship was so intertwined that we even offered to finance part of various projects in order to assure that they implemented all aspects of key solutions. The financial assistance was not completely altruistic but did have a solid foundation on assuring that the client met their goals. We even had some consultants embedded for so long that we were not sure who they actually worked for. For a time, I had an office at the client site and even spent more time there than at home. Working hand in hand with the client also allowed us to adjust our service model to their needs. Outsourcing relationships are not inflexible but often evolve in response to client's requirements (Kishore, Rao, Nam, Rajagopalan, & Chaudhury, 2003). This flexibility could essentially expand to servicing clients from various international locations through offshoring. A key evolutionary factor was that offshoring expanded the benefits of outsourcing globally through a cost seeking objective.

Offshoring is defined when an organization sources processes or resources from another that is located beyond their national borders (Murray et al., 2009 & Peslak, 2012). The **major difference between**

outsourcing and offshoring is that offshoring is a task-based activity performed outside a given country's borders and is closer to a productivity seeking global strategy (Jensen et al., 2012). Air travel and technology advancements have made it easier to perform business at a global scale and set up international locations providing services targeting domestic markets. Through this approach organizations may target the most inexpensive global service provider without forming a strategic partnership that outsourcing usually provides. However, **offshore outsourcing** is defined by the movement of outsourcing-related jobs to a company outside the organization's home country borders (Peslak, 2012). **Offshore out-tasking** is similar as a company will engage with another company outside their country borders to provide nonstrategic services from a country outside their home base. One of the main benefits typically sought by organizations engaging in offshore out-tasking is a cost reduction by taking advantage of lower cost country's labor costs.

5.3.2 *The Future: Backsourcing as a Key Strategic Element*

This section will cover the second part of outsourcing's story of evolution. We will learn how outsourcing is no longer practiced as it formerly was and how it evolved into three different stages with a foundation based on backsourcing. The three stages are **Diversified Outsourcing**, **Hybrid Outsourcing**, and **Hybrid Backsourcing**.

Gottschalk's and Solli-Sæther (2005) research highlighted that overall organizational control is shifting with resources moving from client to vendor organizations. Full legacy outsourcing engagements support this shift in the power dynamic that supplier diversification attempts to dissolve. Supplier diversification as a practice is not new as Feng, Q. and Shi, R.'s (2012) work highlights the benefits of price competition. However, the pharmaceutical industry has taken the idea of using a variety of suppliers to the next level by Diversified Outsourcing. Diversified Outsourcing does not only diversify suppliers but returns control and coordination of suppliers. These recent shifts in control through coordination differentiates as the factor that is backsourced.

Diversified Outsourcing is the procured services from one main supplier to multiple while assuring that the client owns the coordination of various suppliers. The main evolutionary factor is that it diversifies risk from having one main supplier and brings back control to the client.

The associated risk could range from not meeting a specific key deliverable to introducing unplanned perceived hidden cost that were not budgeted. The control factor is the foundational drive behind this strategy as the purpose is to bring back control that the client will not be at risk from the supplier. The control backsourcing is generated through the client having an in-house project management office that coordinates the various suppliers and deliverables in order to assure that they are all aligned and moving toward the expected goal. This strategy has set the foundation for growth as both the Hybrid Outsourcing and Hybrid Backsourcing strategies use it as a part of their model.

Hybrid Outsourcing combines diversified outsourcing with bringing back specially selected key processes that the client has deemed vital to run their operations as well as outsourced the management of various vendors. The last two points are what make it different from diversified sourcing. It is backsourcing not only the control through the diversification but also complete processes needed to have control over to assure success. These processes can differ from industry to industry or even company to company. The underline factor is that they must be vital to their success. The additional key difference of this strategy is that it took the coordination and control backsourcing from diversified outsourcing and elevated it. It took it to the next level by using a third-party provider or subcontractor to manage and coordinate the various suppliers. The subcontractor has complete loyalty to the client as their main stakeholder.

This strategy allows the outsourcing client to have greater flexibility and long-term cost management due to having complete control of their future. Diversified Outsourcing and Hybrid Outsourcing show a significant improvement from the legacy one supplier economies of scale outsourcing model. These two strategies show how outsourcing has evolved through the incorporation of backsourcing as part of the evolution. However, the significant divergent that goes beyond improvements is Hybrid Backsourcing. Hybrid Backsourcing is a completely new stage within the outsourcing evolution because it takes the best aspects of a Client Value-Driven Backsourcing Strategy and a Hybrid Outsourcing Strategy to provide clients with a completely new competitive advantage.

Hybrid Backsourcing allows large organizations independent of industry to take advantage of their international reach. Hybrid Backsourcing also has a foundation of diversified outsourcing. But the model also requires that the company restructures their talent in order to fully implement the two additional pillars that include the implementation of a Supplier Risk Avoidance Support model and maximize internal outsourcing. The Supplier Risk Avoidance Model elevates the management and coordination of various suppliers by temporarily taking control of supplier operations during emergency situations. The additional differentiator is that the company methodologically creates an internal outsourcing organization. Internal outsourcing is when an organization takes advantage of their global reach and sets up international locations at lower cost countries to support the company itself to areas where labor costs are higher.

This internal strategic offshore outsourcing capability provides organizations with long-term cost and process control through fully owning and servicing their international processes. This strategy aims to further limit perceived hidden costs and price variability as well as allowing them the flexibility to quickly respond to prioritized internal requests due to having one macro chain of command. Although this strategy can be applied across industries. It does have the limitation that the company must be large enough to set up their own internal outsourcing organization.

5.4 The Future of Outsourcing Controls

Uncontrolled offshoring strategies to low-cost countries have led to increased costs and risks (Min, Park, & Ahn, 2017). Offshoring has also proven not to be as profitable as once imagined due to associated hidden costs (Mukherjee, 2018). Backsourcing is beginning to thrive as cost reduction results are not significant contributors to success (Qi & Chau, 2015). Although there is an increasing number of cases where cost is no longer a success factor for outsourcing, we can agree that it widely remains a significant reason for outsourcing. However, leading organizations are no longer endlessly chasing the next dollar in savings from indiscriminately outsourcing. New management controls that serve the purpose of key success factors have emerged from the current evolution of outsourcing that will shape the future of global commerce. The fundamental outsourcing success controls that go beyond simply seeking a cost savings advantage now have a foundation based on increasing the quality of outsourced services and mitigating risks which have become a leading reason for organizations to backsource. Organizations are now making a conscientious effort to control their success through **implementing Lean and Agile methodologies as management control tools focused on improving outsourcing quality and reducing risk**.

5.4.1 *Yesterday's Everlasting Cost Reduction Hunger*

Companies have historically sought to reduce their transaction cost through outsourcing. Transactional cost is the associated cost of doing business with an external organization (Coase, 1937). Some of the historical transactional cost considerations that support the decision to engage with external providers are associated with risk, entry barriers, and information processing (Williamson, 1971). **Transaction Cost Economics** (TCE) is the field of study where buying can be more cost effective and desirable than making in-house (Williamson, 1979). The desirability is due to the opportunity to reduce production costs through engaging with an external supplier.

Organizations seeking cost advantages by using external providers have evolved beyond the manufacturing industry and includes outsourcing formerly in-house administrative tasks and management capabilities (Mirghani, 2018). Outsourcing has spread across many industries as it provides services and products at a lower price point than many companies can produce internally. Companies have reduced their operating costs by close to 50% in some cases by engaging with external providers (Pfannenstein & Tsai, 2004). For example, the impact of TCE is especially significant within HR outsourcing for companies seeking to realize cost reductions (Klaas, Clendon, & Gainey, 1999). Healthcare systems and hospitals have taken advantage of outsourcing to reduce costs in response to governmental controls placed on them by the Balanced Budget Act of 1997 to reduce federal spending (Roberts, 2001). Additionally, the contract manufacturing industry also quickly grew as organizations sought to lower their production costs though outsourcing (Gray, Tomlin, & Roth, 2009).

The opportunity to engage with an outsourcer and procure services at a lower price point than the cost to create internally is a significant driver of outsourcing. Historically, outsourcing has been sought to reduce costs where possible while assuring the core competencies stay with the organization. There is a solid body of knowledge supporting outsourcing motivators around core competencies and cost reductions. For example, Gottschalk and Solli-Sæther's (2005) research supports that core competency management is a driving motivator to outsource. However, organizations that seek short-term cost benefits by outsourcing may experience loss of institutional knowledge and innovation, which cost accounting fails to capture (Denning, 2012). Ultimately, organizations have begun to backsource as the costs of outsourcing are greater than they perceived including the hidden costs (España, 2013).

Outsourcing practices are evolving into something much greater than a hyper cost reduction focus. However, the expectations of reducing costs have not evaporated. Chief Financial and Operating Officers across industries are commonly tasked with reducing costs from their operations and continue to seek out outsourcing as a part of that strategy. As Joannides de Lautour (2018) elegantly put it, "The notion of globalisation or a global firm is very often associated with advanced capitalism or financialisation, both appearing as out of control." The outsourcing evolution is in its essence attempting to capture back the control that has been lost due to the perpetual over outsourcing and never satisfying cost reduction hunger that some organizations have craved.

The power shift created by hybrid backsourcing or smart outsourcing strategies have now resulted in cost controls losing their essence as the main driving force behind outsourcing. This has led to cost reduction controls as part of the overall outsourcing strategy no longer being central to the overall success. Cost reductions have simply become an expectation of doing business contributing to the outsourcing success. Outsourcing success is achieved only when an organizational advantage is gained (Grover, Cheon, & Teng, 1996). However, organizations seeking a true competitive advantage are going beyond the limited labor and infrastructure cost reductions objectives (Gerbl, McIvor, & Humphreys, 2016). Hence, the never-ending hunger to reduce costs has resulted in significant quality failures negatively affecting outsourcing relationships.

5.4.2 Backsourcing Success Controls

Global organizations are experiencing major performance failures due to inconsistent outsourcing quality controls (Steven, Dong, & Corsi, 2014). Misaligned quality expectations between outsourcing suppliers and clients have become an increasing reason for reshoring (Uluskan, Joines, & Godfrey, 2016). Backsourcing is now taking place when organizations are balancing costs and risks within outsourcing (Kotlarsky & Bognar, 2012). The **controls around having a successful outsourcing engagement have now further evolved** into having a solid foundation based on quality of service provided by a supplier as well as managing risks.

Future Outsourcing Control 1: ***Service Quality Management Control***

Quality of service provided can range from opening a service ticket to having experienced technical resources who understand specific industry problems and can provide available sustainable solutions. Lower quality service may be associated with having more inexperienced staff who may not be able to address most client concerns and may even need coaching from the client themselves. Additional lower quality level concerns could include temporary solutions not being sustainable, do not fully address the root cause of the issue, or not provided within the needed timeframe. Ultimately, the **quality of service provided** can be gauged by the difference between what the client expected to receive and what was actually provided.

Breakdowns in quality of service provided can lead to increased hidden costs, increased labor costs, and also increased productions costs to name a few. Service quality can also include the quality of the relationship between the client and service provider. Outsourcing success can be achieved through partnership quality (Latif et al., 2018). Quality process controls ultimately help innovation by highlighting roles within an outsourcing relationship (Zarzycka, 2019). Clear goals from the beginning of an engagement with set scope and expectations can help to control and achieve quality expectations throughout the engagement. Having mutually set expectations from the beginning of the engagement can further reduce the potential for cost overruns that could lead to backsourcing.

Controlling Tool 1: Lean and Six Sigma

Implementing lean provides outsourcing organization with interactive quality controls that can complement client's existing systems while fostering innovation (Zarzycka, 2019). For example, Six Sigma has brought extraordinary results to healthcare outsourcing within the last 10 years (Vijaya & Kunnath, 2020). Now more than ever, implementing quality controls through Lean have become key critical success factors when outsourcing (Blijleven, Gong, Mehrsai, & Koelemeijer, 2019). Although Lean Six Sigma is not a novel discovery, its conscious application to increase overall quality within outsourcing is. The benefits of Lean and Six Sigma are now being appreciated within the outsourcing community as a means to control quality of service provided.

I have been part of outsourcing engagements that have written six sigma controls within the contract itself. Being a Six Sigma Black Belt I was initially a bit skeptic when I read that there would be key quality controls associated with Six Sigma from the beginning of the engagement. I originally thought that it was just a sales tactic that no one from the client nor the provider side would genuinely care about. However, I was delighted to learn that both the client and IBM who I worked with at the time, wanted to have controlled cost reductions as part of the year over year price breaks for that prime client. Both the client outsourcing leader as well as our global executive team understood that we needed to do more than promise empty cost reductions that would ultimately destroy quality. Similar contracts from other providers include price breaks year over year as a means to take advantage of the economies of scale. However, cost reductions that are not controlled through a quality system like Lean Six Sigma can have devastating returns that birth costly defects and relationship problems that lead to unsatisfied clients backsource.

Future Control 2: ***Risk Management Control***

The fundamental management of associated risks can be traced back to the origins of transaction cost economics. However, applying risk management principles in outsourcing is a new concept (Shereazad et al., 2012). **Risk management is defined** by dealing with or controlling events, situations, or activities which may lead to potential losses (Qin et al., 2012). Although the body of knowledge around risk management is quite large, backsourcing-based research has only just begun (Gorla & Lau, 2010). Risk management does not necessarily mean the risk scenario will or will not take place but is the process of how to attempt to control such actions or possibilities. Risks need to be minimized when the potential exists leading to undesirable outcomes that result in backsourcing (Denning, 2013) and (Wei & Peach, 2006). Some of the risks which need to be minimized to limit backsourcing include full outsourcing (Nattem & Proveniers, 2012).

Hedging supplier risk was one of the major reasons that drive the evolutionary leap from full outsourcing and offshoring to Diversified Outsourcing. The classic strategy was to outsource wherever possible to reduce costs throughout the organization and allow for greater focus on core competencies. This strategy provided the foundation to justify **outsourcing as a key element** in the outsourcing evolution. However, innovative organizations have begun to backsource as a key element. **Backsourcing as a key element** exists when organizations backsource key elements that directly add value. The major aspect that was backsourced as a part of diversified outsourcing is the decision control of various service providers while diversifying the risk of having one major supplier. Organizations are diversifying their risk through engaging with multiple vendors instead of one major supplier. The decision control has been brought back to the client side through having a loyal company representative to manage and coordinate the various suppliers. A redefining tool that has been growing in popularity due to its ability to help projects more forwards and manage risk is Agile.

Controlling Tool 2: ***Agile***

Agile is a collaborative and cross functional approach to developing solutions through smaller more attainable increments. Agile methodologies became popular through its initial impact on software development and project management. Agile improvement foundation was further adopted by organizations who craved productivity improvements (Cooper, 2016). Additionally, Lean and Agile are not at odds with each other as they can be applied together in order to attain a sustained competitive edge (Kumar, Garg, & Agarwal, 2019). The implementation of Agile project management aims to reduce the time wasted through the classical waterfall approach within outsourcing. Organizations that implement agile project management when they backsource control and coordination from their supplier may be at an advantage. Agile allows them the flexibility to quickly change course if needed as well as maintain the collaborative environment need with their suppliers in order to enact the risk avoidance support model found on Fig. 5.1 of this chapter. There is currently a limited body of knowledge around outsourcing project management and Agile.

The combination of backsourcing decision control and coordination through Agile is giving organizations a new outsourcing competitive advantage. This can arguably be the most important success factor as it allows outsourcing clients with greater visibility and ability to act quicker in order to change direction when needed. Applying agile project management will further help outsourcing organizations shift their focus to either addressing quality issues, unbudgeted hidden costs, or any other issue that may arise in a timely manner.

5.5 Conclusion

This chapter provided us with an overview of the major phases of outsourcing leading to the new Hybrid backsourcing phase. We began the chapter by looking back at two major industries that are currently defining outsourcing as we know it. Both the pharmaceutical and Aviation industry had independent third-party sourcing journeys going back over a century that may help explain why these industries have been able to innovate in such a way that is currently shaping the outsourcing industry.

We looked at how Merck implemented rudimentary outsourcing over a hundred years ago to innovate and compete against companies much larger. We also looked at how subcontracting was used a weapon during World War II to attain greater control over the skies. These stories are significant to the outsourcing evolution because we can see that these industries have been developing vendor management expertise for over a decade which left them in a better position to innovate. The innovation that came out of these two industries such as Diversified Outsourcing, Supplier Risk Avoidance Model, and backsourcing key processes are then explored in greater detail.

We then reviewed the major outsourcing evolutionary leaps and the reason for the jump. Having the significance of the evolutionary growth allows us to see that we are currently experiencing the evolution of the industry and witnessing the birth of a new Hybrid Backsourcing phase. This further helped us to understand that outsourcing has actually been broken out into two sections, beginning with Outsourcing as a Key Element and recently Backsourcing as a Key Element. The classical transaction cost controls are no longer central to the outsourcing decision but have become an expectation of doing business.

Now we see the evolution of outsourcing includes backsourcing as a key element and includes greater scrutiny on outsourcing quality and risk management as the new success controls. We then reviewed two management tools that can help organizations attain greater control of their success. This chapter provides us with a glimpse back in time and review of key historical facts that independently may not show their significance as much as when linked with one another. Ultimately, this chapter helps explain why innovation came out of these two specific industries and how outsourcing is continuing to evolve before our eyes.

Bibliography

Ackroyd, J. A. D. (2011). Sir George Cayley: The invention of the aeroplane near Scarborough at the time of Trafalgar. *Journal of Aeronautical History Paper No*, 6.

Applegate, L. M., & Montealgre, R. (1991). *Eastman kodak: Managing information systems through strategic alliances*. Boston, MA: Harvard Business School.

Arora, S. D., & Mathur, S. (2020). *Effect of airline choice and temporality on flight delays. Journal of Air Transport Management, 86*. https://doi.org/10.1016/j.jairtraman.2020.101813.

Bechthold, M. (2017). Vimy and the Battle of Arras: The evolution of the air campaign. *Journal of Military and Strategic Studies, 18*(2), 66–75.

Blijleven, V., Gong, Y., Mehrsai, A., & Koelemeijer, K. (2019). Critical success factors for lean implementation in IT outsourcing relationships. *Information Technology & People, 32*(3), 715–730. https://doi.org/10.1108/ITP-01-2016-0002.

Bonnassies, O. (2019). IATA anticipates better profits in 2020. *Airfinance Journal*, N.PAG.

Brown, J. H. (2014). Jimmy Carter, Alfred Kahn, and airline deregulation: Anatomy of a policy success. *The Independent Review, 19*(1), 85–99.

Burhop, C. (2009). *Pharmaceutical research in Wilhelmine Germany: The case of E. Merck*. Business History Review, *83*(3), 475-0_9. Retrieved from http://proxy.grenoble-em.com/login?url=https://search-proquest-com.proxy.grenoble-em.com/docview/274406430?accountid=42864.

Chaari, Z. J., & Leclere, D. (2012). THE CONFIGURATIONS OF CONTROL IN THE NETWORK OUTSOURCING. *Journal of Advanced Research in Management, 3*(2), 120–131. Retrieved from http://proxy.grenoble-em.com/login?url=https://search-proquest-com.proxy.grenoble-em.com/docview/1285500602?accountid=42864.

Cooper, R. G. (2016). Agile-stage-gate hybrids: The next stage for product development. *Research Technology Management, 59*(1), 21–29. https://doi.org/10.1080/08956308.2016.1117317.

Coronavirus hit for airlines could reach $113bn: IATA. (2020). *Airfinance Journal*, N.PAG.

Coase, R. H. (1937, November). The nature of the firm. *Economica*.

De Lautour, V. J. (2018). *Strategic management accounting, volume II: Beyond the numbers* (Vol. 2). Switzerland: Palgrave Macmillan.

Denning, S. (2012). A tipping point for foreign outsourcing economics. *Strategy & Leadership, 40*(1), 8–15. https://doi.org/10.1108/10878571211191648.

Denning, S. (2013). What went wrong at Boeing. *Strategy & Leadership, 41*(3), 36–41. https://doi.org/10.1108/10878571311323208.

España, J. (2013). The real costs of offshoring. *Journal of Business and Behavioral Sciences, 25*(2), 40–49. Retrieved from http://proxy.grenoble-em.com/login?url=https://www-proquest-com.proxy.grenoble-em.com/docview/1449610533?accountid=42864.

Feng, Q., & Shi, R. (2012). Sourcing from multiple suppliers for price-dependent demands. Production and Operations Management, 21(3), 547-IX. Retrieved from http://proxy.grenoble-em.com/login?url=https://search.proquest.com/docview/1021424279?accountid=42864.

Frandsen, B. (2017). The birth of American airpower in world war I: Commemorating the 100th anniversary of the US entry into the "great war". *Air & Space Power Journal, 31*(3), 60–73. Retrieved from http://proxy.grenoble-em.com/login?url=https://search-proquest-com.proxy.grenoble-em.com/docview/1937669112?accountid=42864.

Gerbl, M., McIvor, R., & Humphreys, P. (2016). Making the business process outsourcing decision: Why distance matters. *International Journal of Operations & Production Management, 36*(9), 1037–1064. https://doi.org/10.1108/IJOPM-04-2014-0192.

Getz, K., M.B.A. (2018). Clinical trail insights. *Applied Clinical Trials, 27*(12), 12–13. Retrieved from http://proxy.grenoble-em.com/login?url=https://search-proquest-com.proxy.grenoble-em.com/docview/2169221994?accountid=42864.

Gottschalk, P., & Solli-Sæther, H. (2005). Critical success factors from IT outsourcing theories: An empirical study. *Industrial Management & Data Systems, 105*(5), 685–702. Retrieved from http://search.proquest.com/docview/234907751?accountid=42864.

Gorla, N., & Lau, M. B. (2010). Will negative experiences impact future it outsourcing? *The Journal of Computer Information Systems, 50*(3), 91–101. Retrieved from http://search.proquest.com/docview/287966343?accountid=42864.

Gray, J. V., Tomlin, B., & Roth, A. V. (2009). Outsourcing to a powerful contract manufacturer: The effect of learning-by-doing. *Production and Operations Management, 18*(5), 487–505. Retrieved from http://proxy.grenoble-em.com/login?url=https://www-proquest-com.proxy.grenoble-em.com/docview/228723064?accountid=42864.

Grover, V., Cheon, M. J., & Teng, J. T. C. (1996). The effect of service quality and partnership on the outsourcing of information systems functions: JMIS. *Journal of Management Information Systems, 12*(4), 89. Retrieved from http://proxy.grenoble-em.com/login?url=https://www-proquest-com.proxy.grenoble-em.com/docview/218898612?accountid=42864.

Haar, K. G. (1965) *Industry and World War II*. Retrieved from https://www.aia-aerospace.org/wp-content/uploads/2016/06/INDUSTRY-AND-WW-II.pdf.

Haigney, S. (2019). Utilizing analytical services for success in innovation. *Pharmaceutical Technology Europe*, S8,S10–S11. Retrieved from http://proxy.grenoble-em.com/login?url=https://search-proquest-com.proxy.grenoble-em.com/docview/2212626703?accountid=42864.

Holkeri, J. (2019). Outsourcing of aviation technical services—A literature survey. *Journal of Quality in Maintenance Engineering, 26*(1), 33–52. https://doi.org/10.1108/JQME-11-2017-0079.

Jensen, P. D., Ørberg, & Pedersen, T. (2012). Offshoring and international competitiveness: Antecedents of offshoring advanced tasks. *Academy of Marketing Science Journal, 40*(2), 313–328. https://doi.org/10.1007/s11747-011-0286-x.

Kishore, R., Rao, H. R., Nam, K., Rajagopalan, S., & Chaudhury, A. (2003). A relationship perspective on IT outsourcing. *Communications of the Association for Computing Machinery, 46*(12), 87–92.

Klaas, B. S., Clendon, J. M., & Gainey, T. W. (1999). HR outsourcing and its impact: The role of transaction costs. *Personnel Psychology*, *52*(1), 113–136. Retrieved from http://proxy.grenoble-em.com/login?url=https://www-proquest-com.proxy.grenoble-em.com/docview/220141025?accountid=42864.

Kotlarsky, J., & Bognar, L. (2012). Understanding the process of backsourcing: Two cases of process and product backsourcing in europe. *Journal of Information Technology Teaching Cases, 2*(2), 79–86. https://doi.org/10.1057/jittc.2012.7.

Kumar, M., Garg, D., & Agarwal, A. (2019). Cause and effect analysis of inventory management in leagile supply chain. *Journal of Management Information and Decision Sciences, 22*(2), 67–100. http://proxy.grenoble-em.com/login?url=https://www-proquest-com.proxy.grenoble-em.com/docview/2238486105?accountid=42864.

Latif, K., Ismail, M. N., Ph.D., Nazri, M., Ph.D., & Nor, M. R. M., Ph.D. (2018). Conceptual propensity of outsourcing sucecss through robust model development. *Kuwait Chapter of the Arabian Journal of Business and Management Review, 7*(4), 1. http://doi.org/10.12816/0052239.

Lever, J. R. (2007). PET and SPECT imaging of the opioid system: Receptors, radioligands and avenues for drug discovery and development. *Current Pharmaceutical Design, 13*(1), 33–49. https://doi.org/10.2174/138161207779313821.

Loh, L., & Venkatraman, N. (1992). Diffusion of information technology outsourcing: influence sources and the Kodak effect. *Information Systems Research, 3*(4), 334–358.

MarketLine Industry Profile: Airlines in Global. (2019). *Airlines Industry Profile*: Global, 1–46.

Matos, Â. P., Kauffman, A., Vickery, C., Naegeli, K., Strittmatter, L., Sybirna, A., et al. (2020). Synthetic biology category wins the 350th anniversary Merck innovation cup. *Trends in Biotechnology, 38*(1), 1–4. https://doi.org/10.1016/j.tibtech.2019.10.007.

Min, H., Park, H., & Ahn, S. B. (2017). Measuring the supply chain risk in offshoring countries using data envelopment analysis and the analytic hierarchy process. *Benchmarking, 24*(7), 1977–1994. https://doi.org/10.1108/BIJ-04-2016-0054.

Mirghani, N. A. (2018). Outsourcing relationship management: Accounting in the decision mix. *The Journal of Business Strategy, 39*(5), 41–49. https://doi.org/10.1108/JBS-03-2018-0049.

Mukherjee, D. (2018). Hidden costs of offshore outsourcing: An analysis of offshoring decisions. *Journal of Industry, Competition and Trade, 18*(3), 303–318. https://doi.org/10.1007/s10842-017-0259-y.

Murray, J. Y., Kotabe, M., & Westjohn, S. A. (2009). Global sourcing strategy and performance of knowledge-intensive business services: A two-stage strategic fit model. *Journal of International Marketing, 17*(4), 90–105.

Nijboer, D. (2016). *Fighting cockpits: In the pilot's seat of great military aircraft from World War I to Today*. Zenith Press.

Peslak, A. R. (2012). Outsourcing and offshore outsourcing of information technology in major corporations: MRN. *Management Research Review, 35*(1), 14–31. https://doi.org/10.1108/01409171211190788.

Petrillo, A., Bona, G. D., Forcina, A., & Silvestri, A. (2018). Building excellence through the Agile Reengineering Performance Model (ARPM). *Business Process Management Journal, 24*(1), 128–157. https://doi.org/10.1108/BPMJ-03-2016-0071.

Pfannenstein, L. L., & Tsai, R. J. (2004). Offshore outsourcing: Current and future effects on American IT industry. *Information Systems Management, 21*(4), 72–80. Retrieved from http://proxy.grenoble-em.com/login?url=https://search-proquest-com.proxy.grenoble-em.com/docview/214134160?accountid=42864.

Pritchard, J. (1954). The work of the Wright brothers for aviation. *Journal of the Royal Society of Arts, 102*(4916), 112–128. Retrieved July 6, 2020, from www.jstor.org/stable/41365639.

Qi, C., & Chau, P. Y. K. (2015). Relationship or contract? exploring the key factor leading to IT outsourcing success in china. *Information Technology & People, 28*(3), 466–499. https://doi.org/10.1108/ITP-10-2014-0236.

Roberts, V. (2001). Managing strategic outsourcing in the healthcare industry. *Journal of Healthcare Management, 46*(4), 239–49. Retrieved from http://proxy.grenoble-em.com/login?url=https://www-proquest-com.proxy.grenoble-em.com/docview/206722802?accountid=42864.

Sanders, N. R., Locke, A., Moore, C. B., & Autry, C. W. (2007). A multidimensional framework for understanding outsourcing arrangements. *Journal of Supply Chain Management, 43*(4), 3–15. Retrieved from http://proxy.grenoble-em.com/login?url=https://search-proquest-com.proxy.grenoble-em.com/docview/235220905?accountid=42864.

Shereazad, J. G., Gorod, A., & Sauser, B. (2012). Prioritization of outsourcing risks from a systemic perspective. *Strategic Outsourcing: An International Journal, 5*(1), 39–71. https://doi.org/10.1108/17538291211221951.

Shetti, G., & Khanna, V. T. (2019). Role of prescriptions in the pharmaceutical market: A "Willingness to prescribe" study of the generic drugs. *BVIMSR Journal of Management Research, 11*(2), 124.

Siegmund, F. (1990). Competition and performance in the Airline industry. *Policy Studies Review, 9*(4), 649–663. https://doi.org/10.1111/j.1541-1338.1990.tb01071.x.

Statistica, 2020. https://www.statista.com/statistics/784420/share-of-worldwide-pharma-revenue-by-country/.

Steven, A. B., Dong, Y., & Corsi, T. (2014). Global sourcing and quality recalls: An empirical study of outsourcing-supplier concentration-product recalls linkages. *Journal of Operations Management, 32*(5), 241.

Tan, K. M. (2018). Outsourcing and price competition: An empirical analysis of the partnerships between legacy carriers and regional airlines. *Review of Industrial Organization, 53*(2), 275–294. https://doi.org/10.1007/s11151-017-9610-z.

Thornicroft, K. W. (1989). Airline deregulation and the airline labor market. *Journal of Labor Research, 10*(2), 163–181. https://doi.org/10.1007/BF02685262.

Tucker, S. C. (Ed.). (2014). *World War I: The definitive encyclopedia and document collection [5 volumes]: The definitive encyclopedia and document collection*. Abc-Clio.

Uluskan, M., Joines, J. A., & Godfrey, A. B. (2016). Comprehensive insight into supplier quality and the impact of quality strategies of suppliers on outsourcing decisions. *Supply Chain Management, 21*(1), 92–102.

Vijaya, S. M., & Kunnath, N. R. (2020). Six sigma to reduce claims processing errors in a healthcare payer firm. *Production Planning & Control, 31*(6), 496–511. http://proxy.grenoble-em.com/login?url=https://www-proquest-com.proxy.grenoble-em.com/docview/2371168945?accountid=42864.

Wei, J., & Peach, B. (2006). Development of a risk assessment model for global information technology outsourcing. *Journal of International Technology and Information Management, 15*(4), 35-III. Retrieved from http://search.proquest.com/docview/205860147?accountid=42864.

Williamson, O. E. (1971). The vertical integration of production: Market failure considerations. *The American Economic Review, 61*(2), 112–123.

Williamson, O. E. (1979). Transaction-cost economics: The governance of contractual relations. *The Journal of Law and Economics, 22*(2), 233–261.

Zarb, B. J. (2018). Liquidity, solvency, and financial health: Do they have an impact on U.S. Airline companies' profit volatility? *International Journal of Business, Accounting, & Finance, 12*(1), 42–51.

Zarzycka, E., Dobroszek, J., Lepistö, L., & Moilanen, S. (2019). Coexistence of innovation and standardization: Evidence from the lean environment of business process outsourcing. *Journal of Management Control, 30*(3), 251–286. https://doi.org/10.1007/s00187-019-00284-x.

Pending APA formatting of the below: Referring back to the IBM and Novartis deal

https://books.google.com/books?id=IUh5AgAAQBAJ&pg=PA334&lpg=PA334&dq=novartis+outsourcing+IT+ibm&source=bl&ots=FcSINpqcMC&sig=ACfU3U2fPLTPm_l4JlXc4nOwlcIGCxBsUg&hl=en&sa=X&ved=2ahUKEwj4s5SCvvTpAhVPSjABHSzPAdAQ6AEwA3oECAkQAQ#v=onepage&q=novartis%20outsourcing%20IT%20ibm&f=false.

https://www.cio.com/article/3305757/novartis-succeeds-in-managing-it-modernization-journey-with-two-team-approach.html.

EvaluatePharma. (2019). https://info.evaluate.com/rs/607-YGS-364/images/EvaluatePharma_World_Preview_2019.pdf.

Fierce Biotech. (2016). https://www.fiercebiotech.com/it/roche-to-ax-350-it-jobs-u-s-and-europe-shift-toward-offshoring.

Kraus, T. L. (n.d). *The CAA helps America prepare for World War II*. https://www.faa.gov/about/history/milestones/media/The_CAA_Helps_America_Prepare_for_World_WarII.pdf.

FDA.gov. (2018). https://www.fda.gov/about-fda/history-fdas-fight-consumer-protection-and-public-health.

IBM. (1998). https://www-03.ibm.com/press/us/en/pressrelease/2436.wss#feeds. Accessed on June 30.

BBC News, 2014 https://www.bbc.com/news/magazine-29612707#:~:text=There%20were%20over%2050%20different,to%20American%20historian%20Richard%20Hallion.&text=Over%20the%20course%20of%20the,aircraft%20and%20even%20more%20engines.

CHAPTER 6

Strategic Backsourcing as a Powerhouse

Outsourcing as a strategic powerhouse is evolving. The industry has made a significant maturity jump within the last few years that has transformed it from an endless pursue of outsourcing all process areas to as of lately backsourcing as a key competitive element. Organizations are now rethinking their internal vs. outsourced process ownership scope in order to place controls around increasing quality and diminishing outsourcing risks. This chapter opens with an overview that backsourcing is not an individual stage within the evolution of outsourcing but is embedded with the most mature outsourcing strategies today This first section will further cover some initial **backsourcing best practices** as well as implementations steps to achieve successful Backsourcing as a Key Element strategy.

The second part of the chapter covers the **Mederos Backsourcing Quadrant**. This process-oriented model was designed to help outsourcing leaders and organizations understand where in the quadrant they reside at a specific point in time. The quadrant was designed to help organizations understand the major difference from outsourcing strategies of yesterday against those of tomorrow. The third part of the chapter will cover the **Lazarus Decision Model (LDM)**. The LDM is simple to implement and simple to use tool to help organizations understand the Real Value of outsourcing a specific process area. Both models are a direct output of a five-year research that included some of the leading outsourcing minds of

L. A. Mederos, *The Future of Outsourcing*,
Palgrave Studies in Accounting and Finance Practice,
https://doi.org/10.1007/978-3-030-71407-9_6

the twenty-first century. The research included supplier side pioneers that were part of the official origin of the industry and have contributed to its skyrocketing success.

The research captured both sides of the outsourcing story by also including the global outsourcing client-side leaders that are purchasing outsourcing services while simultaneously backsourcing key areas of their business. The result of that research included the two models that will be covered in this chapter. Ultimately, this chapter provides additional layers to the **backsourcing evolutions story where we can now clearly see that it is not solely the opposite of outsourcing**. Backsourcing has embedded itself within the evolution of outsourcing through being a key element of the most advanced strategies.

6.1 Why Are Companies Beginning to Backsource?

Outsourcing has been unceasingly used as a cost saving strategy (Smith et. al., 1998; Blaskovich & Mintchik, 2011; McIvor, 2016). However, while outsourcing continues to show savings for some clients, others have experienced increased costs of doing business (Stoy & Kytzia, 2005; Patil & Wongsurawat, 2015). Increased cost of doing business and quality failures are now some of the main reasons for backsourcing (Gewald & Schäfer, 2017). Backsourcing has become increasingly popular within the outsourcing community, but not as a new independent phase where organizations are simply bringing back previously outsourced processes. We have seen the evolution of outsourcing within the last few years give us a variation of new outsourcing strategies that have backsourcing embedded within them. **The goal of the advanced outsourcing strategies is to backsource long-term cost management, dilute supplier control, reduce supplier risk, and manage quality**.

Classical outsourcing strategies have a foundation of outsourcing as a fundamental key element. This means that a major element driving the outsourcing strategy focuses on "**taking out**" processes from the company. While the advanced outsourcing strategies represent the future of outsourcing and focus on "**bringing back**" processes to the company. The future of outsourcing has a foundation based on backsourcing as a key element which is currently being defined by **Diversified Outsourcing, Hybrid Outsourcing,** and **Hybrid Backsourcing**. Backsourcing as a key element has resulted in aspects of backsourcing being embedded within outsourcing, resulting in new stronger and more resilient outsourcing strategies. The below image describes the three strategies that are currently redefining outsourcing (Fig. 6.1).

Backsourcing as a key element has exposed that the best way to backsource is by not having to backsource in the first place. This means that a well-balanced outsourcing strategy considers a company's internal capabilities by limiting outsourcing in the first place. Don't get me wrong, I am a proponent of backsourcing when needed. I favor the practice because I witnessed clients implement solutions resulting in stronger organizations, lower operating costs, and increased quality of services when they chose to strategically backsource. Ultimately, their strategic sourcing changes led to positively impacting all their global hubs by generating new jobs in local economies. However, I have also seen clients indiscriminately backsourcing all possible processes in response to a failed outsourcing strategy. As one can imagine, the client's strategic changes were executed in a highly politized environment and resulted in that company incurring long-term costs of doing business. Generally, full backsourcing is not the best alternative for a business recovering from their failed outsourcing strategy. Organizations that continue to extract value from their suppliers while combining it with their own internal capabilities are in a much better competitive position. Ultimately, creating a **balanced outsourcing strategy is the best alternative to backsourcing**.

6.1.1 Backsourcing for Value

Backsourcing key areas of the business is the future of outsourcing. The time where an organization could progressively blindly carve out sections of their business by continuously outsourcing are becoming a thing of the past. Business environments constantly change and so are the supplier relationships that lead to strategic advantages. As such, supplier relationships have also evolved, and it is no longer expected to outsource all possible areas to one major supplier. A successful backsourcing strategy is not focused on solely bringing back all areas of the business that were once outsourced.

Backsourcing evaluation measures begin with a list of all the processes and their associated owners. At this point, most processes if not all would historically be owned by the service provider. The company looking to backsource should **review each process in the value chain** to see if they have a direct downstream impact on the end client. The value chain processes that have a direct impact to sales, marketing, or logistics

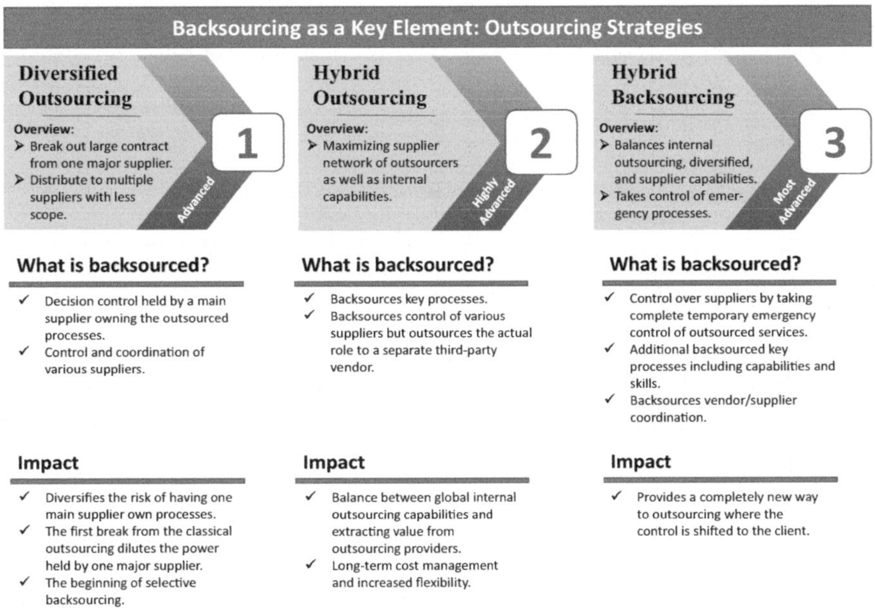

Fig. 6.1 Backsourcing as a key element: outsourcing strategies

should be considered as vital, but it will depend on the individual company's primary business objectives. The company should conduct a **value chain analysis to backsource** each item that can have a ripple effect into a client not purchasing a service or product. **Ripple effect** is similar to the water ripples in a river and defined by the increasing affects created by the initial impact. The backsourcing of value-based processes could range from bringing back the entire production of the process to only the management and control of such process. The management and control of the processes means that an outsourcer would still be responsible for the process itself, but the client would be managing its progress.

Although this perspective allows a company to focus on their core competencies, it is not the focus. Core competency management was popular in the 1990s because it allowed organizations to hand over noncore services to vendors (Gandolfi & Hansson, 2010). We are now 30 years into the future and **outsourcing has evolved to include core competencies within outsourcing strategies**. The value chain analysis can include both core and noncore competencies as long as they add direct value to the end client. For example, this can include supporting functions such as management activities around an enterprise resource planning system that can lead to an end client not receiving their product. Backsourcing for value puts aside the core competency requirement and backsource both core and noncore areas of the have an impact on the client purchasing the product or service. The next section covers the best practices when backsourcing to achieve a well-balanced outsourcing strategy.

6.1.2 Backsourcing Best Practice

The aim of implementing a value-based backsourcing strategy is not to fully backsource all previously outsourced processes. The **aim of backsourcing is to bring value balance to the outsourcing strategy**. The exercise should take advantage of the services and/or products a supplier can provide and balance them with the internal capabilities a company will benefit most by nurturing and developing (Fig. 6.2).

The **first step** that a company looking to backsource should complete is an initial **"as is" assessment**. As with most major initiatives a company must first understand where they are in order to go elsewhere. This is a good time to review the Mederos Quadrant (which will be covered on

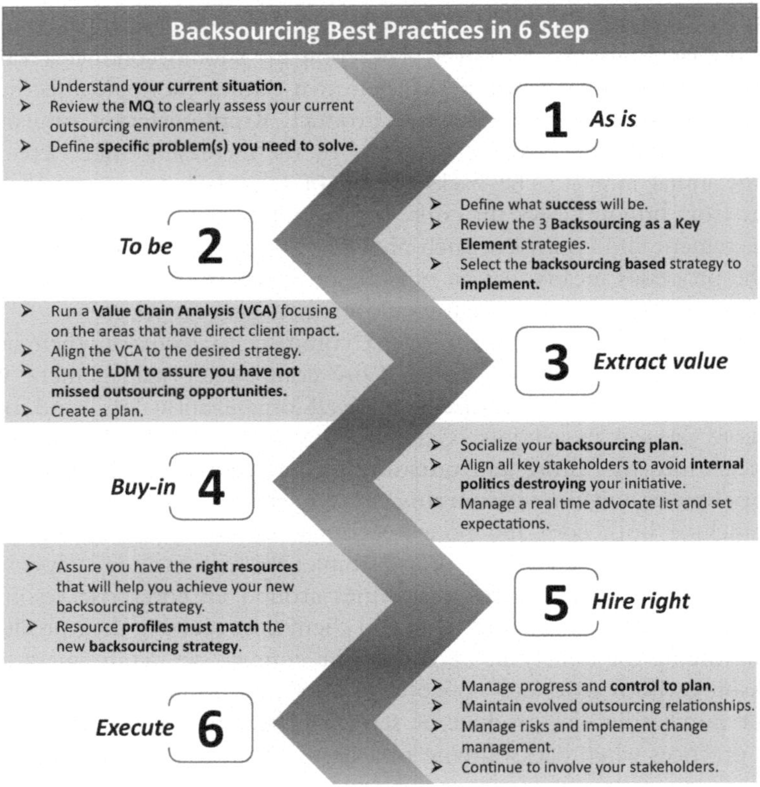

Fig. 6.2 Backsourcing best practices

the next section of this chapter) to assess where they are within the evolution of outsourcing and compare with their current outsourcing maturity. This stage should also include an honest assessment of an organization's problems that need to be solved. After reviewing their current position, a company can then assess whether they want to move toward the future or stay outsourcing in the past. Moving toward the future entails the completion of the **second step** which is a clear definition of **what success will need "to be."**

The "to be" stage requires a review of the three Backsourcing as a Key Element (BaaKE) strategies to avoid the pitfall of backsourcing indiscriminately resulting in an ill sourcing strategy resulting in the same situation they were trying to escape. At this point the company should select a BaakE strategy in order to begin aligning the next steps toward a successful backsourcing strategy. Your organization will now be on **step three** where you can **extract the current value** from your existing outsourcing strategy and supplier network in order to align the key processes to the BaaKE strategy that you have previously selected. It is critical to run a Value Chain Analysis (VCA) during step three in order to not lose the value achieved by your current outsourcing strategy. Balancing the supplier provided value and the company internal capabilities is a critical success factor during the strategy transition in order to not lose the established value provided by the outsourcing services. It is also recommended that you run the Lazarus Decision Model (which will be covered later on this chapter) to help you avoid missing any process outsourcing opportunities. You will now be ready to create a plan that will balance the internal company capabilities against external supplier value provided. Once you have a solid business case and plan to transform the organization is when you are ready to move on to the next step. The **fourth step** directly addresses **stakeholder buy-in** which is one of the leading causes for outsourcing as well as projects in general to fail. Socialization of the plan is not enough. The outsourcing strategy change project sponsor must also create allegiances with key stakeholders that will help the overall initiative move forward without unnecessary delays or letting internal politics destroy the project.

Only after you have a solid foundation of allies and support for the project is when you should move on to the **fifth step** and **hire the right resources**. Although this step is called hire right, it really is assuring that you have the right resources that match the future state strategy. It makes no sense to have the best skilled coders in the world if what you need is a project manager or vice versa. At this point you are ready for **step six** to take back the world. Well, this is assuming that you have a global project. This **sixth step** is where the **execution of the strategy** takes place. This sixth step is similar to managing a large-scale project in that it needs to follow commonly accepted project management monitoring and control processes to assure that the project keeps moving according to plan.

The following image describes the backsourcing evolution critical success process because it covers three major questions that need to be answered before starting a backsourcing strategy and tools to answer them. The next section of this chapter goes over the **Mederos Backsourcing Evolution Quadrant (MQ)** to help answer the **"where are**

we" question dividing outsourcing between past and future industry capabilities. The past provides a high-level overview of yesterday's classical outsourcing, while the future provides outsourcing capabilities for tomorrow. Having a clear separation of the past and the future allows us to further see "**where do we want to go**" by describing four major outsourcing stages. Only after we have a clear understanding of the various options within the outsourcing evolution as part of the MQ is when we can decide whether or not to outsource a process area. The last section of the chapter serves as a tool helping organizations answer the "**should we go**" question by balancing stakeholder value and cost within the outsourcing decision (Fig. 6.3).

6.1.3 Backsourcing as a Competitive Weapon

Outsourcing has been a thriving industry for over three decades showing increasing adoptions rates granting businesses with a fluid competitive advantage. A **fluid competitive advantage** is one that shapes to the independent company requirements. Fluid competitive advantages through outsourcing are applicable depending on individual company requirements as suppliers offer diverse access to niche skillsets, entry into new markets, and staffing flexibility to name a few. Having access to an outsourcing supplier allows organizations to procure whichever competitive advantage they require such as access to lower cost labor. However, a competitive advantage lasts as long as it takes the competition to adopt it. This loss of competitive advantage has been compounded by organizations experiencing an increased loss of process control leading to increased cost of doing business and reduced quality. Failed outsourcing strategies have gained popularity due to business over outsourcing control of what makes them successful. Although we have seen a recent increase in backsourcing, a successful backsourcing strategy is not simply the opposite of outsourcing. A successful backsourcing strategy focuses on backsourcing the key competitive elements of the company that make it thrive.

Backsourcing as a key competitive weapon is the application of Backsourcing as a Key Element (BaaKE) strategies. BaaKE takes advantage of supplier capabilities and only those capabilities. This supplier advantage extraction is further amplified by having a diversified outsourcing foundation where organizations are able to multiply their value acquisition through engaging with various suppliers. BaaKE strategies provide organizations with the ability to assess value add process independent of who

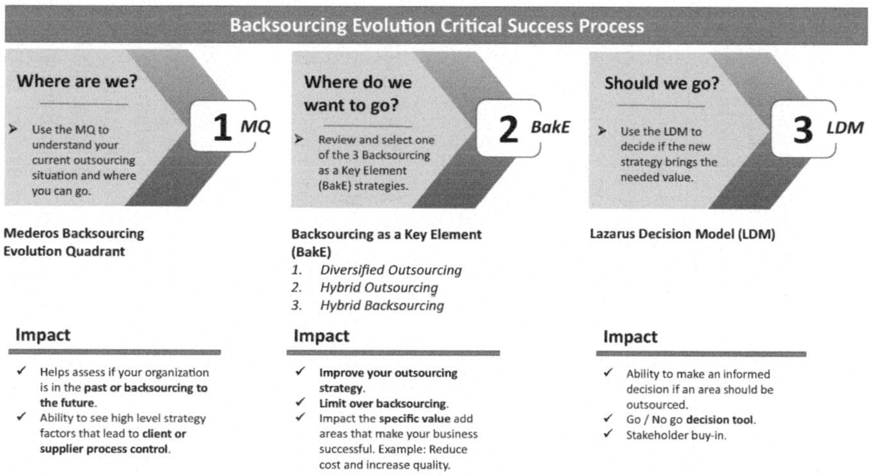

Fig. 6.3 Backsourcing evolution critical success process

owns the entire process. Some of the key outsourcing controls that have been lost through failed outsourcing strategies include manufacturing reworks and lower quality output that resulted in increased production costs. We are seeing what was originally meant to be outsourcing benefits turn into outsourcing risks of doing business with an outside supplier. This supplier risk is now possible to be managed and controlled through BaaKE. BaaKE strategies provide the next level of evolution within outsourcing as it takes the best elements out outsourcing and combines them with the best elements of backsourcing.

Organizations can now implement outsourcing strategies that go beyond simply outsourcing all possible areas of their business to focusing on outsourcing based on supplier value. For example, a company may outsource the manufacturing of a product to attain a lower cost levels, but backsource quality control to assure their products remain competitive. Baake strategies also foster long-term cost management control by backsourcing the coordination of various suppliers and managing progress against budget. Ultimately, BaaKE strategies are fully focused on helping organizations attain a fluid competitive advantage through balancing the right external opportunities with internal capabilities.

6.2 The Mederos Backsourcing Evolution Quadrant

The first model covered in this chapter bears my last name, but it is dedicated to my father. He always encouraged me to pursue higher education and continuously reminded me that knowledge is the one thing that cannot be taken away from you. He was a scholar and political prisoner in Cuba who was only allowed to take his hunger for freedom and the knowledge he had collected through his studies when he finally able to leave the island. Knowledge is at the foundation of the first model as its objective is to empower business leaders with the ability to understand which outsourcing strategy can be the best alternative given their outsourcing capabilities. **The Mederos Backsourcing Evolution Quadrant (MQ) provides organizations with a tool to analyze and apply their outsourcing choices in real time**. Accurately applying the MQ could help organizations evolve their outsourcing strategies together with industry trends in order to remain relevant and competitive.

The MQ takes into consideration the current industry evolution where leading organizations are not focused on progressively outsourcing as much as possible but aim for a balance of backsourcing key areas while outsourcing others. Organizations who align their sourcing strategies to the quadrant should be in a better position to understand where they are in the quadrant and move toward a more advanced alternative when ready. The quadrant is divided between the past and the future to show that there is a current break in the industry. The future strategies take advantage of the key benefits of the past while adding new backsourcing-based capabilities that make them stronger and more resilient. **Backsourcing is helping to define and strengthen the future of outsourcing strategies as seen through this model**.

This section begins by covering the most advanced outsourcing strategies—**Hybrid Outsourcing** and **Hybrid Backsourcing** located in the first quadrant of analysis. These two powerhouse strategies are included together in this part of the quadrant due to their shared similarities and work best when applied at large global organizations seeking a higher level of control over their decision-making, lower supplier risk, balanced cost of doing business, and an increase in quality control. The section continues with a review of the second quadrant and covers the second strategy—Diversified Outsourcing. Although it is the second most advanced strategy, it may be implemented by organizations that have not yet matured into outsourcing. **Diversified Outsourcing**'s significance as a foundation sets the stage to use more strategies as the first way in which to backsource control and coordinate suppliers to diversify risk. This strategy can be implemented by smaller companies seeking to manage cost, improve quality, and backsource decision-making control. The third quadrant covers functional outsourcing. **Functional Outsourcing** is often interpreted as the less advanced and less mature outsourcing strategy to be covered in this section. Companies choose functional outsourcing when they frequently prioritize cost savings over technology or strategic initiatives. The section concludes with **Classical Outsourcing**, the oldest outsourcing strategy that defined many key elements of outsourcing. Although a Classical Outsourcing strategy allows organizations to hand over process control to suppliers, it also provides them with access to low-cost resources, niche capabilities, and key technology to name only a few benefits. The quadrant's content allows organizations a view of their past and possibly future outsourcing strategy options and their relationship. It further provides a high-level overview of aspirational strategies for organizations that remain in the past progressively handing over success controls to their suppliers (Fig. 6.4).

6.2.1 Hybrid (Outsourcing + Backsourcing)

The first quadrant is home of Hybrid (outsourcing + backsourcing) and it includes both Hybrid Outsourcing Strategy (HOS) and Hybrid Backsourcing Strategy (HBS). This is the most coveted position within the quadrant as it represents the most advanced and matured outsourcing strategies. These two strategies share many similarities in that they both aim to have a balance between the internal and external sourcing capabilities with HBS being the evolution. Both strategies endorse backsourcing key processes that have an impact on the end client as well as backsourcing the control and coordination of various diversified vendors that have replaced the former single supplier. They both require full process documentation and improvement with Lean and Six sigma or similar. HBS takes process improvement to the next level as it uses the outcome of the Lean and Six Sigma process outcomes to restructure the organization according to the value of the process. Organizations may have to hire resources that were once outsourced and vice versa due to the restructuring their organization based on value-based processes. Both strategies impact long-term cost management while HBS attempts to fully regain decision control.

The major difference between the two strategies is that HOS takes advantage of nearshoring and national outsourcing, while HBS focuses on building internal outsourcing capabilities. HBS are best applied to large global organizations that already have regional hubs. Instead of backsourcing key processes to the home country of origin, the companies internalize processes throughout the world. This strategy change reduces the risk placed on an external supplier and brings back the responsibility in house while the costs generally remain low through operating at lower cost country. Both strategies recommend backsourcing the control and coordination of the processes provided by the various supplier who have replaced the former one supplier classical model.

The coordination of suppliers further manages the progress of the various processes under contract. However, only HBS has a lever on supplier risk by monitoring progress of suppliers and jumping in and fully taking over supplier processes through funding and additional labor to

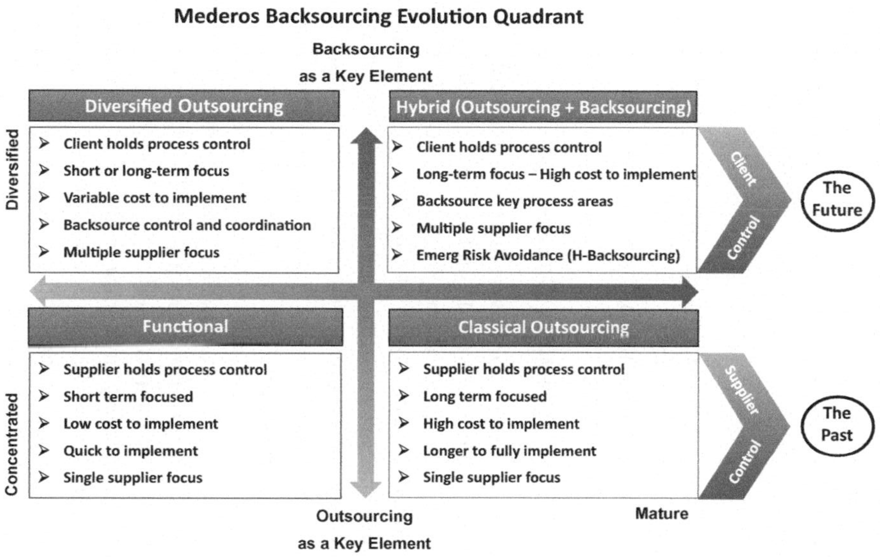

Fig. 6.4 The Mederos backsourcing evolution quadrant (MQ)

assure that the key deliverables are met. This takeover is only temporary with the focus to limit negative client impact. Once the operations are back to normal then the process control and management is transferred back to the supplier. This first quadrant represents the most advanced outsourcing strategies and serves as a goal for large organizations in other parts of the quadrants to strive toward. Organizations that adopt HOS or HBS should have a higher level of decision control, lower supplier risk, balanced cost of doing business, and increased quality control.
Hybrid (Outsourcing + Backsourcing) Key Points:

- **Maturity**: High
- **Diversified v. Concentrated Outsourcing**: Diversified
- **Tactical or Strategic**: Strategic
- **Fundamental Driver**: Backsourcing as a Key Element.

6.2.2 Diversified Outsourcing

The second quadrant is home to **Diversified Outsourcing** which is responsible for providing the first break from the classical full outsourcing options of the past. This strategy is the foundation of both HBS and HOS because its initial purpose is to dilute the power held by one major supplier. This strategy was the direct outcome of organizations that supported and believed in outsourcing but were no longer able to control their success or business outcomes as a result of large global supplier outsourcing engagements that handed over process control to the supplier. This strategy focuses on breaking out outsourced processes from one major supplier and creates smaller more manageable contracts with multiple vendors. Organizations can use local suppliers to continue taking advantage of low-cost countries and regional political complexities.

Clear process documentation and improvement is a critical success factor as processes will be broken out and handed over to various suppliers. As processes are broken out and handed over to suppliers a key requirement is the control and coordination of the various suppliers. The most important backsourcing aspect of this strategy is that the control and coordination capabilities must rest within the client company.

Organizations that seek to reduce outsourcing risk from one major supplier should also review this strategy as it not only dilutes the power held by one major supplier but also dilutes the risk of having so many responsibilities owned by one major organization. Additionally, a diversified strategy can be implemented by any company seeking to take back control of various processes as it manages the overall progress of outsourced services while not fully investing in large-scale backsourcing of processes. It provides an alternative to full (classical) and functional outsourcing with greater decision control weighed to the client.

This is also a good alternative for organizations that have experienced an increase in hidden cost or overall cost of doing business as it can generate a competitive bidding process where multiple suppliers bid for the previously unavailable work. The new contracts could be priced lower as an attempt to gain the business as well as have stronger cost controls to diminish to potential of perceived hidden costthrough previous outsourcing lessons learned. The Fig. 6.5 captures how the diversified outsourcing model transforms information flowing up to the client-side management into control measured flowing down to the multiple suppliers. The relationship between multiple suppliers is coordinated to a point that the stakeholders represented as client-side executive leaders are able to control the various groups and make consolidated decision-making due to the coordination and increased information flow.

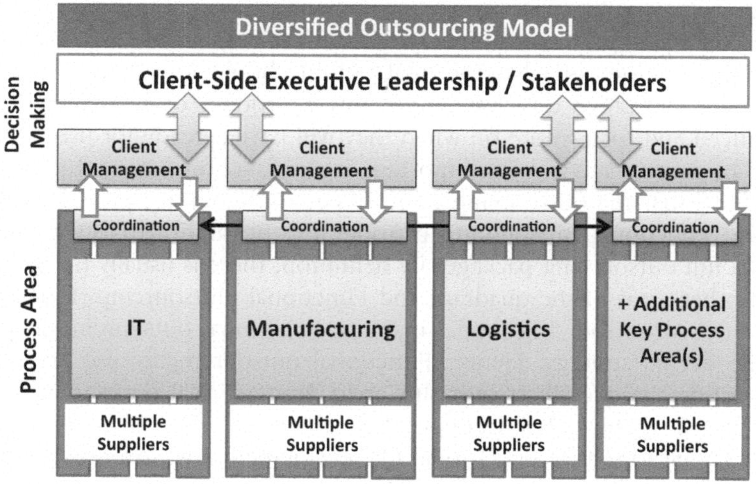

Fig. 6.5 Diversified outsourcing model

Diversified Outsourcing Key Points:

- **Maturity**: Low (can be a jump from functional of classical full outsourcing)
- **Diversified v. Concentrated Outsourcing**: Diversified
- **Tactical or Strategic**: Strategic
- **Fundamental Driver**: Backsourcing as a Key Element.

6.2.3 Functional Outsourcing

The **Functional Outsourcing** section of the quadrant represents the layer of outsourcing where organizations require deep functional area knowledge on a specific process area. There is a need for subject matter expertise often with a myopic perspective. Clients at this stage are seeking a vendor who can fully own a process or functional area. The supplier serves as a strategic business partner who is responsible for providing an overall output. The outsourcing client is not focused on running the day to day operations and is mainly focused on the overall output by the provider. It is important that clients at the functional outsourcing quadrant stage still have flexibility to ramp up or ramp down due in terms of resources in relations to overall service or product demand. Clients at this stage do not focus on training the outsourced staff but are responsible for providing clear expectations of what the final output should look like. Typically, clients at this stage care less about how a product or service is being produced and focus more on when they will have it ready for use.

Management metrics are important at the functional stage due to the blindness that the outsourcing client has as to the service provider operations. Functional outsourcing provides the possibility to offer clients with a full outsourcing package. By definition, there is usually no overlap with other areas of the quadrant and Functional Outsourcing. However, a diversified outsourcing model may use Functional outsourcing as part of the overall strategy. Hence, Functional outsourcing is also aimed at supporting the overall strategy similar to Transactional outsourcing, but it is not a strategy. For example, the overall strategy of an organization may be to reduce operational IT development cost. An organization may engage with an outsourcing provider and step into a functional outsourcing relationship where the provider can take over their IT development function and implement new solutions. Due to the provider owning the processes, most of the control and decision-making stays with the provider for the specific outsourced functional area.

Organizations usually build their trust in outsourcing after engaging in transactional outsourcing experience before they trust a supplier to take over one of their functional areas. An additional benefit sought by outsourcing clients when engaging in a functional outsourcing relationship is not to have to worry about the daily operation and focus on the more profitable or valuable parts of their business that are. Additionally, the outsourcing client has the flexibility to expand their reach or scope now that they do not have to worry about a specific functional area. At this stage cost advantage weighs in as a heavy factor as organizations pursue operational cost reductions in lieu of strategic technological partnerships. Quality does remain important at this stage but is not as significant as cost reduction objectives.

Classical Outsourcing Key Points:

- **Maturity**: Low
- **Diversified v. Concentrated Outsourcing**: Concentrated
- **Tactical or Strategic**: Tactical
- **Fundamental Driver**: Outsourcing as a Key Element.

6.2.4 *Classical Outsourcing*

The fourth part of the quadrant represents **Classical Outsourcing** or commonly known as "full outsourcing" where organizations seek to fully outsource their entire process areas to a single major provider as a part of their overall company strategy. Classical outsourcing goes beyond Functional outsourcing in that it is not solely focused on a functional area but can also be an entire process such as a company's Information Technology or Manufacturing. Organizations seek a low maintenance approach where the provider owns the process, and the client receives the output. It takes longer to fully implement than Functional outsourcing and often the service providers also rely on the company's resources to provide contracted services.

The service provider owns the process and makes decisions to meet their committed output. The service provider may also have participated in the client's decision-making since they control their contracted output. Continuous requirements are open to interpretation and the service provider works autonomously. However, service level agreements can significantly impact finances if not implemented according to the commitments outlined in the initial engagement. Hence, the interaction between the service provider and client are more project readout focused rather than business partner coordinating meetings.

The outsourcing relationship becomes an engagement as the entire service is handed over to one major supplier creating a marriage between both organizations. There is a mutual dependency formed between both parties, but it does not constitute a merger. This could mean that the outsourcing client may not be able to meet their own commitments to their own clients if products or services are not provided in time. This being both the reason for comprehensive service level agreements management and allotting the service provider a voice when making decisions at the client's executive table. Service providers may also treat this complete outsourcing engagement as a business line within their own business by often having its own P&L and executive leadership organization. The aim of this strategy is to outsource as many process areas as possible without affecting the core function. However, there are cases where mature organizations create strong partnerships and outsource their core capabilities.

Organizations at this stage seek specific financial and/or technological benefits from their suppliers. Classical outsourcing suppliers empower organizations to focus on those areas core to their business while providing them with a competitive sourcing advantage over their competitors. Often process area leaders with large teams lose control of their influence scope as their previous employees may then be employed by the service provider. The retained leadership transformation is vital to the success of the engagement as they become relationship managers instead of continuing as process area leaders. Additionally, during this stage successfully focus on managing outcomes and not tasks. This strategy is the most mature in outsourcing and provides a necessary key element before moving to adopt the next strategy.

Classical Outsourcing Key Points:

- **Maturity**: High
- **Diversified v. Concentrated Outsourcing**: Concentrated
- **Tactical or Strategic**: Strategic
- **Fundamental Driver**: Outsourcing as a Key Element (Fig. 6.6).

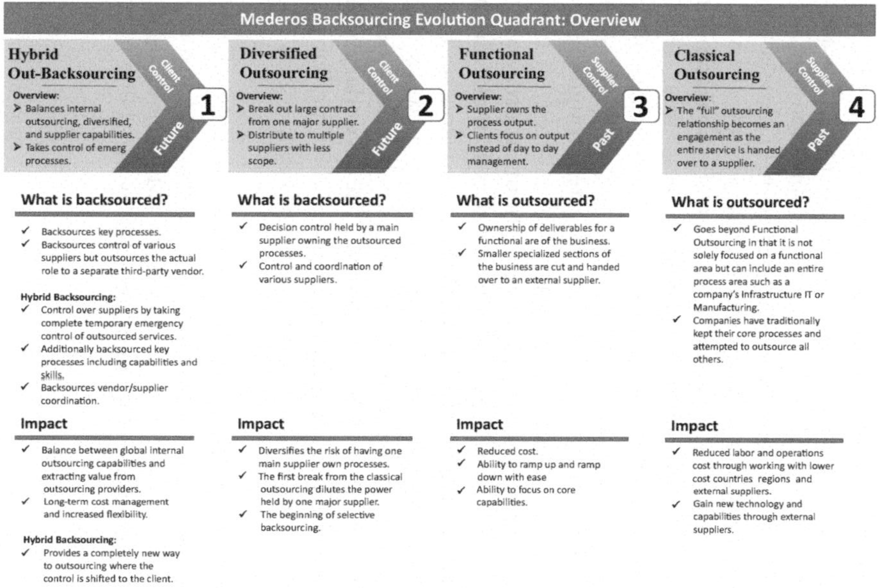

Fig. 6.6 Mederos backsourcing evolution quadrant: overview

6.3 The Lazarus Decision Model (LDM)

Similar to the MQ, the Lazarus Decision Model bears my name. However, it is also a dedication to a family friend who I was named after. I hesitated to name the models similar to my own name, but I felt it was a way to honor those that have positively impacted my life in long-lasting ways. The new outsourcing decision model that will be covered in this section is a combination of lessons learned, tears, and success stories shared by key industry leaders in combination with proven academic theory. The model has been designed to help close a current gap of unavailable outsourcing decision models that are simple to understand and simple to apply. The question it solves is if it **makes political and financial sense to outsource a specific process area**. The new outsourcing decision model is a combination of heart aches, successes stories, and lessons learned by key leading outsourcing professionals with proven academic theory to help organizations navigate through the evolution of outsourcing. The model balances the value placed on business units from stakeholder theory (**do people care about an area**) with the cost sensitivity of transactional cost economics (**does it make financial sense**). **The Lazarus Decision Model (LDM)** shown below on Fig. 6.7 has **two main goals**. The **primary goal** of the model is to extract the real value of outsourcing by balancing planned cost with the value stakeholders place on a given area to be outsourced. The **secondary goal** of the model is to limit the need to fully backsource down the line due to finding the right balance for each individual organization.

1. **Stakeholder Theory**: There has been significant ambiguity in the exact definition of stakeholder theory as it has included anyone who may be affected by the corporate objectives (Mitchell et al., 1997; Miles, 2017). The stakeholder mindset includes the ability to create

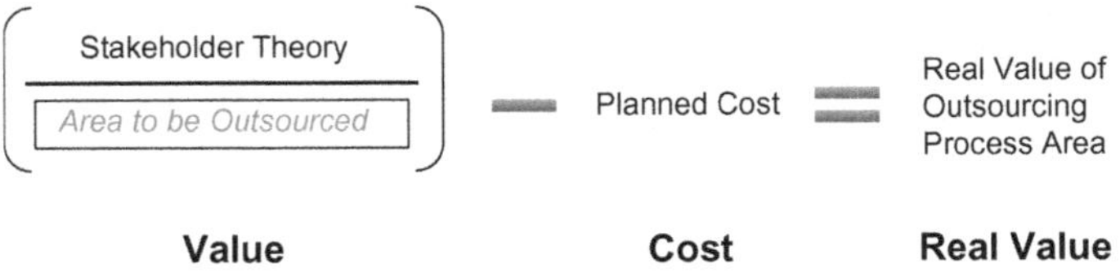

Fig. 6.7 Lazarus Decision Model formula

value from the relationships between communities, employees, financiers, and suppliers (Freeman et. al., 2010). Manager must pay close attention to specific stakeholders to achieve desired outcomes (Mitchell et. al., 1997).

- **Stakeholders to include in the LDM**: Those that have a stakeholder mindset, are familiar with the areas to be outsourced, and have a vested interest in its success.
- **How to acquire the number to use**: Run a short survey of key stakeholders to assess if they care about a specific area and value it as a contributing portion of the business. The survey should be no more than ten questions to assure that the senior stakeholders take it seriously and completely it with caution. Ideally it would be provided in person and not over email. The questions included in the survey should all be kept in scope of understanding the perceived value of a specific area to the stakeholder taking the survey.
- **How to apply the final number to use**: Average out the numbers gathered from the short survey to land on a specific number from one to ten. This landed number is the one that will be included in the model.

2. **Area to be outsourced:** Outsourcing gained significant popularity due to the competitive advantage it offers its clients by allowing organizations to focus on the areas that differentiate them from competitors. Outsourcing is currently going through an explosive evolution and the BaaKE strategies extract process-based value regardless if is internally produced or externally procured. Adding to that value-based core competency view is assessing which of the internal company-owned processes add most value to the organization. A crucial lean tool to access which processes adds value to an organization is the value stream map. A **value stream map** is a diagram that captures the sequence of end to end activities it takes to generate a product (Gahagan, 2007). Value stream mapping helps extract process value for end clients in both manufacturing and services industries (Emiliani & Stec, 2004).

    - **How to acquire the number to use**: Create a value stream map for the process area in question. Make sure to highlight the areas of the business that have a significant impact on the client's core decision to purchase. Each major process should be listed out and included in a value stream map.

- **How to apply the final number to use**: Add the total number of process steps that have both an impact on the client purchase decision and add a core competitive feature to the company. Keeping it simple in the spirit it Lean, the total number of processes should be cross referenced to a simple list ranging from one to ten. One being that the total number of processes do not have any significance on core competitive aspect of the company, while ten being that it is a core competitive feature.

3. **Transactional Cost Theory**: The model borrows from Coase (1937) in that it extracts the cost of transactions performed by a specific process area to later asses if they should be performed by an outside company. Cost of transactions is the foundation of using the LDM because cost management has historically been a significant motivator behind the decision to outsource. The formula takes the forecasted transaction costs of a process area and labels it as planned cost. Planed cost is used because it will be the forward-looking cost that will incur at a future time if an area is outsourced. This section's focus is to capture the future cost of doing business in order to subtract the to-be cost. This section shows best results when the cost is forecasted using an outsourced environment. **The question the user is trying to answer is how much it would cost to have the process area serviced by an outside supplier**.

    - **Cost to include in the LDM**: The outcome of this section should be to come up with a number that sums up the total costs of running the process area being considered for outsourcing and forecasted out by a given time. The time can be quarterly or annually depending on the individual business environment.
    - **How to acquire the specific number to use**: It is recommended to calculate the total amount associated with the process area including labor and material. An easy way to look at this is the forecasted or allotted budget for the given area. Be realistic with including the associated costs such as transition and transformation costs. Another way to perform this activity if you don't have a budget is to take the amount of work completed for a given period and multiply it by the remaining

amount of time needed to complete it at the supplier rate. Ultimately, each cost item associated with doing business should be forecasted as a line item and added to fully assess the planned costs of the area in question.

- **How to Apply the final number to use**: The number acquired by planning out the cost of doing business should then be assigned a number from one to ten. This number is individual to the company giving it weight as it will represent how they perceive the cost of a specific area. For example, one million dollars may be a large number for a smaller sized business, but it may also be assigned a "one" by a large organization. The assignment of the number between one and ten will represent how each specific company perceives the future cost of doing business within the specific area in question.

4. **Real Value (the result)**: This section takes inspiration from Porter (1985) value realization by associating the results of the model on customer centric perceived value from the process area. Anything above zero brings value to the organization and should be kept in house while anything negative does not bring sufficient value and should be outsourced.

    - **How to read the result**: The results of the model ranges from negative ten to positive ten. Positive results above 0.1 recommend outsourcing while anything zero or less suggest keeping the process in house.

The LDM's primary objective is to provide leaders with an outsourcing decision tool while the second is to help cut through the corporate politics fog that destroys many initiatives. The primary objective provides a balanced approach in helping organizations understand if a process area adds sufficient value to keep in house or outsource. The secondary objective is not as overt because it is a byproduct of using the model. This secondary objective is that it specifically highlights the impact of stakeholders and requires their inclusion in the decision. It will no longer be feasible to negatively talk about a project without basis because they will be part of such decision. Applying the model should unite the organization in the decision to either outsource a process area or continue believing in its internal capabilities.

6.3.1 Before Implementing the LDM

The LDM model should be applied when a company is interested in outsourcing a complete process area and not a single role or resource. The model provides best results when organization initially complete an assessment of what makes them competitive through a value stream map and core capabilities analysis. The results from the analysis will help organizations understand the value that an area has to offer as well as areas it could improve if the ultimate decision is to keep it in house. The prior completion of the Mederos Backsourcing Evolution Quadrant is also recommended because it will help organizations align their current and future outsourcing objectives to the exercise surrounding the successful execution of the LDM. Understanding where in the quadrant an organization is situated entails an internal analysis of its core functions in relation to a BaaKE or OaaKE strategy. This analysis is essential, as it will provide direction on what should be outsourced within the organization. The MQ serves as the tool to help organizations understand where they are within the outsourcing evolution and where they can go, before deciding if they want to embark in the journey. The below diagram provides a visual representation of the three major implementation areas that should be completed in order to attain a successful decision (Fig. 6.8).

The pillars shown above represent three fundamental requirements that feed into the LDM. The first pillar describes the completion of a VSM. **Value stream mapping** is a lean tool that became popular in the manufacturing industry because it easily helps to visualize activities within a process area. It has been recently applied to the services industry to eliminate wasted time and non-value-add activities. The VSM should be more than simply writing out the processes and time spent on each. An organization should strategically review all processes involved in a process area that is being considered for outsourcing to assess the true value of an area. The second pillar is closely correlated with core competency management theory by assessing the level of correlation an area has with a business' core competency. A **core analysis** must be performed where all processes within the area in questions are drawn and compared to both the core business capabilities of the company and the buying decision. The comparison should be simple and solely to see if the process area has significant alignment to the core business functions of the company. The third pillar is a peek into the future of outsourcing through reviewing the MQ in order to assess if the company is heading toward an outsourcing

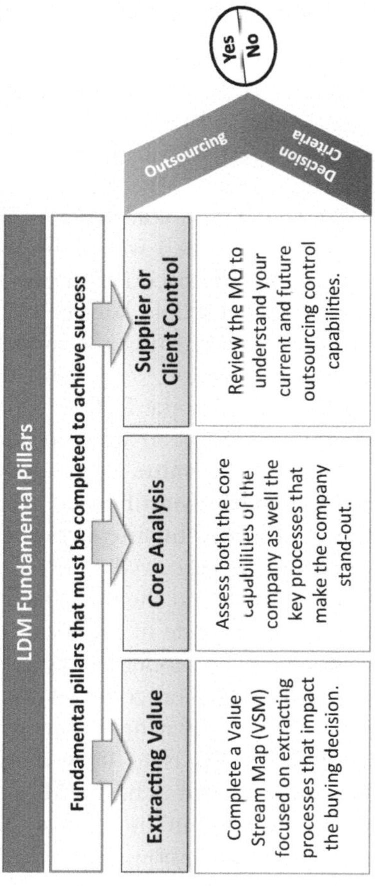

Fig. 6.8 LDM fundamental pillars

strategy resulting in outsourcer or client controls process. The **supplier control** pillar serves as a review of a company's internal outsourcing strategy and reminder that the industry now has additional outsourcing options where the objective is not to outsourcing all possible areas.

6.3.2 *Academic and Management Relevancy*

The LDM further serves as a bridge between academia and management practices in that it is both relevant to the outsourcing management decision but also based on proven academic theory. The model was designed together with key outsourcing pioneers who had been craving a decision tool that had a solid academic foundation. Most of the outsourcing executives that were part of this model creation voiced a concern with limited tools to aid in the outsourcing decision that were founded on academic principles. They strongly championed the need for an easy to apply model with an academic foundation because it would later help them in gaining buy-in from their stakeholders on both trusting the model's process and as well as its final decision recommendation. The result of those lessons learned, and relevant management need is the LDM.

The essence of the LDM is to find out if an area should be outsourced while weighing its value and cost. The **value is gauged according to stakeholder perception divided by the significance given to the area to be outsourced in relation to its core business competencies**. Stakeholder perceived value divided by the perceived value of the area to be considered for outsourcing allows us to find the overall perceived value of the area(s) being considered. The other side of the formula also needs to be considered as it focuses on cost. The model allows us to gauge value and subtract cost from such value. The outcome of the model allows organizations to use decision criteria displaying a view of pure value or lack thereof. **The purpose of the LDM is to have a straightforward decision of whether to outsource or not**. The LDM is an outsourcing decision tool which has three distinct but imperative areas that when combined are vital to the outsourcing decision. The below two diagrams show the direct interpretation of the three main theories that make up the LDM from both the academic and managerial perspective (Figs. 6.9 and 6.10).

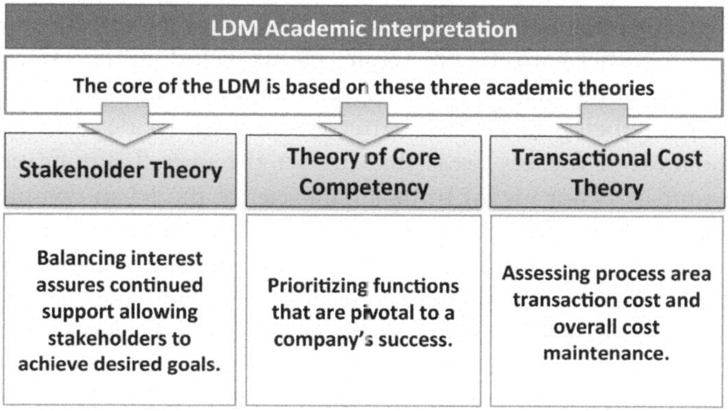

Fig. 6.9 LWM academic interpretation

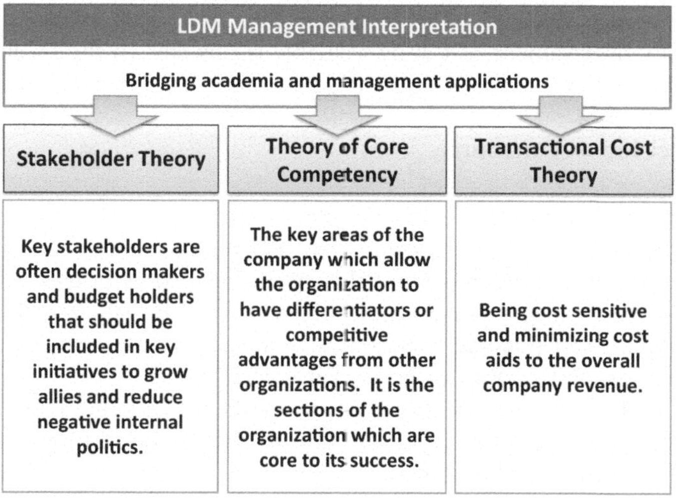

Fig. 6.10 LWM management interpretation

6.3.3 *How to Implement the LDM*

The formula behind the LDM is designed to help organizations think about key forces behind the outsourcing decision. The simple model is not able to capture all possible scenarios and serves as a guide that forces users to complete due diligence of the process area in question. The model together with the pre-requirements including the value stream mapping, core competency analysis, and stakeholder buy-in should result in users already being in a much better position to decide. The model is a consolidation of the key areas that impact the overall significance of a business unit. It is not meant to be a data science model so complex that loses touch with reality. It is ultimately a simple balance of factors based on due diligence. The formula is user friendly and can be easily included in an Excel tab. The formula is represented by using the "= (Numerical Value1/Numerical Value2) – Value 3." Figure 6.11 shows the LDM included in Excel to reflect the ease of use as it relates to Infrastructure IT. The formula is weighted and needs to have a value of 1 to 10 assigned to each section. The person responsible for the model must assign a number to each section in order to fully utilize the decision tool.

- Numerical Value 1 = 10 (do people care about this area)
- Numerical Value 2 = 1 (how valuable is this area to the business)
- Numerical Value 3 = 7 (how expensive will it be to run it outside)
- **Result = 4**
- **Decision = Outsource.**

Stakeholder value: Place a value of 1 to 10, with 1 being the weakest and 10 being the strongest most valued. Place a numerical value on this area depending on how important the specific area to be outsourced is to the key stakeholder(s). For example, the value is "10" for test 1 below. This is the highest possible weight as it represents a core business area as being extremely important to key stakeholders.

Area to be outsourced: Similar to the stakeholder value process, the user would have to place a value of 1 to 10 on how important this area being considered for outsourcing is in relation to its core success. For the "Infrastructure IT" example below, the value is "1" and the lowest because this is not a core business area and not critical to the organization's core capabilities.

Planned/Future cost: Users should apply the planned budget or estimated cost including transition and ongoing operating costs of having the area in an outsourced environment. For example, the "Infrastructure IT" test below shows that the cost is slightly above average for outsourcing the business unit in question when including the associated cost of continuing

Lazarus Decision Model	Infrastructure IT	Human Resources	Service Support	Business Intelligence
Perceived Stakeholder Value.	10	3	10	5
Value of area to be outsourced in relation to the core business capabilities.	1	3	1	1
Future cost - of having the area in an outsource environment.	7	5	1	5
Result	3.0	-4.0	9.0	0.0
Outsource: Yes or No	Yes	No	Yes	No

Fig. 6.11 LDM example

to run it post the signing of the outsourced agreement. This could be due to having to buy IT hardware such as servers or the technical expertise having a premium. This could also include the spike in cost during the transition and transformation stage of the project while processes are handed over to the service provider.

Results (section): The positive numerical results recommend outsourcing while the negative advise against it. The results below show "Business Intelligence" marked in RED reflecting 0.0. The 0.0 recommendation is not to outsource that given area at the moment. Although this decision proposes that Business Intelligence should not be outsourced, it also shines a light that the unit leaders need to work to improving their overall impact and stakeholder perception. The example below also shows that "Service Support" should be outsourced regardless of its high stakeholder perception. The model shines a light where stakeholders believe an area is important to the business but in reality, it adds little value to its core competitive capabilities. Additionally, "Service Support" has an associated low cost when outsourced which leads to the model resulting in a 9.0, recommending the organization to outsource it.

The model has an added feature around risk management. The LDM focuses on the root cause of backsourcing by concentrating on what should have been outsourced in the first place. Implementing the **LDM should result in overall reduction of backsourcing due to a more structured and applicable model limiting the need to backsource in the future**. The LDM marries academic and management theory into practices by allowing organizations to make informed decisions as to whether or not to outsource in the first place.

6.4 Conclusion

Backsourcing has evolved to become much more than the opposite of outsourcing by embedding itself within the evolution of outsourcing. This chapter provided an overview of why major companies are beginning to backsource as well as best practices to attain the right balance between internal capabilities and external opportunities. The chapter then provided an overview of two models designed to help leaders and organizations navigate through the evolution of the outsourcing industry. The first is the MQ which is meant to help organizations understand where in the outsourcing evolution they reside and presents them with four major outsourcing strategies.

Each of the four outsourcing strategies represent in the MQ reflect a major evolutionary break within the industry. The model also describes the major differences between concentrated strategies of the past and diversified outsourcing strategies of the future. The future outsourcing strategies have a foundation based on backsourcing that focuses on bringing back value. The second model is a go/no go decision model to help organizations within the outsourcing decision. The model extracts the perceived value from key areas of the business and provides a weight to help businesses decide if a process area should be outsourced. In conclusion, the chapter provides reasons why backsourcing is taking place, how to best perform a backsourcing strategy and tools to use within the endeavor.

Bibliography

Blaskovich, J., & Mintchik, N. (2011). Information technology outsourcing: A taxonomy of prior studies and directions for future research. *Journal of Information Systems, 25*(1), 1–36.

Coase, R. H. (1937). The nature of the firm. *Economica, 4*(16), 386. https://doi.org/10.2307/2626876.

Emiliani, M. L., & Stec, D. J. (2004). Using value-stream maps to improve leadership. *Leadership and Organization Development Journal, 25*(7), 622–645. https://doi.org/10.1108/01437730410564979.

Freeman, R. E., Harrison, J. S., Wicks, A. C., Parmar, B. L., & De Colle, S. (2010). *Stakeholder theory: The state of the art*. Cambridge University Press.

Gahagan, S. M. (2007). Adding value to value stream mapping: A simulation model template for VSM. In *IIE annual conference. Proceedings* (pp. 712–717).

Gandolfi, F., & Hansson, M. (2010). Reduction-in-force (RIF)-New developments and a brief historical analysis of a business strategy. *Journal of Management and Organization, 16*(5), 727.

Gewald, H., & Schäfer, L. (2017). Quo vadis outsourcing? A view from practice. *Journal of Global Operations and Strategic Sourcing, 10*(1), 2–17.

McIvor, R. (2016). An analysis of the application of process improvement techniques in business process outsourcing. *The International Journal of Quality and Reliability Management, 33*(3), 321–343.

Mitchell, R. K., Agle, B. R., & Wood, D. J. (1997). Toward a theory of stakeholder identification and salience: Defining the principle of who and what really counts. *The Academy of Management Review, 22*(4), 853–886.

Miles, S. (2017). Stakeholder theory classification: A theoretical and empirical evaluation of definitions. *JBE, 142*(3), 437–459.

Patil, S., & Wongsurawat, W. (2015). Information technology (IT) outsourcing by business process outsourcing/information technology enabled services (BPO/ITES) firms in India. *Journal of Enterprise Information Management, 28*(1), 60–76.

Porter, M. E. (1985). *Competitive advantage: Creating and sustaining superior performance*. The Free Press.

Smith, M. A., Mitra, S., & Narasimhan, S. (1998). Information systems outsourcing: A study of pre-event firm characteristics. *JMIS Journal of Management Information Systems, 15*(2), 61–93.

Stoy, C., & Kytzia, S. (2005). Cost of outsourcing versus cost of rental services for office buildings in Switzerland. *Journal of Corporate Real Estate, 7*(3), 246–257.

Conclusion

The book provides a new perspective on outsourcing where we can trace the essence of the industry to key historical events and academics. We begin by going back much further than the widely accepted birth of the industry in the 1980s and see how there are traces of outsourcing going back two centuries. We see how outsourcing is linked to key academics such as Adam Smith, David Ricardo, and Michael Porter. We also see how their consolidated contributions helped define the outsourcing industry we know today. This historical perspective was further exposed through the four stages of management accounting and how it laid the foundation for the outsourcing success controls that we know today. The management accounting controls helped the industry grow to a multibillion-dollar global industry that provided many other businesses with the ability to reduce labor cost, access to global talent, and ability to augment staff when needed. As we saw how significant the outsourcing industry had grown to be, we also begun to see how it was experiencing challenges that were leading to some organizations beginning to backsource. We then theorize on why organizations are beginning to backsource and simultaneously help contribute to the current body of knowledge through three neighboring outsourcing communities being Critical Success Factors, Risk Management, and Outsourcing Strategy.

The contribution to the body of knowledge goes beyond theorizing to include a journey together with industry leaders to uncover the complete

L. A. Mederos, *The Future of Outsourcing*,
Palgrave Studies in Accounting and Finance Practice,
https://doi.org/10.1007/978-3-030-71407-9

backsourcing story. This journey takes form through four case studies that included some of the leading outsourcing pioneers that helped define the industry going as far back as the early 1980s. Together we embarked in a journey reviewing four case studies that provided insight into how outsourcing is currently evolving through the Pharmaceutical, Insurance, Cookware, and Aviation industry. We learned how each industry was backsourcing and applying a variation of a backsourcing for value strategy. We then saw how some industries have an innate advantage over others as reflected through their current outsourcing maturity. This advantage can be seen through how Merck implemented rudimentary outsourcing two centuries ago to gain a competitive advantage against other companies that had greater access to capital in the pharmaceutical industry. We also learned how both the US and Germany engaged aviation subcontractors in a race to gain control over the skies. Both the Pharmaceutical and Aviation industries proved that historically working with external suppliers provided an advantage that would otherwise not have been internally attained. We then saw how these two industries have developed hybrid sourcing strategies that are setting the foundation for the future of outsourcing.

Through the case studies we saw how we are currently going through an evolution where outsourcing is being divided between the past and future strategies. The past represents Outsourcing as a Key Element where organizations continuously seek to hand over as many processes as possible to outside suppliers while concentrating on core capabilities. Conversely, the future of outsourcing focuses on Backsourcing as a Key Element where organizations seek to take back control of what makes them successful. The Backsourcing as a Key Element strategies focus on backsourcing key value add processes that have an impact on the final client decision to purchase. Backsourcing is not a phenomenon that will soon go away, it has embedded itself in the evolution of outsourcing as a key competitive aspect helping organizations seeking an advanced outsourcing strategy that brings back specific value processes. As we learn that backsourcing is now a key aspect of outsourcing, we finish the book by going deeper into the practical aspect of implementing a Backsourcing as a Key Element strategy, including best practices and two models to help practitioners navigate the evolution of the outsourcing industry.

Glossary

Absolute Advantage A concept that a country can produce a good or service at a lower cost than another, thus resulting in a complete advantage over its competitors

Backsourcing The repatriation of processes that were once outsourced. Repatriation in this sense refers to a company and not necessarily a country

Budgets The financial plans that help organizations to manage and achieve future goals. Budgets include the expected target of the expected cost for running the business as well as the financial gains the company is expecting, within a set time frame

Business as Usual (BAU) The normal business practices performed to accomplish daily activities and tasks that help achieve overall operational goals

Client satisfaction As a metric, provides companies with a way to assess their clients' level of happiness following brand interaction or purchase

Controlling The activities and tools that help leaders control the path from plan to actual results with the least possible amount of variance

Corporate Ethical Standards The responsible set of standards and guidance that organizations establish for their members to follow

Cost Advantage Strategy The implementation of a strategy focused on providing the desired market with access to lower costs goods or services than the competition

L. A. Mederos, *The Future of Outsourcing*,
Palgrave Studies in Accounting and Finance Practice,
https://doi.org/10.1007/978-3-030-71407-9

Cost Country Paradigm The reflection that some countries have a higher cost of doing business than others. It exists when outsourcing service providers seek opportunities to supply services at lower operating costs from low-cost countries to organizations in high-cost countries that have a reputation for paying higher wages

Core Competency The foundation of a company's competitive attributes that are not easily replicated

Critical Success Factors (CSFs) The essential elements that must exist for an organization to be successful

Decision Stagnation The act of delaying a decision or support request by not approving it or showing support. Decision stagnation is an attempt to avoid being wrong or show support to the wrong side

Diversified Outsourcing When outsourcing clients distribute the outsourcing services from one main supplier to multiple

Enterprise Resource Planning (ERP) An application solution that integrates all business processes. ERP provides a view of all departments throughout the organization in order to make informed business decision

Financial Accounting The process that records precise economic actions taken by the organization for its external stakeholders, lenders, and/or regulators. (Note: Financial reporting is mandatory for publicly traded companies.)

Global Service Agreement (GSA) A contract that provides a pre-negotiated overall agreement of services and prices to be found within the outsourcing relationship

Global Talent Resources that are able to provide services throughout the world regardless of their home country base location through technology

Hidden Costs The costs, which may not have been foreseen or included in the initial budget, that are perceived to be hidden by clients. Examples include server maintenance or labor activities around specific software upgrades that must be performed by skilled resources

Hybrid Backsourcing Strategy (HBS) An outsourcing strategy that includes backsourcing as part of the overall diversified strategic sourcing relationship

Hybrid Outsourcing Strategy (HOS) A sourcing strategy that begins with a foundation of documented processes and structure that aligns diversified outsourcing, backsourcing key processes, and outsourcing of vendor management as the three main contributing pillars. The output of this strategy is to increase internal flexibility while structuring a foundation of long-term cost control management

Indiscriminatory Outsourcing The continuous outsourcing of processes with little effort on due diligence

Internal Offshoring When a company seeks to offshore their own operations outside the home country borders by setting-up a supply chain to their home country and/or to other specifically targeted markets

Inter-Organizational Relationship This relationship occurs when organizations work together to achieve a common goal. The basis of the relationship is that working together for a common goal will mutually achieve more

Internal Outsourcing When organizations take advantage of their multinational strength by employing their own resources throughout the world to attain services internally at lower market-based costs

IT Core Capabilities The information technology-related abilities that fundamentally provide organizations with a competitive advantage

Liability of Foreignness The cost that organizations face when doing business internationally compared to other local firms. Local firms have the home-field advantage. This is a significant advantage and extends to having access to local politicians, an understanding of the local culture and geographical norms

Lean Six Sigma (LSS) A data-driven methodology that provides organizations with a competitive advantage through eliminating waste and non-value processes. It emphasizes process improvement and standardization, as well as variation reductions to enhance client satisfaction

Legacy Outsourcer The long-standing or incumbent outsourcing service provider

Location Strategy The competitive advantages sought after through outsourcing in a specific geographical location. For example, an organization may seek to produce in a country with lower standard wages to achieve a labor cost advantage

Make or Buy Decision The act that involves whether to produce a product or service in-house through making it versus buying it from an outside company

Managerial Accounting This provides internal stakeholders with an unregulated view of what is currently taking place and how the future may look within an organization. It further encompasses collecting, analyzing, and understanding the accounting information

Outsourcing A strategic relationship in which an external organization brings value to another by taking contractual ownership of another organization's internal processes for a given time. It defines the partnership with an outside service provider seeking a strategic competitive advantage through a mutually beneficial relationship

Offshore-Outsourcing When the company looking to expand their market penetration or sourcing options in a specific country dictates the environment to supply goods or services using an offshore service provider in the preferred country

Operating Cost The cost associated with running a business including the cost of goods sold and overhead. Some examples of operating costs include payroll, rent, and machinery

Out Tasking Repetitive low value and low complexity activities tasked to an outside organization

Outsourced Role Scope The work performed by the outsourcing organization broken down by tasks and overall responsibilities owned by such roles

Outsourcing Core Competencies The practice of outsourcing sections of the company that were once thought of as being the foundation of a company's competitive infrastructure

Outsourcing Cycle The complete life cycle of an outsourcing contract. It refers to the completion of all stages from beginning to end including Transition, Business as Usual, and Termination/Renewing

Outsourcing Maturity The level of experience an organization attains through multiple outsourcing cycles

Outsourcing-Offshore When a company outsources beyond their national borders. Often implemented when a company chooses to outsource a process with the actual location strategy as a secondary consideration. This option may be associated with traditional outsourcing cost-saving techniques when the purpose is to outsource, regardless of where the services are provided

Outsourcing Satisfaction The client's satisfaction levels associated with the outsourcing engagement

Passive Resistance When an employee or group of employees delay a project or milestone by being unresponsive or not supportive of the desired outcome

Planning The process of aligning and organizing activities, people, and processes in order to achieve a desired outcome

Progressive Outsourcing Strategy When organizations implement a continuous outsourcing strategy that seeks to outsource more and more parts of their business with no regard to backsourcing

Resolution Lead Times The amount of time it takes to implement a solution or fix

Restructure for Talent When organizations implement a skills-based strategy change to align themselves to the new business environment

Retained Organization The staff that outsourcing clients agree to retain on their payroll after the outsourcing engagement begins. The retained staff are usually tasked with managing the outsourcing service levels and often serve as the liaisons between various departments throughout the company

Risk Management The process to identify, measure, and limit the impact of unplanned situations that could negatively affect planned outcomes

Robotic Process Automation (RPA) Software that can automate basic repetitive tasks through implementing bots

Service Level Agreement (SLA) The written agreement between the company performing the outsourcing services and the client. The service level agreements generally set the standards of responsibility for both parties involved and can include expectations of service related to quality, lead time, and scope of service provided by each party. An SLA can include a statement defining the percentage of server uptime and lead time expected when responding to a service request

Smart Outsourcing Network An outsourcing strategy that exists when the client steps in and supports underperforming suppliers to decrease the discrepancy between expectation and overall delivery of service

Staff Augmentation A technique involving purely adding labor resources to a project or process for a limited time by an outside organization. The resource addition may be focused on a specific skill requirement or need to achieve a desired outcome

Subcontracting A non-strategic agreement according to which an outside person or organization does not take process ownership while providing contractual support to another to achieve a desired outcome

Supplier Risk Avoidance Support The temporary management of supplier processes in order to limit unacceptable risks. This can also include providing funding and labor in order to assure that deliverables are met

Switching Costs The cost associated with changing suppliers

Transition Costs The costs associated with changing services and processes to a new or different supplier. The transition costs are associated to the Transition Stage

Value-Based Backsourcing A sourcing strategy that focuses on reviewing outsourcing client-side priorities and assuring that the client company owns all value chain processes that directly impact the end client's decision to purchase

Index

L. A. Mederos, *The Future of Outsourcing*,
Palgrave Studies in Accounting and Finance Practice,
https://doi.org/10.1007/978-3-030-71407-9

The manufacturer's authorised representative in the EU is Springer Nature Customer Service Centre GmbH, Europaplatz 3, 69115 Heidelberg, Germany. If you have any concerns regarding our products, please contact ProductSafety@springernature.com

Printed and bound by CPI Group (UK) Ltd, Croydon, CR0 4YY
30/09/2026
02225661-0005